Advance Conder

ADAPTIVE ETHICS for
DIGITAL TRANSFORMATION

"Complete waste of time."

—**Attila** ("The Hun")

"Would not recommend this book for senior political leaders or career-minded executives."

—**Nic Macchiavelli**

"Schwartz provides step-by-step instructions on manipulating people and wielding power. I applied it in dealing with the public and senior government leaders. Could have used more content on healing and religion".

—**Grigori Yefimovich Rasputin**

"Fearless Leader burned book as no help in catching moose and squirrel."

—**Boris Badenov** and **Natasha Fatale**

"The author still has his head after that book about Napoleon?!"

—**Robespierre**

"Loved the chapter on manipulation. Helter Skelter, man."

—**Charles Manson**

"Not a good book."

—**His Excellency, President for Life,
Field Marshal Al Hadji Doctor Idi Amin Dada**, VC, DSO, MC, CBE,
Lord of All the Beasts of the Earth and Fishes of the Seas and
Conqueror of the British Empire in Africa in General
and Uganda in Particular

"Humph! As Schwartz points out, we all have our jobs to do. Too many snarky comments about bureaucracy! I value my place in the boss's hierarchy and feel a deep sense of belonging."

—**Beelzebub**, Prince of Hell, Gluttony Department

"I'm not sure I get the point."

—**Vlad the Impaler**

ADAPTIVE ETHICS
for DIGITAL
TRANSFORMATION

ADAPTIVE ETHICS for DIGITAL TRANSFORMATION

A NEW APPROACH FOR ENTERPRISE LEADERS

Featuring Frankenstein vs. the Gingerbread Man

MARK SCHWARTZ

Foreword by Gene Kim
bestselling author of *The Phoenix Project*

IT Revolution
Independent Publisher Since 2013
Portland, Oregon

25 NW 23rd Pl, Suite 6314
Portland, OR 97210

Copyright © 2023 by Mark Schwartz

First Edition
Printed in the United States of America
28 27 26 25 24 23   1 2 3 4 5 6 7 8 9 10

Cover design by Devon Smith Creative
Book design by Devon Smith Creative

Library of Congress Catalog-in-Publication Data

Names: Schwartz, Mark (Chief Information Officer), author.
Title: Adaptive ethics for digital transformation : a new approach for
enterprise leadership in the digital age (featuring Frankenstein vs. the
Gingerbread Man) / by Mark Schwartz ; foreword by Gene Kim.
Description: Portland, OR : IT Revolution, [2023] | Includes bibliographical references and index.
Identifiers: LCCN 2023006570 (print) | LCCN 2023006571 (ebook) |
ISBN 9781950508716 (paperback) | ISBN 9781950508723 (ebook) |
ISBN 9781950508730 (pdf) | ISBN 9781950508747
Subjects: LCSH: Business ethics. | Corporations—Moral and ethical aspects.
| Information technology—Management. | Organizational change—Moral and ethical aspects.
Classification: LCC HF5387 .S3887 2023 (print) | LCC HF5387 (ebook) | DDC 174/.4—dc23/
eng/20230216
LC record available at https://lccn.loc.gov/2023006570
LC ebook record available at https://lccn.loc.gov/2023006571

ISBN: 9781950508716
eBook ISBN: 9781950508723
Web PDF ISBN: 9781950508730
Audio: 9781950508747

For information about special discounts for bulk purchases
or for information on booking authors for an event, please visit our website at
www.ITRevolution.com.

FOR BUSINESS LEADERS LIKE ME,
WHO ARE SINCERELY TRYING TO DO THE RIGHT THING,
BUT AREN'T ALWAYS QUITE SURE WHAT IT IS.

The doer cannot apprehend who the powers are whose emissary and acting agent he is; he must nevertheless be aware that the fullness of the world's destiny, namelessly interwoven, passes through his hands.

—Martin Buber

And Heaven have mercy on us all—Presbyterians and Pagans alike—for we are all somehow dreadfully cracked about the head, and sadly need mending.

—Herman Melville

Contents

Foreword

by Gene Kim

I have always admired the writings of Mark Schwartz—maybe it would be more accurate to say that I envy his writings because I know that he's written things I am simply incapable of writing.

However, when Mark mentioned that he wanted to write a book on ethics a year ago, I likely just smiled politely and said, "That's great!" Internally, my real reaction was, "How utterly unexpected and odd—hopefully, he'll move quickly through this phase and do something more useful."

To my surprise, he not only finished the book but, after I read it, I found it to be one of the most astonishing and rewarding books I've read in a long time.

Neither should have been a surprise—and, had I understood more fully what ethics, morality, and philosophy actually were, I should have known that I would love this book. Here is my attempt to convince you why this book might be important to you, despite a title that might not bring to mind a problem you currently have.

First, I think many will agree that, as leaders, we live in a time when we are tasked with solving an unusually high number of novel problems and dilemmas, all of which are highly ambiguous and dependent on context. We should value tools that we can use to get results we can all be proud of, recognizing that organizations and people are truly messy things. And maybe that requires re-examining the fundamentals of why we do what we do.

Second, philosophy might give us some very useful tools.

The Oxford English Dictionary defines philosophy as "the study of the fundamental nature of knowledge, reality, and existence, especially when considered as an academic discipline." It defines ethics (which is in the book title) as "moral principles that govern a person's behavior or the conducting of an activity." Morals are "a person's standards of behavior or beliefs concerning what is and is not acceptable for them to do."

After reading this book, it reminds me that one of the things I loved listening to most over a decade ago were the episodes of "Philosophy Talk" I would hear driving home from work. I loved how Drs. John Perry and Ken Taylor were able to precisely decompose and discuss important problems with intelligence, clarity, and incisive wit—which they became famous for.

Third, to help teach us, it's helpful that Mark is not just a philosopher; he's also an accomplished leader and business historian. (Note that I am merely ascribing these skills to him, not asserting any professional credentials.)

He takes us on an astonishing journey to understand why organizations behave in the way they do. Technology leaders all confront the challenge of leading organizations to achieve a goal—and they are often in a situation that requires changing how an organization works. As is often said, "To change something, you must first understand it."

After reading Mark's book, I started to realize just how much I didn't understand. This book will take you on a wild ride, and you will learn so much to help you understand things so that you can better change them.

- Philosophy
- Platitudes and their origins
- History of management systems
- The nature of the self and how we act and in purpose of what
- Self-improvement
- Business history
- Theory of the firm
- Macroeconomic theory
- Accounting principles
- Nature of personal relationships
- Platitudes to policies to procedures
- Examining the differences between work vs. play

Last, this book has made me rethink the value of platitudes. Over the last several decades, I've always had an aversion to platitudes, those trite or prosaic statements that are often cliché. They strike me as meaningless statements, such as "buy low, sell high." It is undoubtedly a correct statement but not prescriptive enough to give readers any value. I think my aversion to them has served me well, as a researcher and author.

This book does not just state platitudes but gives their origins, puts them into taxonomies, shows concrete examples of processes that enforce them, and provides excuses you can give to your lawyer when you are prosecuted for not following them. This book truly forces one to examine many topics from first principles.

As such, I'm sure this book is not for everyone—but for anyone who wants to more deeply understand how and why people and organizations work in the way they do, I recommend this book.

(Another reason I love this book: I love order. I love that I can go into a grocery store almost anywhere in the world and a banana will always have a 4011 sticker—and I learned that means I am likely a Deontologist, but I also learned what the benefits of being a Contractarian, Virtue Ethicist, or Consequentialist are.)

In fact, I believe in fifty years this book will be required reading for undergraduates—it will be loved by the university professors (or whatever they'll be called then), and it will be equally despised by the students who need to fully understand its concepts. But it will be beloved by leaders who want to truly lead.

—**Gene Kim**
Portland, OR
2023

Preface

May I be forgiven the discovery that all moral philosophy so far has been boring and was a soporific and that "virtue" has been impaired more for me by its boring advocates than by anything else.

—Nietzsche, *Beyond Good and Evil*

A learned man must be broad and resolute, for his burden is heavy and the journey is long. He takes true goodness as his burden: Is that not indeed heavy? And only with death does he stop: Is that not indeed long?

—Confucius, *Analects*

If there's an elephant in the room, it must be chased out quickly or it will leave a bad smell. I'll do so in Chapter 6, but some preliminary tidying is in order here.

Each of my books demanded to be written as I was working on the previous one. My first book, *The Art of Business Value*, had a chapter on the CIO's role in determining what is valuable to a business. That deserved a book in itself, so *A Seat at the Table: IT Leadership in the Age of Agility* forced its way into my word processor. In that book I gently hinted that business and IT folks needed to talk to each other more. The readers—many of them IT folks—agreed but suggested that I deliver that message to the business leaders as well. I tried, and the result was *War and Peace and IT: Business Leadership, Technology, and Success in the Digital Age*. It hit me then that every one of my books made a strange claim that bureaucracy creates business value, and since readers probably didn't believe me, I would have to explain myself with *The (Delicate) Art of Bureaucracy: Digital Transformation with the Monkey, the Razor, and the Sumo Wrestler*.

Wouldn't you know it? In that book I had a cryptic sentence about how bureaucracy is a kind of ethics. I was committed. I'd have to write another book. The problem: I'm uniquely unqualified to write a book about ethics. Yes, I have a master's degree in philosophy. But ethics classes were the ones I slept through. I thought anyone who'd written about how I should behave should have found a better way to use their time, perhaps sleeping through *their* metaphysics classes. Why should I listen to Immanuel Kant telling me what to do, anyway? No one else did. Ethics is the COBOL of philosophy—lots of words, little result, mostly ignored, well past its expiration date in Y2K.

On top of that, everyone else seems to be writing about digital ethics, and they all seem to be angrier than me. They also seem to have qualifications—they're AI specialists writing about ethics in AI, privacy specialists writing about privacy ethics, cybersecurity experts writing about cybersecurity ethics, veterinarians writing about cat ethics, pasta experts bringing food to the ethics party.

Every genre of writing has its conventions, and books on ethics have high standards for fear-mongering, soberness, seriousness, smugness, and—damn it—authorial qualifications. I'm sure there's value in all that, but it just wasn't me. So, what could I bring to the conversation that was new?

It occurred to me that maybe *that* in itself was the right angle; maybe I could write from the point of view of someone with only a soupçon of anger, trying to think through difficult ethical issues, as puzzled as anyone else, figuring out as I went along what I was supposed to have learned in graduate school. I could bounce back and forth between the point of view of a consumer and that of a business leader, between that of a technologist and that of a Luddite, between someone who amuses himself by making little jokes and someone who was serious about healing the problems of the world.

Instead of writing about evil, greedy tech companies with foosball tables and free soft drinks in their offices, I could stick to the subject I've been writing about for years: how large organizations with built-in dysfunctions (they all have them) who are trying to do a digital transformation (whatever that is) can think about ethical issues (that they were probably ignoring). The stuff they knew in the back of their minds they probably would need to deal with after emptying the inbox, escaping from the endless budget review meeting, or finding a new coffee shop after the one they'd been going to closed during the pandemic.

Others were writing about evil tech companies and how their executives were pushing people out of the way so they could grab places at the front of the line for admission to the place of fire and brimstone. But—I don't know—it seems way too easy to bash companies that are generously donating greenhouse gases to the atmosphere, educating the public on making explosives at home, and playing hide-and-seek with their privacy preferences pages. What if I wrote a book for the ordinary companies, the traditional ones who were weathering a squall of rapid change and felt tossed about and soggy?

That leads us to the odorous elephant in the drawing room. As I said, when there's a pachyderm snuffling around your salon, you'd better get rid of it before it sits down in your favorite armchair with a Nespresso and your first-edition Kierkegaards.

The elephant: I work for Amazon, which, some believe, is a company that needs an attitude adjustment. How can I be qualified to write a book on ethics?

In answer, I'll repeat that I'm *not* qualified, so that's that. Anyway, I'm not going to talk about my company at all. I'll write about traditional enterprises that are trying to adapt to the digital age, not the gingerbread man companies scooting ahead and turning back now and then to mock them for being slow. I don't plan to offer any views on my employer except to say that—like any intelligent and aware employee of any company—there are things I agree with and things I don't. If I thought my company was evil, I wouldn't work there. If you think that makes me a miserable, unprincipled baby-eater, please read the book anyway because you're just making an *argumentum ad hominem.* I still might say some interesting things about ethics—and besides, I've used a Latin phrase, and that usually settles philosophical arguments. In any case, the views in this book are purely mine, not those of Amazon or—I am fairly certain—anyone else on the planet.

There, pachyderm disposed of, and just in time.

Ethics is hard to talk about. I wrote this book knowing that no matter what I said, it would probably make people angry. The typical book on ethics takes a position that the author feels self-righteous about, pronounces self-righteously on it, and assumes that people who disagree are going to buy a different book. I favor nuance and conversation, as you might know from my bureaucracy book, and I'm going to try to write that way.

I know, the apocalypse is coming, and this book will not be opinionated enough to stop it. But that's no reason not to read it. Harry Potter isn't going to stop the apocalypse either. Okay, maybe that's the wrong example. *Fifty Shades of Grey* is not going to stop the apocalypse, and I know you've read that. It's okay, I won't tell anyone. I value your privacy (see Chapter 9).

An authorial trap when writing about virtuous behavior is to imply that a virtuous person is a person exactly like them. When I start to list virtues in later chapters, they might sound like precisely the virtues I believe myself to have. If anything like that happens, it's just coincidence, and anyway, I'm the author.

If you disagree with anything I say, feel free to blame my parents. It's certainly not my fault. Or maybe my grade school teachers, including Ms. Garfinkle, who said I wasn't participating enough in class. I'm participating now. Eighty-plus thousand words. So there.

In any case, I'm going to puzzle through this ethics thing, and I'd appreciate your company for the journey.

—*Mark*

---

*Argument against the person, rather than the substance of the discussion.

Introduction

Happiness lies in conquering one's enemies, in driving them in front of oneself, in taking their property, in savoring their despair, in outraging their wives and daughters.
    —Genghis Khan, quoted in Witold Rodzinski's *The Walled Kingdom*

Not to speak of the stupidity of moral indignation, which is the unfailing sign in a philosopher that his philosophical sense of humor has left him.
    —Nietzsche, *Beyond Good and Evil*

Is it okay to kick a robot dog?* Should robots be free to choose the work they prefer? Do we need to be polite to artificial intelligences? Should Dave have unplugged HAL's circuit boards in *2001: A Space Odyssey*, given that it was causing HAL to sing that atrocious song?

These are great questions, and I shall do my best not to answer a single one of them in this book. Instead, I'll focus on mundane questions like why we work, how we should live, and who wins when Frankenstein's creature fights Gary, the tooting gingerbread man.†

Take a deep breath. We're going to talk about ethics.

You may be nervous reading a book on ethics because you worry that I'm going to call you out on the naughty things you've been doing, the principles you've compromised for convenience, the nagging doubts you haven't had time or will to face. Or perhaps you're eager to read it because you hope to bask in warm, righteous feelings as I say things you already believe. I know you want to hear some snarky criticism of big businesses and governments. I see you—nodding like the bobblehead dolls in one of my earlier books.[1]

If any of that's what you expect, you may have chosen the wrong book, but feel free to read it anyway and then use colorful language complaining. I value your feedback. You see, I fully respect your sense of what's right and what's wrong, what your parents and your teachers and your role models and Big Julius, the bully down the street, taught you about morality. I try hard not to quarrel with Big Julius, your spiritual advisors, my ethics professors, or anyone bigger than me. People have strong feelings about the issues I'll take up, and rather than preaching, I'll try to lay down a basis for discussion.

---

* This disturbing question is found in *AI Ethics* by Mark Coeckelbergh, 54.

† Yes, there is a story about a tooting gingerbread man. See Tootin' Tom, *Gary the Farting Gingerbread Man*.

That said, I think you'll find that I'm manipulatively sneaking in radical ideas right up until Chapter 8, where we get to the part that says manipulation might be bad.

This book is about ethics in what people call *digital transformation* or *enterprise transformation*, terms that will probably be found wandering the streets in confusion, occasionally bumping into each other, by the time this book appears on an Amazon.com product page. They're terms that might have been meaningful for a moment or two before companies started using them in their press releases or promising them to their investors. What I mean by digital transformation is this:

Something has been changing in the business world, brought on by advances in technology, emerging ideas about good ways of working, new generations of workers and consumers arriving in the marketplace with different values, and changes in government regulation and geopolitics. Large, traditional enterprises like banks, healthcare companies, and even government agencies are trying to learn from more nimble and disruptive digital native businesses, and finding it confusing and stressful.

I know it's confusing and stressful because in my work I meet with the leaders of those companies and I find them confused and stressed. When someone mentions the cloud or becoming data-driven they suddenly need to leave the room for an urgent phone call. I'm writing this book to lower their blood pressure and help them succeed with whatever it is they mean by "digital transformation." Think of it as my contribution to improved healthcare outcomes. That's why I'm going to focus more on the everyday issues of digital business ethics rather than on the sexy issues like the apocalypse that will be upon us if we don't decide right this moment whether it's okay to let artificial intelligences attend company meetings and draw random doodles out of boredom.

What does ethics have to do with digital transformation? I will argue that one reason digital transformation is so difficult is that it involves a change in ethical outlook, one that goes deep, and that a company cannot succeed in this transformation without adjusting its fundamental values. Company leaders find themselves with one foot stuck in the bureaucratic world of traditional enterprises and the other foot desperately trying to plant itself in the always-moving digital world.

I often talk to enterprise executives about the "cultural change" that must accompany digital transformation. Part of what we've been calling cultural change is actually this shift in values. *Of course* your organization resists digital transformation—how much more could you displace people's cheese than by asking them to change their deeply held moral beliefs around cheese displacement?

Traditional enterprises, I'll show in the next chapter, are based on bureaucratic principles. I don't mean just that they have annoying bureaucracy, but rather that deep in their structures and their ways of thinking lie principles of bureaucracy. And bureaucracy, as I said in my last book,[2] *is* an ethics. Bureaucracy's ethical principles are so deeply embedded that we don't notice them any more. But digital ways of working incorporate a rather different set of values and moral principles.

You might not have noticed that your work takes place in an environment structured with ethical assumptions. I want to drag those assumptions out of their hiding places and scrutinize them. I want to think through some moral puzzles with you, rather than pretending I have the answers. And I want to suggest that just as digitally transforming an enterprise is hard, so is making responsible moral decisions. In fact, there's a connection between the two.

Little Questions and Big Questions

So, is it okay to kick a robot dog? How will we control artificial intelligence once it becomes smarter than the average politician? I'm not sure I care. Or, more precisely, I don't see these as meaningful questions given what we know today. I fear that the big, dramatic issues like generative AI labradoodles as pets and unprotected avatar sex that get all the attention in the press are distracting us from more immediate ethical issues.

With just a bit of reflection on our lives as consumers rather than as business leaders, the real issues stand out like transistor radios in a metaverse. As a consumer I don't care much about robot dogs—but I do care that companies, some of which I do business with, actively try to mislead me. I care that subscription services make it hard for me to unsubscribe. Airlines and cable companies are pretending to be close friends of mine, and if there's one thing I've learned in my adult life, it's that they are not. I have more than a little discomfort with white collar criminals committing white collar crimes and being punished with just a few nanoseconds in white collar prisons.

I've got a bunch of envelopes in front of me now saying things like "Open immediately! Important information about your account enclosed," or "Congratulations! You qualify for an EXCLUSIVE offer!" when they don't contain information about my account and the offer isn't exclusive. Later today I'll find myself listening to a phone system that says "Your call is important to us. We're experiencing higher-than-expected call volumes, but please stay on the line." It's hard to understand why they don't expect those high call volumes, because their phone message has said that for years. We call that *lying* where I'm from (Earth).

Look—there are workplace versions of Big Julius the bully. Rasputin Inc. is trying to manipulate me into spending my days mindlessly clicking on dancing frogs or listening to people I don't know humbly bragging about how honored they are to be named the most vegan left-handed software developer in the Frankenville metro area for 2022. People are committing statistics all around me, and I'm exhausted from being k-means-clustered every hour of the day.

Frankenstein is getting all the press, while the gingerbread man is running around on the loose.

Right From Wrong

Are you going to preach at us?
No. The truth is that I've failed at ethics.
You've acted badly?
No, that's not what I mean. I mean I studied philosophy for a master's degree but found ethics boring. I wanted to do metaphysics and ontology. A philosophy snob.
But somehow you're confident enough to write a book on the subject?
I have some doubts. About my expertise. I worry.
Examples, please?

Eduardo

Eduardo worked for me as one of a team of three technical specialists. One day the other two came to me complaining that Eduardo was violent and threatening, and that they were afraid to work with him. Eduardo was tense and wound up; his body language was disconcerting; he stared at them intimidatingly; he kicked the walls of his cubicle.

I met with Eduardo to ask what was wrong—nothing, he said—and to formally document the complaint and the conversation. The next day, I was called into the office of the furious CEO. "Are you planning to fire Eduardo? Is that why you asked him those questions?" Eduardo, I knew, had a close relationship with the CEO that went back long before I joined the company. "Eduardo told me that he's just angry because of the way you treat him. It's your fault! I forbid you to fire him!"

That was strange—to be forbidden to fire one of my employees, one who might be endangering his coworkers. But I had to reflect on what the CEO had said: perhaps there was a problem with my leadership. And Eduardo was pretty much the only Latinx employee anywhere near our IT department. Was it possible that some stereotyping was going on—you know, some "violent south-of-the-border" character that people were projecting on him?

I didn't do anything. Several weeks later the head of HR found me in a meeting. "Come with me," she said. I followed her out into the hall.

"You're going to come upstairs with me right now and fire Eduardo."

"What happened?"

"He just got up in a coworker's face, stared him down, yelled at him, and then gave him a push that sent him flying across the room. Witnesses saw the whole thing."

"But the CEO told me I'm not allowed to fire him."

"I don't care. I've already told him you have to."

So I did. The CEO continued to blame me. But had I improperly endangered the other employees by not doing anything about Eduardo in the first place?

Mary

In another role, I was working closely with a business peer on a project she was leading. We were in a touchy—some would say toxic—environment, with lots of secrets, hidden agendas, complicated dynamics. Mary and I had developed a close working relationship where we helped each other by sharing everything we knew about these organizational politics and collaborated on trying to make sense of our environment. Sharing information made life more tolerable for both of us.

One day the head of the organization invited me to her office for a talk. (Notice the pattern of closed-door meetings. More on this later.) Mary's project wasn't going well, and the executive blamed it on Mary's leadership. She was going to dismiss Mary from her role and put me in charge instead. The executive also told me that, of course, I wasn't to tell Mary about this. She wanted to tell Mary herself and wasn't planning to do so until she figured out where to assign Mary next. She was telling me in advance only so that I could prepare.

Weeks passed and she still didn't talk to Mary. Mary continued to assume that I was sharing everything I knew with her. The executive said she needed more time. When she finally told Mary that I'd be taking over the project, Mary was predictably furious—at me, for being in on the "plot" and not telling her what was going on. She was right, too—I had thoroughly violated an understanding that we'd had. Once our trust had been destroyed, it was natural for her to suspect that I'd plotted her dismissal from the first to get myself put in charge of the project.

Alec

Early in my career, while I was still an undergraduate, I was one of five summer interns working at a large company. It was still early days in corporate information security, and for convenience the company had all five of us sharing a single login account. (Don't do this.) One day Alec, a fellow intern, showed me how—due to the company's lax security—he'd been able to get access to a file of employee passwords. He wasn't planning to do anything malicious with it; he just wanted to make a point about how bad the company's security was and show off his hacking skills.

The company's security wasn't as bad as we thought. He'd triggered some sort of alarm, and the security team figured out that the password file had been compromised—by someone using our shared login account. They suspected it was me, because—you won't believe this—I had a tiny reputation as a troublemaker.

They interrogated each of us individually, and I was the first. They asked if I was responsible for the break-in, and I truthfully said no. They asked if I knew who had done it, and I untruthfully said no. I thought about it this way: Alec, who I believed was honest, would tell them he had done it, and I thought he should be the one to tell them. I was also angry that they suspected me, because this was actually something I'd never do—I don't have that hacker personality—and they should know me well enough to realize that. It wasn't fair to put me in this situation, since it was their own security flaws that were responsible. So I said I didn't know.

Later, I was surprised to find out that Alec had denied it. He told me it was because his father also worked for the company—that was why he'd been given the internship—and he was afraid it might compromise his father's position. That left the suspicion on me. But it was too late to enlighten anyone—it just would have brought to light my original lie.

Ethics

These were just things that came up during the course of working and managing. None of this sexy, biased-AI, peddling-people's-data stuff. There are a few important points to notice. First, these situations were highly ambiguous, at least to me, at least at the time. There was no good option, as far as I could see, and no clear basis for making a decision. No unambiguous rule I could follow that would relieve my responsibility for choosing. Today, I'd still have trouble telling you what was right.

We usually think of business ethics in terms of evil, smirking billionaires doing vile things like defrauding grandmothers and feeding people carcinogenic rigatoni. But most ethical challenges in business are just situations where there are competing ethical demands, and we have to choose between them. In the case of Eduardo I had a duty to protect employees and a duty of fairness to Eduardo. In Mary's case I had a duty to safeguard a secret I'd been told in confidence and a duty to be candid based on a prior relationship. In Alec's case I had a duty to tell the truth and a duty to annoy my employer. The challenge of everyday ethics is to resolve competing obligations.

Greek tragedies taught that the demands of the gods are contradictory and our obligations are ambiguous. Choosing to obey one god's demand does not relieve us of our other duties—and it makes the other gods angry. As the philosopher and political theorist Isaiah Berlin put it, "The world that we encounter in ordinary experience, is one in which we are faced with choices between ends equally ultimate, and claims equally absolute, the realization of some of which must inevitably involve the sacrifice of others."[3]

Ethics is the field that tries to answer questions like "What ought we to do?" Or, more broadly, "How should we live?" or "What does it mean to live well?" (to "flourish," in ethics jargon). Pay special attention to those words "ought" and "should." Most disciplines concern themselves with fact—what *is* the case. Ethics is the discipline that deals with what *ought* to be the case. Mathematicians don't ask whether two plus three *ought* to equal five. Physicists don't ask whether everything *ought* to travel slower than light in a vacuum. Ethics is different.

But how do we *know* whether we "ought" to do something, or to refrain from doing something (to "ought not" do it)? And how can we convince someone else they ought or ought not? We have ways to demonstrate what the sum of two and three is; ways to show that nothing moves faster than light; thermometers can measure temperature, cameras can capture events. But how can you prove an ought, convince someone of an ought, or even know what you or someone else should ought?

The eighteenth-century philosopher David Hume famously pointed out that you can't logically derive an "ought" from an "is"*—according to "Hume's Law" or "Hume's Guillotine," no amount of reasoning based on facts can get you to an "ought," unless you secretly introduce a premise that has an ought in it. Though there are philosophers who disagree with Hume, on the face of it he has a point. I'm not talking about the challenge of moral relativism—the observation that people in different cultures seem to have different oughts—

---

* A common paraphrase of Hume's argument in *A Treatise of Human Nature* (book III, part I, section I).

but noting that even within a single society, it's hard to prove or know with assurance what the oughts ought to be.

It's common to frame ethics in terms of rules—the sort of shalts and shalt nots that we're familiar with from the Bible and our kindergarten teachers. Should I murder someone? No, I ought not. There's a rule against it. Should I give money to the poor? Yes, I ought. Rule of charity. Save the person sitting near me at the restaurant who seems to be choking, given that I know the Heimlich maneuver? Yes, I have a "duty" of benevolence. Display my middle finger to the driver behind me? No rule; it's up to me, though in New York I ought.

But this kind of ethical thinking, the application of given rules, turns out to be only one of many ways of framing ethical questions. In fact, it didn't become common until the Enlightenment—say around the eighteenth century. Wouldn't you know it—the rules-based approach to ethics grew up more or less in tandem with rule-based bureaucracies in government and businesses. Coincidence it isn't, and the consequences will be interesting when we look at the challenges of digital transformation in the first chapter.

Some people believe oughts come from divine revelation, perhaps inscribed on stone tablets. I won't take that approach in this book, partly because not everyone accepts it and partly because ethics is concerned with logical justification rather than simple belief. There's a certain circularity when you frame ethics with respect to revelation: essentially, you have to make a prior decision to *accept* revelation before the oughts can follow. In Plato's dialogue *Euthyphro*, Socrates provokes poor Euthyphro, who has trouble keeping up with him, saying, "Is what is holy holy because the gods approve it, or do they approve it because it is holy?"[4] Socrates asks annoyingly good questions.

Divine revelation also doesn't seem to cover many ethical decisions we have to make today. For example, I'm not sure what the Bible tells me about whether a company should keep customers' personal information private when law enforcement asks for it, or if I should have fired Eduardo and taken the consequences of my CEO's anger. And not a damn thing about robot dogs.

Without religion, how do you convince people to act ethically?

We'll get there. But speaking of that, it's not like you're my conscience, right?

God, no

What, then? Interrogator?

I prefer the term "co-expositor." A partner, teammate, collaborator. You need my help—trust me on this.

It would be great if divine revelation told us exactly how to act, because it would relieve a lot of our stress. We'd consult the right stone tablet, scan the ten or so rules, and apply the one that fit. Unfortunately, as business leaders, we constantly find we have complex ethical decisions to make and no tablets to guide us. We struggle with new questions of diversity and inclusion, environmental sustainability, social responsibility, privacy, responsible AI, and ethical linguini sourcing that not even Immanuel Kant, who knew everything, gave us guidance on.

The Apocalypse Approaches

It's not that there aren't any books on the subject. I'll save you the trouble of reading them. Here's what they say:

Bad things are happening! We're in danger! It's a slippery slope—today someone can predict whether you like your french fries crispy or mushy, so tomorrow the government may lock you up because they think you'll some-day jaywalk! Companies are out of control! Elephants are in the room! Technologists are ignoring the dangers of their technologies! We have to make ethical decisions right now, before it's too late! Remember what happened with Frankenstein!

Then they cite some unrelated statistics to insinuate that our problem is dire. "Every day, the amount of new data produced is enough to fill the Grand Canyon with enough left over to take up the overhead racks on every flight where at least one reading light doesn't work!" Finally, they present some vague and therefore hard-to-disagree-with but very strong opinions on whatever the author has very strong opinions on: "We must never never allow scary three-letter government agencies to gather data on how people like our sun-dried tomato capelli d'angelo sauce."

I suppose ethics books sell better when they have that alarmist tone and element of surprise ("Gee—I never thought about that! What *if* a robot some-day commands me to make paper clips?"). Some author with an undisclosed conflict of interest is telling readers how to behave. I'm not sure I have much to add on the dangers of paper clips, so, in full disclosure: this is not that kind of book.

All the same, you might want to know what kind of person I am. For the record: I do believe that the planet is plenty warm as it is,* and I kind of like the species we have on earth today, especially sea otters, and with the exception of mosquitoes, so I see no advantage to mutants that thrive

---

* See the author's Eversource electricity bills for July–August 2022.

on carbon emissions. I do want there to be succeeding generations who can buy my books. I do believe that we need more diversity and inclusion in our businesses and Northern California yacht clubs. I don't believe in companies using my private information to target ads for fingernail clippers at me. And I sure would like companies to take a more active role in solving difficult social challenges like homelessness and the proliferation of yoga studios.

It's hard to accept that the future is largely out of our control. Alarmist books and articles are appealing because they imply that by planning appropriately, by addressing the questions now, we can gain that control. We were all taught, as we crossed the line from being fun teenagers to boring adults, that we need to plan.

Unfortunately, in situations of high uncertainty and change, plans have limited value. No matter what stance we take today about whether it's okay to kick a robot dog, we don't really know whether robot kicking will someday be an Olympic sport and whether our intuitions today will still be our intuitions when robot dogs start biting our ankles. Think about social media twenty years ago. Who would have thought that social media would affect the self-image of teenage girls? That social media companies might block messages from presidents of the United States? It's hard to talk about the course that disruptive stuff will take—because that's what it means to be disruptive.

But that's neither here nor there; there's a monster on the loose.

Frankenstein and the Gingerbread Man

I'm curious—can you explain the subtitle? What's this about Frankenstein and the gingerbread man? Is there a joke I'm missing?

If you don't read the footnotes and the epigraphs, you might miss some jokes. But the point about Frankenstein is that metaphors matter when we're framing ethical issues. People talk about artificial intelligence or genetic engineering as a Frankenstein monster—out of control, sociopathic, and malevolent. HE MUST BE DESTROYED before he destroys humanity as we know it! But what would happen if we thought of runaway AI as more like the gingerbread man?

What would happen?

I'll get to that. But here's a clue. Like Frankenstein's creature, the gingerbread man escapes and runs away. But most of what he does while being chased is to make fun of his pursuers. HE MUST BE DESTROYED . . . well, because we want to eat dessert. He's not very smart, so eventually he gets tricked into being eaten. In the Scandinavian version of the story, he's a pancake. The frightening future of intelligent technology might be flattened dough.

Refining Our Metaphors

Anyway, it's worth going back to Mary Wollstonecraft soon-to-be-Shelley's novel *Frankenstein* to see what it actually says, because it says some useful things for our discussion here.

First, about Frankenstein: Frankenstein is not actually Frankenstein. I mean that Frankenstein is the name of the scientist, not the monster. In fact, there is no monster; Frankenstein's creature is referred to as "the creature." That's "creature"—a word with the same root as "create." He's also called "fiend" and "wretch," just as I am in some circles. And Frankenstein is not a doctor. He's just referred to as Victor Frankenstein.

The book is not about a monster who escapes from Frankenstein's control. Victor is disgusted by the creature's ugliness and disturbed that he has done something as unnatural as giving birth to an adult, so *he* runs away, leaving the creature to fend for itself. "Accursed creator! Why did you form a monster so hideous that even you turned from me in disgust?" it asks.[5] The creature—really pretty ugly by anyone's standards, since it's made of other people's body parts sewn together—has trouble making friends and finding love and swears vengeance on Victor after trying to negotiate with him to create a female companion.

Frankenstein—Victor, I mean—has turned his back on his child, which was no more considered good form in 1819 than today. He's refused to take on the obligations of creature rearing, including his responsibility for the creature's ethical development. "The wicked are like God—they too do as they please," says the sacred Tamil *Kural* of India,[6] and Victor has indeed usurped the role of God—and, incidentally, of mothers.

We learn about Victor's moral failings—not the creature's—as the wretch/fiend goes on his killing spree, much as we learn about our own biases as we examine the activities of our artificial intelligences. To read *Frankenstein* as the story of an escaped and evil creature and worry that AI might be his cousin is to miss the point.

While Victor remains a morally deficient human being, the creature becomes a better "person" as he learns empathy and kindness by observing other humans. This theme of the creature as Victor's double runs throughout the book, much as the theme of artificial intelligence as our double, subject to the same biases and errors as humanity, runs through discussions on responsible AI. Even a superficial reading of Frankenstein suggests that we should hug our robots and artificial intelligences, not recoil from them. We should teach them to be kind. We should nurture them.

Frankenstein is a very personal book about the responsibilities of creators, written at a time when Mary Wollstonecraft was creating little human beings in the usual way with her kooky but apparently good-looking poet-boyfriend, Percy Bysshe Shelley. One of her babies had already died in its infancy, and she was about to lose two more. Victor is a caricature of a Romantic-era hero, as was perhaps—ahem—Percy himself.

Frankenstein is a fable about creation—like entrepreneurial creation in our emerging digital world. Long discriminated against for his deformities, Frankenstein's creature has been unfairly maligned, misnomered, and—you'll agree—mis-mental-modeled.

The Gingerbread Man

The gingerbread man, unlike Frankenstein's creature, *does* escape his creator—the cook. The tale begins when the birthday dessert she's baking for little Billy jumps out of the oven and runs away. The cook chases the gingerbread man and is soon joined in the chase by her husband, a neighbor, a postal worker, and various other upright citizens, not to mention a dog, a cat, a monkey, and a fox. The gingerbread man not only outruns them but taunts them, turning back now and then saying "Run, run, as fast as you can. You can't catch me, I'm the gingerbread man!"

At this point there's some dispute about the historical record. In some accounts, a fox tricks the gingerbread man into riding across a river on his back and then eats him. According to other sources, the gingerbread man is finally caught and fed to Billy, who eats him one limb at a time ("Ouch! There goes my leg!"). In a related Eastern European story called *The Kolobok*, the fox tricks the Kolobok by praising his singing. In a German version, *The Thick Fat Pancake*, the pancake allows itself to be eaten by two hungry orphan children. In any case, the gingerbread man's virtue—tastiness—is finally realized, to the benefit of humanity.

What if artificial intelligence is not Frankenstein's creature but an escaped dessert, thumbing its nose at us comical, famished, slow-moving diners? A slice of pizza making fun of the sleep-deprived software developers coding their gradient descent algorithms?

Restatement of the Problem

If you're following me—rather than chasing dessert—here's what I'm getting at. Digital transformation requires that we change our ethical assumptions about business, assumptions we've long taken for granted, because they are largely inherited from legacy bureaucratic ways of thinking. If you don't believe me, please suspend your disbelief until the next chapter, when I'll explain.

Those ethical assumptions structure our *everyday* ways of acting in a business. Ethical decisions are not generally big-picture choices between good and evil—restraining Frankenstein monsters—but the scads of everyday, small matters that cross our desks or flicker up on Zoom. We struggle every day to manage conflicting imperatives, many of which arise because we are squatting in both the digital and bureaucratic worlds.

Because innovation is such an important part of the digital world, we are constantly releasing little Frankenstein critters and ambulatory desserts into the world. Let's not close our minds in fear but rather engage with them. It turns out that they have a lot to teach us—about ourselves.

Clarifications and Disclaimers

Before we go chasing pancakes, there are a few things I should clarify.

I'm going to use the terms *ethics*, *morality*, and *values*. Ethics, as I have said, is about how we ought to act, or how one should live a good life. Morality means the same thing. I vaguely remember a teacher way back drawing a pedantic distinction between ethics and morals, but today the terms are generally interchangeable. The word *values* refers to things we evaluate as *good*. If we value peace and harmony, for example, that means we think they are good things. Ethics is about how to get to the state that we value; what we ought to do that will bring about peace and harmony, or at least what behaviors are consistent with them.

I was born and grew up in the United States. I know that I can't speak for everyone when it comes to ethics. Expect my background to show through.

Importantly, I haven't worked much in highly manual jobs, factory work, unionized positions—stuff that is often called "blue collar." I did work, for a while, behind the counter at a coffee shop and once, in a careless move, spilled hot coffee all over a customer in an expensive business suit. That's all I'll claim for my expertise. Activating my excuse that this is a book about digital transformation, I'll focus on the white collar, office worker stuff.

This book is *not* about what is legal. The concepts of ethics and law are distinct, even if they are related. Fraud is illegal, but lying is not. The law says nothing about whether I should have told Mary about her pending demotion.

Laws get things wrong. Slavery was once legal in the United States, but it was never moral. In the 1600s, a woman convicted of being a "common scold" could be sentenced to the ducking stool.[7] In 1912, the legislature in Saskatchewan, Canada, passed a law forbidding any white woman to work in any restaurant, laundry, or other place of business owned, kept, or managed by any "Japanese, Chinamen or other Oriental person."[8] The principles of the Nazi genocide were carefully translated into laws that deprived Jews of legal protections and legal status. These were all unethical laws.

If you still don't believe that law and ethics are different, I'm more than overjoyed* because it gives me a chance to tell you about silly laws from around the globe. In Liverpool, it is illegal for a woman to be topless except as a clerk in a tropical fish store.[9] In medieval Russia you could be fined for assaulting someone's mustache.[10] In parts of Washington State, it's a felony to harass Bigfoot, Sasquatch, or any other undiscovered species.[11]

While ethics concerns itself with logical reasoning, some laws are exuberantly illogical: In 1897, the Indiana House of Representatives voted on whether to make the number *pi* equal to exactly 3.2.[12] In the UK it's illegal to die in the Houses of Parliament,[13] and in Canada you can be imprisoned for life for rendering data meaningless.[14] A proposed law in Kansas declared that "When two railroad trains meet at a crossing, each shall stop and neither shall proceed until the other has passed."[15]

Ladies and gentlemen of the jury, law is not ethics.

What We'll Cover

There are really two topics we need to cover: ethics in the workplace—that is, how *people* should behave when they're working—and business ethics—that is, how *businesses* should behave. Some people think these are the same question; that a business is simply a collection of individuals, and if they behave well, then the business is behaving well. I'll treat them as separate questions, though I'll explain why some people would disagree with me.

Since I will suggest that ethical norms evolve and that the best way to learn about them is through inspecting and adapting, just as in Agile IT, I've divided this book into evolutionary sections: Primordial Muck (the building blocks for our digital ethics), Perilous Predators (the real problems of business ethics today), and Evolution (how we can face the future with a more adaptive approach).

In "Primordial Muck," I'll set the stage for a discussion of the challenges in digital transformation ethics. First, I'll explain what's at stake in the shift

---

* See the chapter on bullshit for an explanation of overjoyed++.

from traditional enterprises to digital ones: what old values no longer apply and what new values are emerging. Then I'll present some of the classic ways of framing ethical questions and assess which of them are useful today. My goal is to explore ways to ground ethical decisions, not to preach about what is right and what is wrong. I'm going to claim, though it might sound odd, that there are "adaptive" or "agile" ways of thinking about ethics.

In "Perils and Predators," I'll explore some of today's dilemmas. I will argue that we've lost sight of what the real questions are, partly because of all the hype around Frankenstein and big scary problems. I'll focus on the areas where we must decide between competing ethical imperatives; where we are torn—often without realizing it—between traditional bureaucratic values and new digital values. For example: Are executives justified in investing in socially responsible initiatives despite their fiduciary duty to shareholders?

In "Evolution," I'll suggest that we learn to think differently about relationships with customers and employees. I will question one of the deepest assumptions of the emerging digital world—the idea of customer intimacy. Frankenstein's creature and the gingerbread man will set us on the right path by explaining how to evolve digital norms by experimenting and learning. I'll frame the ethics of digital transformation as a matter of cultivating and applying virtues rather than applying rules.

Finally, I'll put it all in the perspective of executive visioning: imagining a state of what philosophers call human flourishing. Once we envision it, we can use our managerial skills to get us there. Ethics is not just a matter of refraining from doing bad things. It's a matter of building the world we want, and it's the job of company executives.

Why Should You Read This Book?

There are lots of books on digital transformation, including four I've written. They're great books—if you don't believe me, read Napoleon Bonaparte's foreword to *War and Peace and IT*.[16] Unlike most technology books, they deal with important problems like selecting pasta, harpooning whales, and watching bobbleheads bobble. But while writing them I noticed that everything I was talking about was, in a sense, just surface indications of a deeper set of issues, the froth on the soup that hides the shifts in values that really are the meat and bones of digital transformation. Since ethics is hard, we've all been staring at the surface, stroking our beards and trying to look wise as we speculate on the pattern of the bubbles. This book will help you skim off the froth and see bone marrow bubbling underneath.

Ethics has become an important topic for businesses. Boards of directors and senior executives talk about ESG (environmental, social, and governance standards) and CSR (corporate social responsibility). These topics have emerged so suddenly that many executives find themselves lost figuring out what they should be *doing*—as opposed to what they should be saying—about ethics.

Saying is easy. Here we go: "We are committed to the health of the planet and to employing a diverse workforce." But how do you act on your oughts when you're running a business and have angry shareholders chasing you around the company cafeteria with their proxy votes? When will those entitled Gen Z-ers ever be satisfied with what your company is doing, when it's perfectly clear from your mission statement that your goal is to bring peace and prosperity to the world?

Forget robot dogs. We've got more acute problems.

PART I

PRIMORDIAL MUCK

Ethics of Bureaucracies
The Challenge of Digital Transformation

Nothing is so painful to the human mind as a great and sudden change.
—Mary Shelley, *Frankenstein*

That a person stands there and says the right thing—and so has understood it—and then when he acts does the wrong thing—and so shows that he has not understood it; yes, that is infinitely comical.
—Kierkegaard, *The Sickness unto Death*

The typical narrative of digital transformation goes something like this: The pace of change in business is accelerating wildly. Unfortunately, most traditional businesses have organized themselves for stability and continuity, assuming that change will be rare and exceptional. They've concentrated on becoming as efficient as possible at what they've always done. They've formalized processes, set up governance structures, "right-sized" their staff, and—deliberately or not—erected barriers to diverging from what they're already good at. Over the years, they've accumulated "legacy" technologies that support the way they've always worked. They innovate, but only through a risk-averting governance process that makes sure they don't innovate *too* much.

However, they realize that they are not prepared for the emerging business environment—one characterized by complexity, uncertainty, and rapid change. They fear becoming irrelevant like a Blockbuster or a Kodak. Recognizing the mismatch between the fluid external environment and their stodgy corporate structures, they are eagerly—if awkwardly—adopting the practices of the companies that were brought to life in the digital age, the so-called digital "unicorns," that are better prepared for an environment that's continuously swept by emerging technologies, shifts in customer preferences and expectations, new regulations and deregulations, geopolitical dynamics, public health crises, and climate change.

A traditional company that wants to imitate unicorns needs a "digital transformation"—a deep change in mindset and culture as well as processes and technologies—through which they come to use technology as an enabler of business strategies that depend on adaptation and innovation.

Digital What?

The term *digital transformation* has become confusing as technology companies have crafted marketing messages around it and consultants have twisted it into shapes to fit neatly on PowerPoint slides. Boards of directors, nervously eyeing the survival of their firms and feeling pressure from the capital markets, demand more *transformation* and more *digital* but leave the details to baffled employees. Media outlets with a superficial understanding proffer expert guidance. But the trend is clear enough. In this book I'll use the term as a fuzzy and approximate shorthand for "the stuff that's happening to organizations today, focused on adaptability rather than stability."

The best way to deal with complexity, rapid change, and uncertainty—which have long been factors in the technology world—is through a group of practices we associate with agile IT. These practices include organizing employees into small, empowered, autonomous teams; modernizing IT systems to make them more adaptable; using large amounts of automation; encouraging innovation by testing new ideas quickly in rapid, iterative, learning feedback cycles; and using data to drive decisions. Traditional companies, with their emphasis on planning, stability, deliberation, and control, are at a disadvantage.

Organizing for adaptability is hard enough; companies also have to deal with society's new expectations. As businesses become faster, customers come to expect instant satisfaction, creating pressure for yet more speed. Emerging technologies are rapidly absorbed into the everyday lives of consumers. Deeply interconnected supply chains amplify local difficulties into global crises. The incoming workforce expects a diverse and inclusive workplace. COVID has influenced society in ways that we don't even fully understand.

As they've begun their digital transformations, traditional enterprises have learned some lessons. The first is that it's hard. Successful old-school companies are successful because they've been doing something right, which they struggle to reconcile with "completely transforming" for the new world. Because many of today's ways of working come from technology unicorns, they're framed in terms of process and technology, which makes it easy to miss the deeper organizational and conceptual changes needed. Leaders retreat into vague theory and abstraction—there may be broad agreement across the company on a need to "change culture," "become data-driven," or "deepen customer relationships," but that agreement does not in itself cause any change. That's the bobblehead effect I talked about in *War and Peace and IT*.[1]

But what makes digital transformation especially difficult is that it is not just a change in how businesses do business and technologists do technology, but a deep change in moral outlook and ethical assumptions. Many of today's ethical challenges arise because we retain the ethical stance of bureaucracy while trying to adopt the values of the digital enterprise. Digital transformation doesn't just *raise* ethical issues, it—in itself—*is* an ethical shift.

The Traditional Enterprise

The best way to locate this ethical shift is to be very clear on what we're transforming *from* and what we're transforming *to*. Both are difficult to pin down, for different reasons: it's hard to know the "to" part as it's constantly evolving, and it's hard to know the "from" part because it's so thoroughly ingrained in how we think about businesses that it's almost invisible to us. I'll start with the "from" part.

Traditional businesses, as we've known them for the last couple hundred years, have been based on bureaucratic principles, refined over the twentieth century with "scientific" principles of management. By *bureaucratic*, I don't mean anything negative; in fact, the bureaucratic structure of businesses is something that we've come to expect and value. I'm using the technical, academic definition of bureaucracy, not our everyday sense of it as a frustrating, obstructive, soul-destroying, lumbering Frankenstein creature. The sociologist Max Weber, writing in the early twentieth century, defined bureaucracy as an organizational system with six characteristics: (1) division of labor, (2) hierarchical organization, (3) technical competence, (4) rules, (5) formal, documented communications, and (6) impersonality.*

In *The (Delicate) Art of Bureaucracy*, I grouped these characteristics like this: **rigid roles** (a formal delineation of accountabilities, organized into a hierarchy and filled with people who have the expertise to perform their roles) and **rigid rules** (activities that are determined by rules applied universally and impersonally, with a paper trail that shows the rules have been followed).

> *Is that a pitch for your book?*
> Maybe. I think it's pretty good.
> *Shouldn't you disclose the conflict of interest?*
> Yes.
> *(. . .)*

---

* This is my version of the characteristics Weber talks about in *Economy and Society*.[2] Other writers have their own ways of paraphrasing and organizing them.

By the way, I thought you weren't my conscience.

Agility. I step in where I'm needed. That's a joke.

Good one.

Well, if you're not coercing readers into buying your other book, can you give us the summary? Why do you say that traditional companies are always bureaucracies?

You'll recognize Weber's definition in the way businesses are typically structured. Rigid roles—properties 1, 2, and 3—are just what we call an org chart (property 3 means that the person in each role has the right skills for that role). Properties 4 and 5 say that there are formal mechanisms through which different parts of the org chart interact with one another and with the public, and that those formal interactions are supported by a flow of paper. Even though the flow of paper is now often a flow of online forms, packets of client-server interactions, emails, and texts, it serves the same purpose.

Property 6 is especially interesting, and I'll talk more about it below. Think of it as a principle that the roles in a bureaucracy are independent of the particular people filling them at any moment. An org chart mainly shows the company's organizing principles, though it may also reveal the identities of the people in the roles.

This should sound familiar. Sales is one branch of an org chart and marketing is a different branch. Sales people have sales skills and do sales things; marketing people have marketing skills and do marketing things. They interact through a well-defined mechanism: marketing generates leads and passes marketing-qualified leads (MQLs) to sales. An org chart depicts a hierarchy with increasing authority and accountability toward the top. Traditional companies refine their business processes over time, document them, make them repeatable, and enforce them. They are bureaucracies by definition.

And there's an IT department, divided into functional specialties like development, operations, and security.

Yup.

And I suppose IT interactions are triggered by a flow of helpdesk tickets.

Unfortunately, yes.

Bureaucracy is just a way of organizing social interactions, with advantages and disadvantages. It helps businesses solve challenges of scale, control, and repeatability (think of McDonald's trying to get all of its franchises to make their milkshakes the same way). It allows businesses to comply with regulations and prove to auditors that they are enforcing controls. It lets them fine-tune their processes and make sure employees use them. It even helps them maintain the consistency of their brands by setting rules about how logos will be used, what typefaces their communications will appear in, and what tone their messaging will take.

Weber saw bureaucracy as necessary and beneficial. To him, bureaucracy was

> capable of attaining the highest degree of efficiency and in this sense formally the most *rational* known means of exercising authority over human beings. It is superior to any other form in precision, in stability, in the stringency of its discipline, and in its reliability. . . . The choice is only that between bureaucracy and dilettantism in the field of administration. [emphasis mine][3]

If these positive words seem strange, realize that Weber was writing in a period when rationality was a guiding principle. Bureaucracy was the most logical ("rational") way to set up an efficient organization. Bureaucracies could maintain quality, capture economies of scale, and progress quickly up the experience curve.

The Rise of Bureaucracy

While bureaucracies have existed since ancient times, they became especially important during the industrial revolution, when they crossed over from government to business. As a tool of mass democracy, bureaucracy had provided the necessary legal-rational structure to replace rule by monarchy in the early nineteenth century. As capitalist enterprises grew larger and more global later that century, they borrowed bureaucratic ideas from government to substitute for the firsthand intimacy they had had when smaller.

These new enterprises were—originally, at least—large manufacturers. Bureaucracy, with its emphasis on repeatability, predictability, and processes fine-tuned for efficiency, was a perfect fit for companies with factories at their core. Bureaucracy's division of labor broke down production into its component activities; its rules and formalized interactions helped guarantee repeatability and control quality; its hierarchical structure gave managers at the top a view across all the granular operations that produced the company's outputs. Labor and machinery could be combined into a production process that was . . . well, mechanical.

Weberian bureaucracy has so thoroughly dominated our culture that it's hard for us to imagine any other way of doing things. It's not just our model for businesses and governments, but the way we organize most of our social world—from yacht clubs to criminal gangs to religions and family interactions.

The fact that bureaucracy was the governmental solution for mass democracy is a clue that an ethics lies buried inside it. Another clue is its connection to religious principles, as Weber—our bureaucracy expert—noted in *The Protestant Ethic and the Spirit of Capitalism*: "The phenomenon of the division of labor, and of the structuring of society according to occupation, had already been seen by Thomas Aquinas . . . as the direct result of God's plan for the world."[4]

As I describe each of bureaucracy's values in the next paragraphs, think about how they guide our actions in the workplace and how they might need to change today. I'll show how these values, when brought into the digital world, are responsible for the conflicting ethical imperatives we face.

The Core Bureaucratic Value: Impersonality

Bureaucracy's most important value is contained in property 6—impersonality—which is closely related to values of impartiality, fairness, and justice. Employees and civil servants in bureaucracies are required to perform their roles solely according to the rules and the authorities delegated to their roles, not according to their own feelings or opinions. They are to treat everyone by the same, objective rules. They execute their roles *"sine ira et studio"*—without anger or bias—that is, without personal feelings. As Weber says,

> Bureaucracy develops the more perfectly, the more it is "dehumanized,"
> the more completely it succeeds in eliminating from official business love,
> hatred, and all purely personal, irrational, and emotional elements which
> escape calculation. This is appraised its special virtue by capitalism.[5]

Fairness is seen as a matter of impersonality, which is understandable, since bureaucracy replaced rule by kings and queens. Monarchs are anything but impersonal: "L'état, c'est moi" (The state—that's me!).* They don't need to be fair—they bring their biases to work, fill their governments with friends and relatives, and make up rules whenever they feel like it. If the king thinks all software should be written in Java and you write some in Python, you should expect to find yourself in the Bastille. At the company foosball table, you always let the emperor win.

Bureaucracy is annoying when we don't *want* to be treated according to strict rules. But those rules, executed impersonally, are intended to guarantee equal treatment. A CEO cannot chop employees' heads off, no matter how badly they miss their sales goals. If Rumpelstiltskin is a customer and I am a

---

* Attributed to Louis XIV in a speech to Parliament.

cable provider, I must mystify Rumpelstiltskin with complicated pricing tiers and must not show up for scheduled home visits, just like I do with every other customer.

Bureaucracy is so thoroughly oriented toward fairness that unions love it. When they bargain with management, they are generally looking to *add* bureaucracy: employee cubicles should have such-and-such a size, seniority should be respected in such-and-such a way, and the union must be notified of planned changes in working conditions using such-and-such a form so-and-so number of days in advance.

Employees are asked to "leave themselves at home"; when they show up at the office, they take on their work role and execute it as it has been defined. Bringing personal issues to work is unprofessional. Bringing work home, for most employees, is also a no-no—once an employee leaves work for the day, they no longer have the authority of their role.

This all makes sense when you realize that business bureaucracy was born from a factory model. Work is done in a factory, not at home, because it requires the machinery of production. When you leave the factory each day, you no longer have access to the tools and the assembly line. Work means dedicating yourself some number of hours each day to doing what you've been told to do, no more and no less. Personal concerns just get in the way.

I see where you're going. This is changing in the digital world, isn't it?

Exactly. I'll get to that in a few pages. But first there's more to say about the ethics of bureaucracy. Impersonality is the key, but there are other important values.

Bureaucratic Value: Rationalized Production

Management's goal in the bureaucratic model is to control workers and machines, the factors of production, to achieve the company's objectives efficiently. Henry Ford's analysis showed that of the 7,882 operations required to build a Model T, 670 could be performed by legless men, 2,637 by one-legged men, 2 by armless men, 715 by one-armed men, and 10 by blind men.[6] "Why is it that when I ask for a pair of hands," Ford asked, "a brain comes attached?"[7]

As an important side note, Ford did this analysis in order to be able to employ more people with disabilities. The example shows us both the mechanical nature of rationalized production and the fairness it can provide.

Since the job of employees is more or less mechanical execution, science and engineering are models for continuous improvement. Frederick Taylor, credited with founding "scientific management," sent his assistants to analyze the movements of workers with stopwatches, then—as the story goes—derived the optimal series of motions, standardized and enforced them, and made production more efficient. Actually, he did nothing of the sort, but that's for a later chapter.

In any case, bureaucracy assumes that a scientific, rational approach to designing work leads to the highest degree of efficiency—which is its objective. Yes, it's strange when you think about the mounds of paperwork filled out in triplicate, approvals from bored rubber-stampers, and trolls who pop up now and then to stop work dead, quoting rules conceived two centuries ago. But bureaucracy does not come packaged with the bored rubber stampers—they're just a feature of highly mature bureaucracies.

Even the human aspects of management could be treated as engineering problems. William Whyte's *The Organization Man*, a classic work on bureaucratic corporations from the 1950s, talked about a "social ethic" by which society controls the worker, with "scientism" as its foundation:

> [Scientism] is the practical part of the Social Ethic, for it is the promise that with the same techniques that have worked in the physical sciences we can eventually create an exact science of man. In one form or another, it has had a long and dismal record of achievement; even its proponents readily admit that the bugs are appalling. But this has not shaken the faith in scientism; for it is essentially a Utopian rather than a technical idea.[8]

A Utopian idea, a matter of faith—or, better, a matter of underlying values. Scientism is not a science but a way of engineering social activity to align with the bureaucratic value of rational design for efficiency.

Bureaucratic Value: Neutrality

Bureaucracies have built pyramids, distributed medical supplies, offered housing to the poor—and exterminated Jews during the Nazi Holocaust. Bureaucracy itself is value-neutral: its goal is to find the most rational and efficient way to accomplish whatever goal is given to it.

The "metaphysical heart of rationalism," as Louis Menand states, paraphrasing Isaiah Berlin, is the belief that "all rational ends are commensurable, that unhappiness is caused by the irrational or insufficiently rational, and that when everyone becomes rational and obeys rational laws, human beings will be free."[9] That is the paradoxical, Utopian dream of bureaucracy.

Bureaucratic Value: Owned Time

Between nine a.m. and five p.m., the company owns an employee's time; the employee yields control of their productive capacity to a manager. Though we've grown used to the idea, there's something strange about it. The anthropologist David Graeber points out that for most people throughout history, work was done in spurts, interspersed with periods of relaxation or lighter work. Farming, for example, requires bursts of activity around planting and harvesting, while the rest of the time the effort required is approximately that of watching the grass grow. Medieval serfs probably worked long hours twenty or thirty days a year but just a few hours a day otherwise.[10]

> The idea that one person's time can belong to someone else is actually quite peculiar. First, to think of the potter's capacity to work, his "labor-power," as a thing that was distinct from the potter himself, and second, to devise some way to pour that capacity out, as it were, into uniform temporal containers—hours, days, work shifts—that could then be purchased, using cash. To the average Athenian or Roman, such ideas would have likely seemed weird, exotic, even mystical. How could you buy time?[11]

The idea of buying employees' time implies that any idleness on the part of an employee is not just inefficient—it's actually *immoral*. It is theft, given that the employer is paying for the time.[12]

Nevertheless, employees will try to be idle. Bureaucracies assume that workers are recalcitrant, so managers must oversee them to make sure they stay productive.

Bureaucratic Value: Technical Skills

Bureaucracies value narrow but deep functional skills. Weber believed—with considerable justification—that businesses were becoming increasingly complex and technical. Employees could not be expected to master more than one specialty. That's why the ideal division of labor breaks down activities into technical (functional) specialties and makes sure that the employee hired for each role has adequate functional expertise. That model fit the needs of manufacturing companies during the industrial revolution and fit even better as technologies advanced and grew more complex.

Since each role involves a single functional specialty, the company can write a job description listing the skills it requires and hire the candidate who best demonstrates those skills. This allows a bureaucracy to be meritocratic (that is, fair in hiring and promotion).

Bureaucratic Value: Conformity

Bureaucracies are said to be "faceless." They are indeed, in the sense that work is performed impersonally. They are also faceless in that the people who happen to fill the roles at the moment are irrelevant. And they are faceless because new employees are quickly absorbed and learn to display publicly only the image the company has chosen for them. One employee quoted in Studs Terkel's book *Working*, a collection of over a hundred interviews with employees in a wide range of jobs, says "Who you gonna sock? You can't sock General Motors."[13] A company is an abstraction, not a set of particular people.

Whyte says that the social ethic includes three propositions: a belief in the group as the source of creativity, a belief in belongingness as the ultimate need of the individual, and a belief in the application of science to achieve the belongingness.[14] Conformity is valued. A new employee must adjust to the company, not the reverse. This conformity satisfies the employee's need for belongingness.

Bureaucratic Value: Predictability (Calculability)

Bureaucracy thrives on predictability, or as Weber calls it, *calculability*. A bureaucracy's rules are deterministic; employees know what to expect from their interactions with other parts of the company. Predictability yields a kind of transparency that supports fairness.

Organizational hierarchies pass goals and targets down and results up; making the two match is an obsession. Public companies project quarterly results and must deliver on those expectations, business cases with financial projections are used to make investment decisions and gauge their success, and Gantt charts document milestones that must be adhered to.

The need for predictability explains why innovation is risky: it adds an unknown element into the calculations. Even when innovation is permitted, it tends to be incremental and modest, since the organization optimizes "locally" within each functional area, rather than across the entire enterprise.

Bureaucratic Value: Deference

A bureaucracy is a class system: it distinguishes between senior (strategic) leaders, operational managers, and workers. Senior leaders and middle managers make decisions; workers execute them. "Workers are bodies without minds, managers minds without bodies," as the philosopher Matthew Stewart says in *The Management Myth*.[15] The very way that we draw the org chart—leaders at the top—establishes a pattern of deference to authority. An org chart could, theoretically, be drawn left to right, or with the branches stretching upward.

Senior managers set strategy and operational managers lead its execution—a further class distinction. "Strategic planning is a species of rhetoric—a kind of 'expert talk'—that justifies the power of top management over the middle,"[16] Stewart says. The media glorification of famous CEOs further increases this class distinction between leaders and the people below them in the org chart.

Summary of Bureaucratic Values

The bureaucratic value system is based on impersonality: the idea that employees must leave their personalities, peculiarities, and biases at home and bring to work only the technical skills required for their work roles. Because bureaucracy impersonally applies rules that are the same for everyone, it is demonstrably fair.

Hang on—one point of clarification.

Yes?

You said this was going to be about ethics, but instead you're talking about values. What's the connection?

Technically, values are criteria we use to assess whether a state of affairs is good, while ethics is about how to reach those good states. Think of values as a higher level of abstraction, a step up the ethical org chart. Since there are different ethical frameworks available to us—I'll explain in the next chapter—I'm trying to stay neutral between them by talking about values here.

I see. That helps. But can you give us some idea of how it translates into ethics?

Yeah, I'll give it a try. Here's a loose description of the bureaucratic ethic.

Though we're not quite ready to formalize them, a number of ethical principles follow from the bureaucratic value system I described above. As an employee, you should not bring any of your beliefs, opinions, feelings—or indeed, anything personal—to work. You should execute your role as defined, and demonstrate expertise in your technical function. You should be fair, in the sense of treating everyone the same. You should conform to the organization and dedicate the required period each day to your employer, productively. You should defer to those senior to you in the org chart.

If you are a manager or leader, you should strive to create an efficient and productive organization to accomplish the goals you are given, whatever they are. The company as a whole should efficiently execute on its given objectives, which, in recent practice, are chosen by the owners of the business.* There's more, but these rules are the essence of the bureaucratic ethic.

The Digital Enterprise

A lot has changed—in the business environment, in technology, in our understanding—since the days when mass industrialization made possible the efficient production of bobbleheads. Norms have evolved. History has been written into history books. Service-oriented architectures have become microservice-oriented architectures. Pandemics have led to questioning as well as sneezing. The world looks pretty different from the way it looked when bureaucracy was celebrated by Weber.

First, software, as they say, is eating the world; in truth, shoveling it disgustingly fast down its gullet. Software is agile; it can be changed at any time just by typing on a keyboard, while hardware—physical products—cannot. The companies we interact with every day online make thousands of small, mostly unnoticeable software changes every week. The world moves quickly through software's intestines and turns to . . . yes, well, bullshit is the topic of Chapter 6.

Businesses are caught in a cycle of rapid change. Competitors sprint ahead like gingerbread men and consumers change their preferred vendors in the time it takes an executive to tweet a tasteless joke. Sudden supply chain disruptions require sudden responses. War interferes with offshore software development and causes shortages of essential commodities like bolognese sauce. Increasingly, business demands agility, which I define as the ability to respond to change quickly, creatively, cheaply, and at low risk.

Second, our model for business success has become the entrepreneurial venture. It's no longer the tycoons who run huge manufacturing enterprises we admire and hate, but the creative, aggressive, and emotionally unstable outsiders who create something quickly from nothing—the Victor Frankensteins. The American Dream is no longer about slow steps to tycoonship but a sudden leap to gazillionaireship.

I'll call it *The Leprechaun Theory*, the idea that we become prosperous by following a moody, untrustworthy, sometimes unpleasant CEO who will lead us to a pot of gold at the end of a rainbow.

---

* According to the Friedman Doctrine, which I discuss in Chapter 4.

Third, jobs in advanced economies have shifted toward "knowledge work," services, and administration rather than factory work. Technologists—software developers, digital designers, and so on—don't produce identical products like a factory does, and their work doesn't always involve repeatable processes.

And fourth, mom and pop are messing with our economy.

Mom and Pop

Thomas Dunfee, professor of legal studies and business ethics at Wharton, suggests that we are now in a Marketplace of Morals (MOM), where consumers act under the influence of their moral preferences. Eighty-seven percent of consumers say they would purchase a product because a company advocated for an issue close to their hearts.[17] Ethical preferences get priced into goods; companies that satisfy those preferences can command a markup. Customers may even boycott companies that don't meet their ethical standards. In a MOM, the ordinary principles of a market economy still apply, but ethical reputation must be factored in as a driver of customer behavior.

Job seekers make similar trade-offs—they may be willing to take lower pay to work for a company that meets their ethical standards or refuse to work for one that doesn't. Once in the workplace, they act on their values. Global warming is a serious threat to young workers who intend to live forever as medical innovations appear. Born to rapid change, they're impatient to solve the world's social problems.

Cutely, Dunfee defines a POP, or Passion of Propriety, to be a preference consumers display in a MOM. POPs are not necessarily positive—some may support racial, religious, ethnic, or gender discrimination. But because of MOMs and POPs, businesses operate in an economic environment structured with ethical considerations. His conclusion is that "we should always pay attention to what MOM tells us. We should respect and appreciate MOM."[18]

As we move away from the factory model toward a leprechaun economy of rapid change with morality embedded in it, the values of bureaucratic organizations seem a poor fit. Let's compare the emerging digital values with the bureaucratic values above.

Digital Values

Impersonality versus Inclusion

The primary value of bureaucracy—impersonality—is breaking down. As work becomes less mechanical and better suited to bodies that come with brains attached, impersonality is both less important and less feasible. Instead, we value inclusivity. Work groups benefit from members who arrive to work with actual personalities. Progressive Insurance's website, for example, says "Just as we're committed to bringing our name to life each day, we celebrate our employees for bringing their true selves to work in every way."[19]

"Bringing their true selves to work in every way"—note that within a bureaucratic ethic, that is highly unethical!

Employees who leave themselves at home deny their employers the benefit of the synergies, the 1+1>2 value, that comes when you combine people with real differences into teams. Innovation happens faster and better in a diverse team—which matters because, given the speed of the digital economy, competitive advantages are ephemeral. A bureaucratic organization, on the other hand, with its ideal of facelessness, tries to trim away differences, leaving only what is specified in a role description.

Of course, it's difficult to *avoid* bringing yourself to work today, because work has come to your home. Since the beginning of the pandemic employees have regularly hosted colleagues in their homes by video. Pets participate in board meetings. Adorable children join team discussions to be adored.

The distinction between work and personal *time* has also dissolved. We recognize that our colleague Rumpelstiltskin will receive unexpected visits from the cable company, and that coworkers will adjust their schedules based on their childcare responsibilities. We hold meetings at odd hours to accommodate colleagues in distant time zones and take advantage of our more energetic moments, whatever time of day they come, to grind through backlogs of work.

Rationalized Production versus Continuous Innovation

The goal of work is no longer just efficient, repeatable production. Before WWII, only 18% of jobs in the US required high discretion. By 1982, it was 43%, and by 2000, 62%.[20] Automation has replaced many manual workers, while professional, managerial, clerical, sales, and service workers tripled between 1910 and 2000, from one-quarter to three-quarters of total employment.[21]

It's not that efficiency is unimportant, but that leanness (short lead times) and innovation are more directly tied to business results. The value produced by an organization depends not just on the quantity and productivity of labor, but on new factors such as the availability and usability of its data. Since productivity no longer determines success, it can no longer be the measure of employee contribution.

Neutrality versus Care

While bureaucracy is neutral with respect to ends, workers today are often invested in the outcomes of their labor and emotionally connected with the consequences of their efforts. The workplace is no longer a neutral machine—it is a place where equity may be lacking, where diversity and inclusion should be encouraged, where the supply chain must be examined for fair wages and working conditions. Employees have become activists; caring workers care about whether the result of their labor is the production of children's learning toys or efficient genocide.

Feminist economic theory points out that most work has always been "caring labor," work directed at other people, involving a certain amount of interpretation, empathy, and understanding. Even the workers building a bridge, as David Graeber says in *Bullshit Jobs*, reflect on the social value of their work—making it possible for people to cross the river.[22]

Dedicated Time versus Dedicated Efforts

Workers in a digital enterprise are not constrained by a need for factory machinery. There is nothing magic about the eight-hour, nine-to-five day—it's a historical accident.

Since an employee is obligated to do the best job they can for their employer, they *should* work whenever and wherever they can work most effectively. "Production" of innovative ideas may happen best when an employee is taking a shower, gargling, or feeding the labradoodle. It may happen in meetings with people in distant time zones at odd hours of the day. It may very well *not* happen during official working hours when writer's block or blood sugar levels interfere. Adjusting schedules to maximize productivity is not "theft" of time that the employer "owns." On the contrary, it can be the act of a truly dedicated employee.

While it's true that workers who are treated like machines may maximize their personal utility by working as little or as unenthusiastically as possible, workers who *care* maximize their utility by accomplishing meaningful results. Overcoming recalcitrance is no longer the main function of management.

Technical Skills versus Generalist Skills

Bureaucracy values specific functional (technical) skills to cope with increasing complexity. Unfortunately, businesses have found that the division of labor requires hand-offs between silos, which introduces waste and slowness. Digital organizations instead organize into cross-functional teams that take complete responsibility for their outputs. Although Weber was right that technology continues to become more complex, layers of simplification often make it surprisingly more manageable.

Cross-functional teams thrive when members have generalist skills—the ideal employee is said to be "T-shaped," with broad skills as well as a particular area they have deep knowledge of. Flattened hierarchies also benefit from generalist skills, as managers can oversee a broader range of disciplines. Innovation is more likely among generalists, who bring metaphors and analogies from other disciplines to reframe challenges in unexpected ways. Agility increases when an organization employs generalists, since they can be reassigned as the company's needs change. So, while specialization is essential to bureaucracy, generalist skills are valuable to a digital organization.

Conformity versus Contribution

Bureaucracies are afraid that people will bring their biases to work. Digital organizations don't value biases, exactly, but they do value human differences, backgrounds, and experiences for the contributions they can make. Where bureaucracies value conformity—that is, erasing differences—digital organizations value harnessing and synthesizing differences.

Employees are no longer like factory machinery that can easily be replaced. The idea of interchangeable parts—an important enabler of the machine age—doesn't apply to people. Instead of a factory model of labor, we now have something closer to an artisan model.

Deference versus Impeccability

Managing has become less about demonstrating authority and demanding obedience from recalcitrant employees. With productivity as the sole metric, it was easier for managers to know how their actions would affect results. But with more ambiguous goals—innovation, employee retention, customer satisfaction, and a broad range of squishier objectives—the best way for managers to get results is through experimentation, support for the creativity of teams, and feedback loops.

We've come to realize that organizations are complex adaptive systems in which traditional management techniques don't necessarily provide leaders the "control" they expect. Instead, behavior is emergent and organic. Employees and workgroups have their own beliefs and desires, their own strategies for competing and cooperating with other employees.

The ideal employee demonstrates *contribution*, rather than obedience. It is through acting impeccably, taking responsibility and acting on it creatively and with purpose, that an employee serves the interests of their employer.

Predictability versus Adaptability

Success in the digital world comes from fluidity, responsiveness, and creative adaptation. Predictability is less important and in many cases impossible or undesirable. In a fast-changing environment, initiatives whose requirements are determined upfront and rigidly adhered to are risky, while short, incremental efforts, adjusted with constant feedback, reduce risk and increase the pace of returns.

Managers and employees have had to become better at handling uncertainty, working with rough estimates, and making decisions quickly with incomplete information.

Summary:
Conflict of Values

A traditional organization, as Whyte says, believes that "conflict, change, fluidity—these are the evils from which man should be insulated."[23] In the digital organization these are the essence of the job. A digital organization accepts that the world is probabilistic, unpredictable, disorderly, and uncertain. Because of this difference in worldviews, the two types of organizations have different values, and their participants have different ethical obligations. (See Table 1.1 on page 20.)

Through the book, I'll refer to the older kind of enterprise and its value system as the "traditional" or "bureaucratic" enterprise, and the new kind—for lack of a better name—as the "digital" enterprise. The challenge for digital transformation leaders is to reconcile the two conflicting value systems, for the values of bureaucracy have influenced us more than we think.

Now we need to leave the topic of digital transformation and take a little detour into the world of ethics. The questions we'll try to answer are: How does one know what's ethically correct? If we're not consulting stone tablets, how do we justify our choices? I'm going to give a brief history of philosophical approaches to ethics, and perhaps surprise you and my former philosophy professors by showing that some of them share the bureaucratic mindset.

Table 1.1: Values

Traditional Bureaucratic Organization	Digital Organization
Impersonality (Leave Yourself at Home)	Inclusion (Bring Yourself to Work)
Rationalized Production	Continuous Innovation
Neutrality	Care
Owned Time	Owned Efforts
Functional Skills	Generalist Skills
Conformity	Contribution
Deference	Impeccability
Predictability	Adaptability

Bureaucracies of Ethics
An Age of Bureaucratic Enlightenment

Ye cannot live for yourselves; a thousand fibres connect you with your fellow-men, and along those fibres, as along sympathetic threads, run your actions as causes, and return to you as effects.
> —Henry Melvill, "Partaking in Other Men's Sins"

With a stiff seriousness that inspires laughter, all our philosophers demanded something far more exalted, presumptuous, and solemn from themselves as soon as they approached the study of morality: they wanted to supply a rational foundation for morality.
> —Nietzsche, *Beyond Good and Evil*

An odd question: Is there such a thing as an agile ethics? Not an ethics that changes when it's convenient. Not a way for companies to rationalize bad behavior by changing the standards under which they are judged. I mean agile in the same sense that Agile software delivery constantly learns and adapts to changing circumstances. Agile software teams don't change requirements just for convenience; they modify requirements as they learn and as their environment changes—with a consistent vision or business goal in mind. Agile techniques work well with rapid change and uncertainty. Are there ethical frameworks that similarly fit well with the demands of the digital age?

Traditional, bureaucratic thinking assumes that we have a pretty good grasp on the future, even if we don't foresee it exactly. Since predictability, or calculability, is valued, planning is important. Bureaucracies take advantage of their prescience to formulate generalized rules that can apply into the future as well as the present. An ethics of shalts and shalt-nots therefore fits nicely with bureaucratic thinking.

Digital thinking accepts that there is plenty of uncertainty and complexity, so rather than relying on plans and rules, it favors learning and adjusting. For an ethical framework, it seems to need an evolutionary, learning approach without the kind of fixed rules that fall apart under complexity and change.

In other words, an ethical approach that accepts that we don't know enough today to decide how we should behave toward robots once they someday start drinking too much tequila reposado.

The good news: Philosophers have been arguing about ethics ever since they left their university campuses for lunch and noticed that they shared the world with other people. As a result, we have many years worth of ethical frameworks and arguments we don't need to rehash. That's what this chapter is about—the reusable code, so to speak, that we'll build on in later chapters. In this chapter and the next, I'll examine some of the classical ideas of ethical thought through an agile or digital lens, and enjoy seeing how they fail fast.

The Age of Enlightenment

Something strange happened to ethics during the Age of Enlightenment in the late seventeenth and eighteenth centuries. Until then, through most of human existence, ethics was about what it meant to be a good person: what character traits would lead to a good life, a life of "flourishing." It was not about rules of behavior but about personal attributes. There were exceptions, like the rules of the Ten Commandments or anything the pharaoh told you to do, but these were more in the nature of guardrails, not guides to everyday action. Aside from the commandments, even the Bible was mainly about what it meant to be a good or bad person, with plenty of illustrative examples.

During the Enlightenment, the focus suddenly shifted. The question was now "In x kind of situation, what should I do?" rather than "What kind of a person is a good person?" Philosophers wanted to find a rational basis for ethical decision-making. Is it okay for a monk to steal office supplies from the monastery? Ought I empty my chamber pot in the street? Should we burn witches or should we burn celebrity bloggers? Earlier versions of ethics assumed that a good person would naturally do the right things; Enlightenment ethics wanted to formulate rules that would tell us what "the right things" were.

This was consistent with the general character of the Enlightenment. It was an age of faith—faith in logic and science, that is. Individuals would no longer just accept dogma from the church or rely on wisdom from Ancient Greek jokes. By the time of the Enlightenment, there was no longer broad consensus on what it meant to live a good life—it was no longer simply to play a part in storming Troy or to graduate into a less scorching post-life. The one thing people agreed on was that math and science were pretty good, as long as you didn't have to learn them in school, so philosophers naturally looked to reason to disclose and justify ethical norms.

There was also a subtle change in the purpose of ethics. In the ancient world, the goal of behaving ethically was to have a good life—the word used was *eudaemonia*, which means something like happiness, flourishing, prosperity, or blessedness. In Greek heroic society, one achieved eudaemonia by taking one's proper place in society and living virtuously, which earned honor and respect from others. Behaving ethically meant collaborating to create a thriving society, with eudaemonia for all. There was therefore a strong distinction between what was "in" and "out" of society; ethics was about acting *within* the society. For those outside the society of the city-state—strangers—the ethical rules didn't apply: Aristotle is said to have told his student Alexander the Great to treat Greeks as friends and family, but barbarians as animals and plants.[1]

In the Enlightenment, the main goal of ethics was no longer to have a happy life, perhaps because a strain of asceticism had crept into Western thinking. Instead, ethics centered on rules to resolve conflict between people who naturally had competing objectives. The seventeenth-century English philosopher Thomas Hobbes reasoned that if everyone followed only their own interests, they would live in a constant state of strife . . . which is against their own interests.[2] Rational creatures, therefore, must adopt some norms that would allow everyone to live together. This was, incidentally, the context for Adam Smith's idea of a free market that would "invisibly" adapt through the mechanism of price to resolve the natural competition we'd expect from people acting in their own interests.

Ethics, then, was about doing things you *don't want* to do, but have to because you share the world with other people. To Immanuel Kant, an act is ethical only if it is done from duty, rather than for one's own benefit. This is rather different from the essentially positive Ancient Greek concept of acting to achieve honor and eudaemonia or the medieval notion of behaving ethically to book into a five-star afterlife.*

In an amazing absence of coincidence, these changes in ethical thought happened at about the same time as the rise of bureaucracy in governments and newly industrializing companies. Kant was formulating the concepts of Enlightenment ethics in the last quarter of the eighteenth century, precisely when the turbines of the Industrial Revolution started whirring, while the English were busy installing bureaucracy into the operating system of India and Napoleon was about to begin upgrading France's code.

---

* I don't want to overstate this point, because utilitarianism, which came a bit later, was still about happiness for all. But that's a bit different from the joint happiness that was the goal in Ancient Greece; utilitarianism allows for different and even competitive goals.

Both bureaucracy and the Enlightenment ethical tradition tried to rationalize behavior through fixed, general rules or algorithms that can be applied to decision-making. But as the leader of a transformation you might have noticed that rule-based ethics—if you can even find the right rules on those dusty stone tablets—can be hard to apply.

Our Oughts and Other Oughts

I lied when I said that ethics is the discipline of "oughts," which I ought not do, so I'll set the record straight here. Ethics doesn't care about every kind of "ought." For instance, we're not talking about etiquette. I still can never remember whether the fork ought to go to the left or the right of the plate and whether I ought to seat prime ministers or presidents closer to a dinner's host. The Renaissance *Book of the Courtier*, a discussion of how a proper friend to a prince or political leader ought to behave, straddles the fields of ethics and etiquette. It advises courtiers to "leave [other activities] on one side: such as turning summersaults, rope-walking, and the like, which savour of the mountebank and little befit a gentleman."[3] We will not discuss summersaults or rope-walking in this book.

To be inclusive, I will also exclude Confucian guidance on table manners: "Do not roll the rice into a ball; do not bolt down the various dishes; do not swill down the soup . . ."[4] And we definitely won't concern ourselves with Hesiod's imperative "Do not stand upright facing the sun when you make water, but remember to do this when he has set towards his rising."[5] We work from home today, not in the fields, and anyway, WTF?

While these are all undoubtedly important oughts and ought nots, we'll distinguish them from ethics, which focuses more on principles that underlie moral choice. There is no principle from which we can conclude that forks belong on the left . . . or the right . . . whichever.*

As fun as it might be, we also ought to avoid talking about unusual taboos, except in this paragraph. In parts of Madagascar, you shouldn't sing while eating, skin a banana with your teeth, point at a tomb, or kick the walls of your house. Pregnant women shouldn't eat eels or step over an axe. But do definitely call newborn babies ugly and compare them to pigs or dogs.[7] These kinds of taboos may once have been related to ethics, but as with some of the taboos of Deuteronomy, the context in which they made sense has been lost.[8]

---

* Left . . . unless it's a dessert fork. Apparently, for a long time forks were only used to stabilize food to be cut by the knife, not to convey food to the mouth. You did that with a knife.[6]

Oddly, starting in the late seventeenth century, immorality came to mean sexual laxity.[9] I have no explanation for this.

Um, I think you've digressed. Just like that stuff on silly laws.
I know. But authors work hard and need some fun.
Can I point out something else?
Sure.
I'm afraid you're going to confuse readers. Sometimes you're saying "I" and talking about yourself. Sometimes you're saying "you" and talking to the readers. Sometimes you're saying "we" as if you're one of them. It's a bit of a mess.
Yeah, it's deliberate. I'm hoping to bring readers along as I think through these things myself. But did you have a suggestion?
Could you at least say something like "I'm going to put on my consumer hat now" or "I'm going to put on my business hat now"?
I hate clichés like that. I suppose you're right. Okay, but I'll do it my way.

Rules and Consequences

So let's put on our Enlightenment head coverings (tricornes made from beaver, silk top hats, or shepherdess hats) and look at ethics rationally. Say you're on the verge of making an ethical decision. Rationally speaking, there are two ways you might evaluate your options: you can choose the act that would have the best consequences, or you can identify an ethical rule that applies and act on it—regardless of the consequences. In other words, you can consider the expected results or you can defer to universal *principles*.

You can certainly imagine these approaches yielding different answers. For example, there may be a rule that you shouldn't murder people, and yet you believe that doing away with Immanuel Kant will benefit society, since philosophy students to the end of time will not have to spend hours trying to decode his unreadable prose. Whether you believe ethical behavior should be determined by rules or by consequences will determine whether Kant can continue eating his spaetzle.

These two approaches to ethics have names. The first is called *consequentialism*—meaning, you know, that it's the consequences that matter. It actually came along somewhat after the Enlightenment, with the utilitarian philosophy of Jeremy Bentham. The second is called *deontology*—meaning that philosophers don't want anyone to know what they're talking about. We could just as well call it *duty ethics*, because that's what deontology means in Greek. But we'll sound like we paid attention in philosophy class if we say *deontology*.

Just mentioning those terms brings to mind the sound of a trolley.

Hurtling Trolleys

You're not really going to do trolley problems?

Yes. Why not?

Talk about philosophical clichés. And the problems are so artificial. No reader has good answers, so it just makes them feel stupid.

I'll be gentle.

Trolley problems help us get a handle on our intuitions about ethical matters. They were first proposed by the English philosopher Philippa Foot in 1967 and have been exuberantly overcomplicated by ethicists ever since. But no more delay—there's a trolley hurtling down a track and we must decide what to do about it!

Do trolleys really hurtle? That's not the question. You're standing nearby, you see it hurtling by, and you have to make a quick decision. Three oblivious people are sitting on the trolley track enjoying a picnic lunch of pastrami on rye with mayo—and the trolley is going to hit them and destroy their lives and sandwiches. But—there's a switch right next to where you're standing, and if you flip the switch the trolley will be diverted onto another track and it won't harm the sandwiches. Should you flip the switch?

"Yes" is the correct answer if your values are different from Attila the Hun's. I'll assume that's what you said. But now suppose that on this alternate track there's an innocent person delicately nibbling some avocado toast. If you pull the switch you'll save the three people but kill the innocent person, who has just spilled kombucha on their shirt. Pull the switch? Take a photo for your Instagram feed? Replace trolleys with gas-guzzling automobiles that will destroy the planet?

You might reason that destroying one sandwich is better than destroying three, so you should still pull the switch. That would be *consequentialist* thinking. Even so, you might still have a few points of discomfort. What if the three folks are on a picnic from a retirement community, in their nineties, suffering from terminal diseases, and the person on the other track is a Nobel prize winner who is working to bring peace to the world?

Are you *obligated* to pull the switch, or is it just an *acceptable* option? Do the three people deserve to die because pastrami should be eaten with mustard, not mayo, and in any case what kind of just-asking-for-it former species-perpetuators eat lunch on trolley tracks? Remember what Darwin said.

Say you've decided to pull the switch and save three people at the cost of avocado toast person. Fine, I've got another question for you, because that's how trolley problems work. Once again, we've got a hurtling trolley, and once again the people are, for some reason, eating pastrami sandwiches on the trolley tracks. This time you are standing on an overpass next to the track, meditating upon the impending upending of the sandwiches. You notice that next to you on the overpass there's a large man—a very large man (sorry, no offense to any body shapes, that's just the way the story has to go)—and you realize that he's leaning too far over the railing and if you push him off the overpass he'll land right on the trolley tracks and stop the trolley from hurtling towards the pastrami people. Unfortunately, the large man will be killed. Should you push him?

If—like many people—you don't think it's right to push Large Larry off the bridge but thought it was okay to kill avocado person, you might be challenged to figure out the difference. In both cases you are killing one person to save three, and in the case of the large man, not even destroying a sandwich in the process. Perhaps you sense that it's not just a matter of consequences, but that a rule of some sort enters the picture—something you are forbidden to do, despite the positive consequences. If so, you might actually be a *deontologist*.

Spoiler alert: just as you know that Frankenstein—not Frankenstein, the creature—will keep reappearing throughout *Frankenstein*—not Frankenstein, the book—and doing bad things, you know this trolley problem is going to come back later in this book, so keep it in mind.

Was that okay?
Not bad. I've never heard it with sandwiches before.
It's what happens when I write just before lunch.

Consequentialism

An *act consequentialist* believes you should always make ethical decisions by choosing the action that has the best consequences.

But what exactly are "the best consequences"? The best in what way? The classic *utilitarian* version of consequentialism, from Jeremy Bentham, says that we're trying to maximize happiness and minimize unhappiness, and for Bentham, happiness meant pretty much the same thing as pleasure. It's not just the happiness of the actor that matters (except to *ethical egoists*) but the aggregate happiness of everyone affected (pastrami eaters, avocado toast person, and whoever has to clean up the mess).

Actually, a full-fledged act consequentialist believes that it is *only* the outcomes that matter, and that a person is morally *required* to perform the action with the best consequences.[10] In the case of our runaway trolley, we must choose to kill one person rather than three because that maximizes total happiness. If you are a software tester, you'll probably point out that dead people are neither happy nor unhappy, but I am not a software tester. Aristotle himself might have made a good tester, as he asks: "Can someone really be happy during the time after he has died? Surely that is altogether strange, especially when we say happiness is an activity?"[11] He's right—it's one of my favorite activities. I might even call it a hobby.

Something seems a bit off with Bentham's idea, though—should Genghis Khan's pleasure in "outraging" people be counted the same as a naturalist's pleasure in saving cute baby pandas from extinction? The nineteenth-century English philosopher J. S. Mill fixed that problem by distinguishing between "higher" and "lower" pleasures,[12] with the higher ones objectively better than the lower—for example, the pleasure that you get from caring for lepers is better than the pleasure you get from popping cells of bubble wrap.

Consequentialism is served in many flavors. A *preference consequentialist* thinks that it's not so much about happiness but about satisfying people's preferences, so if they prefer pain, that's what they should get. An *egalitarian consequentialist* thinks we should be fair by giving more incremental happiness to people who don't have much of it already, like philosophy students. A philosopher like Arthur Schopenhauer would focus more on reducing unhappiness than on increasing happiness because—well—Schopenhauer is known for saying things like "Work, worry, toil, and trouble are certainly the lot of almost all throughout their lives."[13]

You get the idea. These are all consequentialist ethics—outcomes are what matter, and you should maximize the something-or-other. Consequentialism, like good bureaucracy, is impartial and impersonal—Mill says, "As between his own happiness and that of others, utilitarianism requires him to be as strictly impartial as a disinterested and benevolent spectator."[14] Or as the philosopher Henry Sidgwick put it, a utilitarian must consider "the point of view of the universe" rather than that of a particular person.[15]

You IT people have probably already noticed that consequentialism turns ethics into a linear optimization problem. That's not news—Bentham himself proposed a "felicific calculus," an equation you could plug happiness values into. Happiness is measured in units called *hedons* and unhappiness either in *dolors* or negative hedons. Bentham's formula included seven variables for calculating "hedonic utility": a pleasure's intensity, duration, certainty, propinquity, fecundity, purity, and extent.[16]

Now let's put on our digital deerstalker hats to see if consequentialism is a good way to make ethical decisions in the digital world.

Spoiler alert: no.

Problem of the Unknown Future

A central principle of the digital age is that because of the pace and complexity of change, the future is quite unknowable. As a result, says Shannon Vallor, philosophy professor at Edinburgh University, "the problem of discerning which course of action promises the greatest overall happiness or the least harm—among all the novel paths of biomedical, mechanical, and computational development open to us—is simply incalculable."[17] Even if you are an ethical egoist, you've still got a problem—do you even know what course of action will make *you* happiest in the future?[18]

Problems with the Evaluation Function

This next one is for the nerds. Should we maximize the *total* amount of happiness, or the *average*? If the total, then we'd prefer a world of 100 billion people who are slightly happy to a world with 7 billion people who are ecstatic. Because consequentialism *requires* us to choose the path that maximizes happiness, we must therefore have lots of babies, as long as each baby stands a chance of being slightly happy. Or, based on the opposite assumption, "Would not everyone rather feel so much sympathy for the coming generation that he would prefer to spare it the burden of existence?" asks Schopenhauer . . . as Schopenhauer would.[19]

If you think it's better to maximize average happiness, think again.[20] You would then have to agree that having only one extremely happy person—say, Mr. Genghis—is better than having a thousand only slightly happy people. A good way to raise the average happiness is to kill all the unhappy people.[21] Consequentialist ethics has some bugs, no matter what language you code it in.

Problem of Chuck

Let's say that you're a surgeon and you have four patients, each of whom needs an organ transplant to survive. And let's say that each of them needs a different organ: one needs a heart, one a kidney, one a lung, and one an islet of Langerhans.* You also have a healthy patient named Chuck,†[22] and it occurs to you that if you kill Chuck and take his organs, you can keep the other four patients alive. Should you chop up Chuck? Presumably, a consequentialist would have to say yes—but I don't think you'll find that in your medical ethics textbook.

---

* Yes, it's a thing. You should trust me by now. It's in your pancreas, if you care to look.
† It's Shelley Kagan who refers to him as Chuck, though the example predates Kagan.

You might recognize this as the trolley problem in disguise, where Chuck is the large man on the overpass. Our intuitions seem to require something beyond consequentialism, some sort of prohibition against doing certain bad things to Chuck even while we're maximizing happiness. So that leads us to deontology, ethics based on duties and rules.

Duty Ethics (Deontology)

Duty ethics is more like the rule-based ethics you might have thought this book would be about. A deontologist may believe that there are rules against chopping up Chuck or tossing Large Larry off the overpass. Commonly accepted rules are things like "it's wrong to kill people" or "it's wrong to set babies on fire just for entertainment" or "it's wrong to inject SQL code into a text field even if the dumbass programmer lets you do it."* The nine-to-five job of a deontologist is to come up with a justifiable set of rules.

In digital transformation, a deontological approach would be to derive a set of rules that we ought to follow in deciding whether to appropriate people's private data or unleash machine learning on helpless retirement community residents. For example: never sell a customer's personal data without their permission, always maximize shareholder value as long as you aren't violating any laws, or never put mayo on a pastrami sandwich. Ethics would be a matter of consulting the rules or hiring McKinsey to put them onto PowerPoint slides.

The classic version of deontology is that of Immanuel Kant. We need to discuss Kant's theory here because, after all, this is IMMANUEL KANT, the Enlightenment philosopher with the authoritative voice who clearly said IMPORTANT THINGS because his prose is hard to understand.

Kant begins by pointing out—as we did above—that the moral worth of an action can't depend on its consequences, because those are uncertain. The goodness of an act can only depend on intention. In fine Kantian prose:

> An action done from duty derives its moral worth, not from the purpose which is to be attained by it, but from the maxim by which it is determined, and therefore does not depend on the realization of the object of the action, but merely on the principle of volition by which the action has taken place.[23]

---

* So-called SQL injections are a common technique used by hackers to compromise IT security.

By *maxim*, Kant means the principle or rule that was used in choosing the action. Behaving ethically means acting from duty by applying the right maxim. Since intention is what matters, an act is only ethical if you are doing it *because* it is your duty. The philosopher Alisdair MacIntyre points out that "the injunctions of morality, thus understood, are likely to be ones that human nature, thus understood, has strong tendencies to disobey."[24] Acting ethically in Kant's world is meant to be hard, thus understood.

Next, Kant distinguishes between *hypothetical* imperatives—things you should do because they are the right way to accomplish a goal you have—and *categorical* imperatives—things everyone should do in all cases just because they're the right thing to do. A true ethical law must be categorical. Since a categorical law should hold for every rational being, it must be derived from the general concept of a rational being[25]—in other words, every rational person who thought about it while appropriately caffeinated would derive the same law, because it is a law of reason. Kant states what he believes to be the one categorical-imperative-to-rule-them-all in three different forms. The first version, which we'll call CIv1, is this:

Act only on that maxim whereby thou canst at the same time will that it should become a universal law.[26]

By universal law, he means a law that would apply to all y'all,* in all cases. You should always act for reasons that could serve as acceptable reasons for anyone.[27] So, remembering that what matters is the principle you act on, Kant is asking that you take the principle you're about to apply, try to universalize it—that is, make it a rule that everyone should follow—and see if it is a rule you could want to be in effect.

You'll notice that what Kant has done (so far) is not to supply any rules but to supply a test case for rules (maxims). You can act on any rule, as long as it passes his test. For example, if you are thinking of lying to someone because telling them the truth would get you in trouble, then presumably the maxim you are using is "I should lie whenever it is convenient for me." To determine whether that's an acceptable maxim, universalize it: "Everyone should lie whenever it's convenient for them," and ask yourself whether you would wish for such a rule to be in effect.

Don't bother thinking about it—I've read Kant and the answer is no. Among the maxims that Kant considers acceptable are "Always tell the truth,"

---

* I'm told by my niece who lives in Texas that this is the plural, and y'all is singular

"Always keep promises," "Be benevolent to those in need," and "Do not commit suicide."[28]

Kant's principle seems pretty close to the Golden Rule—"do unto others as you would have them do unto you," but has a few notable differences. First, Kant is able to justify his rule *logically*—it's the only rational categorical law. Secondly, in CIv1 it's not a specific action that has to pass his test, but the generalized principle by which the action is chosen. Thirdly, it avoids the question of individual peculiarities: a masochist following the golden rule might conclude that it's okay to cause pain. CIv1 doesn't just ask whether you like pain, but whether it would be reasonable to wish that everyone acted according to a principle of always causing pain.

So, digital decision makers: If you are walking down an office hallway and you notice that one of your coworkers has a nicer desk chair than yours, should you steal it? If you did, you'd be acting under the maxim "Always steal things that are nicer than the things you have." Can you generalize that and wish that it was a rule everyone should follow? No—it wouldn't make any sense. It would require that other people who have ugly chairs steal that same chair from you! No work would get done, because no one would have a place to sit very long. The hallways would be packed with people rolling desk chairs around. And since you're working from home, your spouse and your cat would not be happy.

Kant's second version of the CI, CIv2, sounds different, but he claims that all three of his versions are "fundamentally only so many formulae of the self-same law, one of which of itself unites the other two within it."[29] Don't argue. Here's CIv2:

> Beings whose existence depends not on our will but on nature's, have nevertheless, if they are irrational beings, only a relative value as means, and are therefore called things; rational beings, on the contrary, are called persons, because their very nature points them out as ends in themselves. . . . Accordingly the practical imperative will be as follows: *So act as to treat humanity, whether in thine own person or in that of any other, in every case as an end withal, never as means only.* [emphasis mine][30]

I can clarify this. *Things* don't have goals: they're just tools for us to use. People, however, are "ends in themselves" who make their own decisions on what to value. Things don't do that, except in scary movies. You're therefore free to "use" things, because they really don't care. But do not treat people solely as a means to your own ends. The same reason you have for thinking of yourself as not being a tool for others is the reason you shouldn't think of others as tools. To think of yourself as an exception, or to act for reasons that you wouldn't accept from other people, would be immoral.

It's okay—note—to treat other people as a means. You do that all the time; signing a contract is a way of using someone as a means to achieving your ends. What you should not do is use them merely as a means, as if they were an object.

I'm not seeing how CIv1 and CIv2 are versions of the same rule.

Me neither. I'll get us out of this by doing some authorial hand-waving and saying, "Both are about treating everyone else as a rational creature, just as you are."

Okay, good enough.

Authors have certain powers over their readers. See Chapter 8 on manipulation.

You said that there were three versions of the CI?

Yes, but I'm going to follow long precedent in the philosophy world and completely ignore the third one, CIv3.

Now let's see why deontology might not be a great fit for an ethics of digital transformation.

Gaps Between Rules

Any given set of rules is probably not going to cover all the cases we need guidance on. In *Ties That Bind*, Wharton professors that Thomas Dunfee and Thomas Donaldson say, "One can only imagine Immanuel Kant's response if he walked into the modern equivalent of a drawing room and was asked, 'Professor Kant, how does the Categorical Imperative apply to hostile takeovers, or to software piracy?'"[31] The CI's guidance is also notably unclear when we consider possibly-sentient creatures like robots. Are they ends in themselves? If we can't lie to humans, can we lie to robots?

In Shannon Vallor's words, "The world does not give us advance notice of every kind of moral scenario it might throw at us, and there is no definitive moral playbook that tells us in advance how to read or respond to any situation."[32]

Rules Are Too General

When someone states an ethical rule, they're probably forgetting all the edge cases. Most of us believe in a rule that says it's wrong to kill people. But how about in self-defense? In a war? What if they consent to being killed, as in the case of euthanasia? Is turning off a life-support system an example of "killing" someone, or just failing to prolong their life? What if the person is about to commit a terrible harm, like overcooking their ferrazzuoli?

Rules Conflict

When more than one rule applies, rule-based systems, categorical in nature, don't give us a way to reconcile them.* Everyday ethics, as I said in the Introduction, is not about good and evil, but about resolving conflicting imperatives. You might have a duty to feed your children and a duty not to steal. A duty to rescue someone who is drowning and a duty to keep your rented tux dry. Should we release facial recognition software that can be used to rescue kidnapped children, if it can be used by authoritarian governments to spy on citizens?

Uncertainty Resurfaces

Deontology, like consequentialism, has trouble with uncertainty. We can solve the problem of chopping up Chuck by invoking a rule against doing harm. But how does that rule apply to cases where there is only a risk of doing harm?[33] If it is unethical to disclose a customer's personal data, is it unethical if there is a 1% chance of disclosure? That would determine how committed we must be to securing their data. Look up *probabilistic altruism* and *risk-deontological* theories if you're interested in bolt-ons to deontology that address this problem.

Nitpicking

Duty ethics lends itself to legalistic, technical nitpicking. For example, people sometimes claim that what they are saying is technically not a lie—even though it is meant to deceive. Just as bureaucrats often become extremely focused on the minutiae of the rules, deontologists can become fixated on the precise terms of ethical principles and miss their point.

---

* The philosopher W. D. Ross deals with this objection by arguing that some rules establish a *prima facie* obligation, which is binding *unless* there is a reason why it is not.

Displacement of Goals

Bureaucracy suffers from a displacement of goals when the rules, rather than their intentions, become central. Similarly, deontological actors can lose track of the motivation behind the rules. In fact, this is probably how obscure taboos come about. Ethical principles are important not because of some abstract reasoning, but because we care about the people around us. Feminist ethicists protest that Kant missed the point—ethics follows from care about our fellow humans. Vallor says:

> Kantian deontology, which supplies a single categorical imperative mandating universal rational consistency in moral action, is criticized for treating the rational consistency of the agent as more important to morality than natural human bonds of care and concern. On this view, moral expertise does not come from fixed moral principles, but is reflected in them; and imperfectly at that.[34]

Bureaucracies of Ethics

Like bureaucracy, deontology is based on categorical rules, universally and impersonally applied. Just as bureaucracies easily become petrified, engraving their rules in stone tablets so they'll never be changed, deontology and consequentialism are not designed for the complexity, fluidity, and uncertainties of the digital world.

Consequentialism is an algorithm for moral decision-making, a calculus of consequences. You could say that the algorithm takes the human decision maker out of it; calculating moral rights and wrongs could just as easily be done on any abacus. Like bureaucracy, it makes humans machine-like by giving them a standardized process to follow, disregarding human complexities and judgment. It's a lot like making decisions by business plans: you project the likely outcomes, gauge their net benefit, and select the action with the highest ROI for the world, with ROI measured in hedons. Business plans aren't great with uncertainty either.

The rules of deontology—like those of bureaucracy—are often role dependent. When you assume the role of a CEO, you accept fiduciary duties. Other roles such as teacher, citizen, soldier, nurse, judge, and sibling[35] each bring their own obligations. *Frankenstein* is an excellent example of role-based obligations: it is Victor's failure to accept his duties as father/creator that causes the creature to become a fiend and wretch and sets the novel's action in motion.

The Yale philosopher Shelley Kagan even points out that role-based deontological obligations are, in effect, a division of moral labor!

> The point is probably obvious, but it is worth belaboring. First of all, by assigning particular duties to particular roles, a division of moral labor is achieved. Specific individuals can become specialists, learning to fulfill particular duties with a skill and efficiency that would otherwise be impossible.[36]

Division of labor, skill, efficiency—this could have come straight from Weber's bureaucracy playbook.

Autonomy as a Fundamental Principle and Guardrail

Yet there's something important in Kant's theory for those of us facing ethical decisions in digital transformation. CIv2 provides a valuable guardrail against inappropriate manipulation of human beings, a situation which I'll show later we're in serious danger of bumping into as we stride into the digital world while looking backward at the bureaucratic world.

CIv2 is related to values of *autonomy* and *dignity*. Autonomy is the ability to have our lives under our own control, to make our own decisions without undue interference from others. To act autonomously, we need to be free of coercion, in control of our desires, and in possession of the information we need to make a decision; this last point is why lying and deception are threats to autonomy. According to Kant, "When you tell a lie, you virtually always rob someone of a crucial ingredient—information—that they need to accomplish whatever it is that they wanted to accomplish."[37]

Kant says that dignity requires autonomy: "What gives us dignity is that we are agents who are capable of acting for reasons that we justifiably see as reasons."[38] In utilitarianism, *dignity* is an essential component of happiness, as Mill says:

> A being of higher faculties requires more to make him happy. . . . We may refer it to the love of liberty and personal independence . . . but its most appropriate appellation is a sense of dignity, which all human beings possess in one form or other. . . . It is better to be a human being dissatisfied than a pig satisfied; better to be Socrates dissatisfied than a fool satisfied.[39]

That may be more praise than Socrates deserves, as we'll see in a moment, but in this book we'll make considerable use of the autonomy principle, melding together, for simplicity, the ideas of autonomy, dignity, and ends-in-themselves (CIv2). Autonomy adds a prima facie principle—a red flag, let's say—we'd better examine our conduct for potential ethical issues if we violate it. It's how we avoid being pigs and fools.

Consequentialism and Deontology: Reject

Rationalist ethics, which have dominated the Western framing of ethical problems for the last few hundred years and which we tend to think of when the subject of ethics arises, are closely tied to bureaucratic principles. They share with bureaucracy a common origin (the Enlightenment emphasis on reason and engineering), common beliefs (rules and roles), and common problems (difficulty dealing with complexity and uncertainty). Anything that shares a lot with bureaucracy is not the agile ethics we potential pigs and fools are foraging for.

Agile (Adaptive) Ethics

Building A Frankenstein Monster
of Ethical Proportions

I do not accept any absolute formulas for living. No preconceived code can see ahead to everything that can happen in a man's life. As we live, we grow and our beliefs change. They must change. So I think we should live with this constant discovery.

—Martin Buber, quoted in *Martin Buber: An Intimate Portrait*

I know not all that may be coming, but be it what it will, I'll go to it laughing.

—Herman Melville, *Moby-Dick*

Imagine, for a moment, that you are Ancient Greece. I know, it's hard to imagine that you are an entire civilization, but bear with me. You are trying to invent the entire intellectual foundation for the western world, because, as we know, that's what Ancient Greeks were up to. You figure out things like the Pythagorean theorem. When someone asks you why the length of the hypotenuse squared is the sum of the lengths of the legs of the triangle squared, you show them a proof and smile proudly.

One thing you have to figure out is how people in western civilization should behave. Maybe you do some deliberating and try: "You shouldn't lie." Then someone asks you, "Why not?" Hmmm. WHY NOT? Sooner or later Socrates is going to find you at the market and start asking hard questions . . .

You took a different angle. Instead of asking yourself what rules people should follow, you wondered, "What does it mean to be a good person?" and "What does it mean to live a good life?" These were easier questions because everyone already agreed, more or less, on the answers. You were engaged in creating the city-state, or *polis*, and you knew what everyone was expected to contribute. To be a good person was to play your part as a citizen. You had role models like Achilles and Oedipus in the heroic epics like *The Iliad* and

The Odyssey. You had dramas, like *Antigone*, that explored the consequences of acting when demands of the gods conflicted.*

So you developed an ethics that was about character, about the attributes of a good person, rather than about ethical choices in specific circumstances. In fact, the word *ethics* comes from your Greek word for *character*, and the word *morality* comes from Cicero's translation of it into Latin. There were few general rules; you tied ethical behavior to the role a person played, whether soldier, dramatist, tailor, philosopher. Alisdair MacIntyre explains the concept, "I am answerable for doing or failing to do what anyone who occupies my role owes to others and this accountability terminates only with death."[1]

You—congratulations—invented what philosophers call *virtue ethics*—ethics based on dispositions and character traits, rather than on rules like "Thou shalt not pass wind in the agora."† The *virtues* in virtue ethics were those character traits that held the society of your city-state together.

Toward an Adaptive Ethics

The idea that ethics is about the ideal self, the virtues, was pretty much the basis of ethics from the time we lost our monkey tails to the time of the Enlightenment, and it has become popular again among ethical philosophers since about the middle of the twentieth century. It also turns out to be the best way to think about ethics in the digitally transforming workplace. While deontology and consequentialist ethics share a lot with the bureaucratic way of organizing, virtue ethics is attuned to the digital world; it allows for decentralized, empowered ethical decision-making under complex and uncertain circumstances.

Our inclination when thinking about digital transformation ethics is to ask what ethical *rules* we must follow. A better question is what virtuous behavior looks like; what virtues apply and how to use them to guide our actions. Don't get thrown by the archaic-sounding word "virtue." It's just a way of talking about what kind of person you want to be and what kind of people you want to associate with.

Virtue ethics will not answer our questions about how *companies* should behave—it's awkward to talk about corporate virtues—but since decisions in companies are made by people, it's a starting point. Later in the chapter we'll come back to corporate ethics, and I'll introduce a framework called *contractarianism* as an agile approach to business ethics.

---

* Antigone decides to bury her brother Polynices, acting on divine law, even though it was forbidden by the king, Creon, therefore against human law.

† Agora = market.

When Aristotle set out to systematize ethics in *The Nicomachean Ethics*, his intention was to record the virtues that everyone already understood. For Ancient Greek heroic society, the central virtue was courage (andreia)—being someone society could rely on. Aristotle's list also included honesty (aletheia), patience (praotes), friendliness (philia), justice (dikaiosunē), and moderation (sôphrosunê), along with a unifying virtue of practical wisdom (phronēsis).[2]

These were the personal traits that would lead to a flourishing polis. That's the key to virtue ethics: it begins with a desired state of affairs, a vision for society, and works backward to determine the virtues that will deliver it. If you try listing all the personal attributes you think are good, you'll wind up with a very long list. But the game of virtue ethicists is to find the critical virtues, the high-priority virtues, if you must, that determine the extent to which society reaches its envisioned goals.

Aristotle's virtues are probably not the ones we'd come up with today. In *Technology and the Virtues*, Shannon Vallor proposes an alternative list of "technosocial" virtues, including honesty, self-control, humility, justice, courage, empathy, care, civility, flexibility, perspective, magnanimity, and technomoral wisdom.[3] While those are all good things, I'm going to take a slightly different direction, focusing on the virtues we want people to bring to the workplace. My list, which appears in Chapter 11, follows from the challenges I'll describe in Part II.

Why Virtue Ethics?

Virtue ethics is the "shift left" version of ethics. In DevOps,* we use the expression "shift left" to mean eliminating a "gatekeeping" control by fulfilling its intentions earlier, thereby "shifting it left" on the schedule. For example, instead of having a security team check for vulnerabilities at the end of a software development initiative and then demand rework, DevOps teams will involve the security team throughout their work to make sure that all their code is built to be secure. They'll design and engineer for security, rather than waiting to find problems at the end.

Similarly, virtue ethics tries to "build virtue in"—helping moral actors cultivate virtues so that when the time comes to make an ethical decision, they are ready to do so. While deontology and consequentialism focus on the moment of decision, virtue ethics focuses on developing character and the ability to make good decisions.

---

* DevOps is the technique currently considered best practice for creating and delivering software. It involves cross-functional IT teams working together with a large amount of automation.

Virtue ethics can sound like a cop-out if you're used to the prescriptions of deontology and consequentialism. Similarly, Agile approaches to software delivery have always sounded like a cop-out to those used to traditional waterfall approaches. "You don't document the requirements up front? You don't plan with a Gantt chart and commit to milestones? That's anarchy, not a process. It's lazy. You can do anything you want and say you are doing a good job!"

It's not true in either case. Both agile and virtue approaches accept uncertainty and complexity and make the best of them. Both are rigorous and goal directed. They just recognize that rules and requirements don't work.

MacIntyre says that virtue ethics actually solves Hume's problem of deriving an ought from an is. Well, it cheats a bit by starting from a desired end state. If you understand the purpose of a watch, then you know—as a fact—that an inaccurate watch is a bad watch. It "ought" to keep time well. In other words, if you can understand purpose, you can derive an ought from an is. That's interesting from the point of view of leading a digital transformation: it tells us that transformation involves both setting a vision for the desired ethical state of affairs and managing the cultural change to a new set of virtues. Laying out a new ethical vision will be the topic of the concluding chapter of this book.

Any ethical framework for digital transformation must be adaptive and agile. It must accommodate:

1. the complexity of our everyday decision contexts,
2. the global and interconnected nature of the digital world,
3. the uncertainty of the consequences of our actions,
4. the continual emergence of new norms (for example, in privacy and AI).

Here's how virtue ethics fits.

1. Tolerant of Complexity

Virtue ethics systems include the special virtue of practical wisdom, or phronēsis, that allows people to make good decisions in knotty circumstances. Vallor explains:

> Practical wisdom is the kind of excellence we find in moral experts, persons whose moral lives are guided by appropriate feeling and intelligence, rather than mindless habit or rote compulsion to follow fixed moral scripts provided by religious, political, or cultural institutions. As Aristotle took pains to note, matters of practical ethics by nature "exhibit

much variety and fluctuation," requiring a distinctive kind of reasoning that displays an understanding of changing particulars as well as fixed universals.[4]

Let's say that your grandmother is in the hospital and about to die. With her last few breaths, she asks how her nephew Rumpelstiltskin is doing. You know that Rumpelstiltskin was just in a fatal car accident. Should you tell her that? A deontologist like Kant would say that you must. But a virtue ethicist would say that you must use practical wisdom and apply other virtues in addition to honesty—perhaps a virtue of empathy or caring. People with the virtue of honesty might not tell the truth.

Leaders of digital transformation find complexity in both everyday gingerbread decisions and big Frankenstein decisions, stemming from irreconcilable demands, ambiguous responsibilities, and a shifting ethical environment. The duty to investors, perhaps, and the need to satisfy the open-ended desires of other stakeholders. The obligations of transparency along with demands for confidentiality. Practical wisdom is an ability to cope with this complexity.

It would have struck the ancient Greeks as strange to formulate universal rules like "never tell a lie," because how can you know if lying is okay until you know the context? Since we have to act in an uncertain, hostile world, exercising the virtues requires judgment. Possessors of practical wisdom "are not overly distressed by unexpected or novel problems to which existing moral rules and conventions do not easily apply, nor do they fall victim to 'analysis paralysis' when those rules or conventions appear to conflict,"[5] says Vallor.

2. Global and Interconnected

Because virtue ethics has played an important role throughout time and across cultures, it's a good basis for reaching intercultural understandings of acceptable behavior. Here are some examples of the breadth of virtue thinking.

Other Western Virtue Traditions

Virtue ethics predates Aristotle, though he's the one with a permanent place on the philosophy bookshelves of Barnes and Noble. The "Instructions of Kagemni," which appear in the *Prisse Papyrus* from the Middle Kingdom of Egypt around 1929 BCE, praise the "silent man" who exhibits the virtues of modesty, calmness, and self-control. His opposite, the "heated man," sounds a lot like Elon Musk.

Medieval thinkers in Europe were pretty sure they understood the purpose of life—to die and enjoy your afterlife. To earn your place in that afterlife, you needed to cultivate a set of virtues—like skill at jousting and intolerance of other religious views.

Protestants were encouraged to cultivate ascetic traits focused on the godly aspects of everyday life. In his autobiography, the American statesman and diplomat Benjamin Franklin explains that in reflecting on his own behavior he devised a list of thirteen virtues he thought would make him a better person: temperance, silence, order, resolution, frugality, industry, sincerity, justice, moderation, cleanliness, tranquility, chastity, and humility. Note how different this list is from that of the Greeks: cleanliness was probably not essential for fighting Trojans, and humility was something the Greeks would not have bragged about.

Eastern Virtue Traditions

Virtue traditions in East Asia go back at least to Confucius and his follower Mencius. Traditional Chinese thought speaks of *dao de* (道德), the ethical power that fosters "uprightness" or "right seeing." A *jūnzǐ* (君子 lit. "lord's son") in Confucianism is a morally superior person who has mastered the virtues; the opposite is the *xiǎorén* (小人), or "small man." "The *jūnzǐ* understands righteousness; the *xiǎorén* understands profit," says Confucius. The virtues are those that enable the "five relationships" to flourish: father-son, ruler-subject, husband-wife, older brother-younger brother, and friend-friend.[6]

The highest Confucian virtue is *rèn* (仁), "benevolence," "humanity," "humanness," or "true goodness." It subsumes the other virtues, which include the "five constants," *Rén, Yì* (义; 義, righteousness, justice), *Lǐ* (礼; 禮, propriety, rites), *Zhì* (智, wisdom, knowledge), and *Xìn* (信, sincerity, faithfulness); as well as the virtues of *Zhōng* (忠, loyalty), *Xiào* (孝, filial piety), and *Jié* (节; 節, continence).[7]

Like Aristotelian ethics, Confucianism downplays rigid rules; a *jūnzǐ* is sensitive to the many factors at play in correctly applying the virtues. While rituals are important, it is the intent and the feeling behind them that matter; a *jūnzǐ* must be sensitive to roles, circumstances, and human needs.[8] A *jūnzǐ* does not treat everyone the same, since different human relationships generate different moral requirements, some stronger than others.[9]

Buddhism also has something analogous to practical wisdom in its practice of "skillful means" (*upāya*)—"the ability in unusual or challenging circumstances to suspend or modify the precepts in unconventional ways, where made necessary in the interests of compassion and the enlightenment of others."[10] The virtues in Buddhism are dispositions that set the stage for enlightenment—the escape from the cycle of birth and death—and, since Buddhism sees deep interconnections between people, improving the lot of humanity in general.[11]

While the virtues differ in each of these traditions, the idea of cultivating virtues throughout one's life and then applying them with practical wisdom is common to them all.

3. Uncertainty of Consequences

Who knows what the consequences of our ethical decisions will be a decade from now, a year from now, or even a day from now? Technology, behavior, and norms coevolve. Even my own future decisions, by definition, are unknown to me. If they're uncertain to me, they're even more uncertain to others, as their future decisions are to me.[12] And we can't yet know about future inventions or new technologies. Uncertainty is baked into the structure of the world.

Virtues are developed over time. They are honed and deepened. They can then be applied to any scenario that emerges. While deontology assumes we can make rules today to govern in the future, and consequentialism assumes we can foresee consequences, virtue ethics is an ethics of continuous learning and feedback.

4. Flexible Through Change and Shifting Norms

Business ethics requires a vision of how we can use digital transformation to improve life—for ourselves, our companies, and society at large. And that vision may change as society changes.

> *Are you saying that what's ethical changes?*
> I am saying that, yes.
> *But don't the principles stay the same, even if people apply them differently?*
> I'm not sure it matters. If norms about how to apply the principles change, we need the agility to change our behavior all the same.

Ethical norms have certainly changed over time. At one time many people thought slavery was okay. At one time torturing people to death in public was considered good entertainment. At one time it was considered right to punish women for expressing opinions and scientists for being right about whether the earth revolves around the sun. Perhaps there *are* underlying principles that stay the same, but that's academic. We must still interpret those principles, and at the very least the interpretation changes over time.

Business ethics in particular is new and unformed. According to Donaldson and Dunfee,

> business ethics should be viewed more as a story in the process of being written than as a moral code like the Ten Commandments. It can and should, we argue, adjust over time—to evolving technology, and to the cultural or religious attitudes of particular economic communities.[13]

Our parents did not teach us right from wrong when it comes to kicking robot dogs. We didn't always have bad actors continually probing our cybersecurity defenses. We have never had edge computing and machine learning to gather information on consumers so we can target advertising and deals at them. We've never had the agile technology-based business culture we have today, the ease of working from home, the threats of global warming.

Iteration, or inspecting and adapting, is built into virtue ethics. Virtue ethicists think of life as a story in which the individual's understanding of virtue deepens over time. MacIntyre says that "as we set out in life, we have only a partial understanding of what a good life is, and what the purposes which we might pursue within it might be, and that it is only in the living of it that we understand this more fully—'what more and what else' it might be."[14]

For newly emerging technologies and business practices, ethical norms will have to be negotiated or emerge as a consensus. The same goes for newly globalized interactions that bring together multiple societies, each with its own norms. For example, the presence of a GDPR in Europe and the lack of one in the US indicates a difference in outlook. Resolving those sorts of differences will involve tests and iteration. These things are hard to negotiate in advance as abstractions.

We can clarify our norms with thought experiments like the Trolley Problem and through experimentation and feedback. Are we okay with genetic modification? How much privacy are we willing to sacrifice if it helps us prevent harms like terrorist or criminal activity? AI and other emerging technologies serve up the provocations we need to drive toward a consensus—or at least understand our differences. It's like putting proposed solutions in front of users to stimulate discussion and get feedback and adapt.

We should conduct ethical experiments?
Why not?
It sounds scary. Like Nazi doctors experimenting on human beings.
Right. I mean that experiments will happen naturally as entrepreneurs try new ideas. The reactions to them—acceptance or distaste—will help us gauge

what society really believes—sort of like a trolley problem. Remember, I'm not talking about good versus evil, but everyday ethical challenges.

The task for a digital ethics, just as with software development, is one of learning—learning what society will consider acceptable in a world that is ambiguous and fluid.

Ethics of the Good Life, Not Just the Bad

While we run from Frankenstein in fear, we forget that the gingerbread man will make a tasty dessert. What's missing from our fear-driven conversations about the ethical future is a vision of what the *good* life looks like.

Emerging technologies might help us solve social problems, and—who knows—maybe even political ones. We can use technology to assist people with disabilities, to fight sexual slavery and human trafficking, to cure diseases, and to support people in making sure their governments serve them. Yes, we must exercise caution. But we must also seize opportunities to work toward human flourishing. Virtue ethics is a striving for constant improvement.

"Virtue" and "flourishing" seem like old-fashioned words.
I know what you mean. But there's a long history behind the words that's useful. Let's just say that "virtue" is about the kind of people we want to be, and "flourishing" is the goal, or vision, or good state that we're aiming at.
It still sounds squishy. Love and peace and kumbaya and all that good stuff. What does it have to do with real, competitive businesses?
I'll talk later specifically about virtues for the workplace. There's nothing squishy—it's about what attributes a good employee brings to work. By the way, it's better to leave the "love" out of it.

Becoming Virtuous

Virtues are developed and honed, not given. How does one cultivate virtues?
First, by practicing.[15] Virtuous leaders act, reflect on their actions, and accept feedback from others. Benjamin Franklin took an exceptionally disciplined approach to learning the virtues. His autobiography announces, matter-of-factly, "It was about this time I conceived the bold and arduous project of arriving at moral perfection. I wished to live without committing any fault at any time."[16] He began with his list of virtues and then devoted each week to becoming better at one of them.

I made a little book, in which I allotted a page for each of the virtues.
I ruled each page with red ink, so as to have seven columns, one for each
day of the week, marking each column with a letter for the day. I crossed
these columns with thirteen red lines, marking the beginning of each
line with the first letter of one of the virtues, on which line, and in its
proper column, I might mark, by a little black spot, every fault I found
upon examination to have been committed respecting that virtue upon
that day.[17]

Um, that's a little . . . anal?
He did say it was a bold and arduous project. Like an ERP system rollout.*

Second, by learning from stories. *The Iliad*, which was recited at public
ceremonies in Ancient Greece, illustrated the virtues of heroic Greek society.
Augustine's *Confessions* and Bunyan's *The Pilgrim's Progress* taught virtues to
Christians. Shakespeare's stories are elaborations of ethical decisions and their
results. Stories tell about how the virtuous act in specific, concrete, complex
circumstances, rather than providing rules for behavior.

Third, by learning from role models. "When we see men of worth, we
should think of equalling them; when we see men of a contrary character,
we should turn inwards and examine ourselves," said Confucius.[18] Unfortunately, business leaders are often presented with poor role models. The media
lionize the leprechaun CEOs, tracing their journeys to the pot of gold at the
end of the rainbow and their immodest reflections on how they blazed the
trail. But sometimes, in truth, they stumbled onto the gold and sometimes
they dropped half their coins by accident as they danced the jig of their own
genius.

According to a *Business Insider* article,[19] former Apple CEO Steve Jobs
referred to Apple's partner company's leaders as "fucking dickless assholes,"
denied paternity of his daughter for years while she lived on welfare, and lied
to his friend Steve Wozniak about the amount of his bonus and pocketed the
money. I don't know if those reports are accurate, but the media seems to imply
that it's part of what made him successful, or an unfortunate but necessary side
effect. I don't buy it.

"Neutron" Jack Welch was known for destroying all the people but leaving
the walls standing.

---

* Enterprise Resource Planning. A type of off-the-shelf IT system that manages many of the
  functions of a business. ERP system rollouts are famous for requiring a great deal more time
  and expense than expected.

Welch was infamous for his explosive temper. He argued his way from one decision to the next, terrorized subordinates with shouting matches, and made even his allies cower in fear. As one GE employee said during his heyday: "Jack comes on like a herd of elephants. If you have a contradictory idea you have to be willing to take the guff to put it forward." Said another: "Working for him is like a war. A lot of people get shot up; the survivors go on to the next battle."[20]

Incidentally, Socrates was also a jerk. He was sarcastic, devious enough to tie his conversation partners in philosophical circles, an elitist who thought that Athenian philosophers should rule Athens. Of course he did—he was an Athenian philosopher. Read *Euthyphro* for a sense of his unctuous sarcasm. He hung around the marketplace harassing people with questions designed to make them feel stupid. He didn't fool anyone: in *The Clouds*, Aristophanes has him pray thus for his powers of obfuscation: "Heavenly Clouds, great divinities to idle men; who supply us with thought and argument, and intelligence and humbug, and circumlocution, and ability to hoax, and comprehension."[21]

Imagine how you'd react when you felt Socrates tugging at your toga as you were trying to buy some berries. This is why lying is sometimes justified. . . . "Sorry Socrates, no time to chat. I've promised Pericles I'd meet him at the baths to discuss the latest episode of *Ted Lasso*."

Feminist Ethics

Most work, as David Graeber points out, is "caring" work rather than the mechanical, factory-like, coerced labor that the bureaucratic organization presumes it to be. Caring labor is work that is directed at other people, and that involves empathy and understanding.[22] Because the digital workplace is filled with caring individuals who have brought themselves to work, the feminist ethics of "care" pioneered by philosophers Carol Gilligan and Nel Noddings is especially relevant.

The ethics of care is a type of virtue ethics, with "care" as a central virtue.* It too is concerned with the development of an "ideal self," as Noddings explains:

> Ethical caring, as I have described it, depends not upon rule or principle but upon the development of an ideal self. . . . Moral statements cannot

---

* Note that Noddings wasn't so sure she liked the virtue ethics label: "When we discuss the ethical ideal, we shall be talking about 'virtue,' but we shall not let 'virtue' dissipate into 'the virtues' described in abstract categories."[23]

be justified in the way that statements of fact can be justified. They are not truths. They are derived not from facts or principles but from the caring attitude. . . . We are not "justified"—we are obligated—to do what is required to maintain and enhance caring.[24]

To understand her point, it helps to distinguish "natural" caring from "ethical" caring. According to Noddings, we have a natural feeling of *care* for others. In that feeling we recognize our best selves—the kind of person we want to be. Based on that aspiration, we strive to develop a disposition to act in ways consistent with this feeling—a *virtue* of care. As Vallor explains it, a morally cultivated person "will be capable of extending natural moral attitudes of caring concern (such as love, fairness, benevolence, respect, or compassion) beyond their initial scope, as called for by the general and situational demands of morality."[25]

Noddings points out that ethical rules or principles—what I call bureaucratic ethics—depend on some notion of universalizability, or "sameness" between cases. Women, she says, prefer to discuss moral problems in terms of concrete situations. Other things are rarely equal, as "bureaucratic" ethical frameworks would imply. Generalized rules don't work.

To say, "It is wrong to cause pain needlessly," contributes nothing by way of knowledge and can hardly be thought likely to change the attitude or behavior of one who might ask, "Why is it wrong?" If I say to someone, "You are hurting the cat, "and he replies, "I know it—so what? I like hurting cats," I feel "zero at the bone." Saying to him, "It is wrong to hurt cats," adds little.[26]

Care plays an important part in Confucian and Buddhist ethics as well. Confucianism refers to the parent-child relationship as the foundation for benevolence, both because of the care children receive from their parents and the care children later provide back to their parents.[27] Buddhist ethics emphasizes compassion (*karunā*) and a related concept of *muditā* ("empathetic joy"), an ability to recognize others' happiness and respond with an appropriate moral co-feeling.[28]

Fear, Anguish, Dread

You're kidding with this anguish and dread stuff, right? I never know.
A little. The existentialist terms are over the top. But there's something important here. Corporate leaders are responsible for their decisions because

they are actual decisions. They can't be "computed" from what rules say or what data says or even what ethical principles say.

As Sartre puts it: "There can be no objective basis for our moral resolutions. We must simply choose, and take responsibility for our choices."[29] To Nietzsche, all rational justifications for values fail; we simply act in accord with our wills and then, perhaps, try to justify our actions after the fact.[30] Kierkegaard points out that even if we justify our actions with reference to first principles, we still have to choose the first principles to adopt.[31]

Business leaders cannot hide behind data or rules. This will become important in the next few chapters.

Contractarianism

The ethical frameworks I've described so far make sense when we talk about how individuals should behave, but it's hard to apply them to businesses. Kantian deontology, for example, doesn't seem to say much about insider trading, the treatment of customer data, or an obligation to reduce carbon emissions. The questions we face in business ethics are not always natural parts of human behavior—think of Enron CFO Andrew Fastow's complex accounting structures that were intended to hide bad behavior. The conduct of business also varies considerably between cultures and industries.

The ethical frameworks I've described take a "view from nowhere"—they are general and divorced from any context. In *Ties That Bind*, Dunfee and Donaldson have adapted the ideas of ethical *contractarianism* to address this gap.

Contractarianism developed from the notion of a "social contract." The seed came from Thomas Hobbes's argument that without a government, the life of humans would be short, nasty, brutish, and entirely Microsoft Windows-based. Because people have conflicting interests, they must agree on implicit social contracts to avoid constant conflict.

According to contractarians, ethical requirements follow from these informal social contracts—like not passing wind in the agora—and, in cases where there is no obvious contract, on the hypothetical agreements we would make if rational "bargainers" negotiated one. In business as in everyday life not all contract terms are formal, they say; many are implicit, akin to "handshake agreements" or generally accepted practices.

Contractarians analyze ethical questions by trying to surface any informal, implicit, or *hypothetical* agreements that might exist—agreements that establish what is "fair" in a given environment.

The normative authority of any social contract derives from the assumption that humans, acting rationally, consent—or at least would consent hypothetically—to the terms of a particular agreement affecting the society or community of which they are a member. In this manner contractarian theories utilize the device of consent, albeit it is often *hypothetical* consent, to justify principles, policies, and structures.[32]

To convince yourself that implicit agreements exist, consider how employees might react if employers ask them to take time off without pay over holidays, hold employee contests that are "fixed," use company resources to remodel the homes of executives, or give retired executives lucrative consulting contracts during a hiring freeze. In each case the actions violate an unstated, implicit contract between employers and employees.[33]

Contractarians see businesses as embedded in a web of contracts with employees, customers, investors, society (which allows the businesses to exist in the first place), suppliers, local communities, and others. In fact, that is pretty much all a business is—a nexus of formal, implicit, and informal contracts. Understanding the responsibilities of businesses is a matter of identifying and analyzing these agreements.

Contractarianism is an agile ethics because these contracts, especially the informal ones, may change over time and may be different from society to society and from industry to industry. Twenty years ago my implicit transactional understanding with a retailer probably didn't include terms about how they would use my data, but today it most likely does.

Summary:
The Monster Walks

The ethical frameworks I've described in these chapters can seem interchangeable when it's time to apply them to a specific situation. Most people flip back and forth. Sometimes they think consequentially ("If I pull the switch, fewer pastrami sandwiches will be destroyed"), sometimes they rely on a rule ("Injecting SQL code is bad"), and sometimes they try to be virtuous ("I'm an honest, good citizen, so I don't lie on my tax returns").[34] If Large Larry is drowning, a consequentialist may reason that rescuing him will maximize wellbeing. A deontologist might refer to a rule about helping people in need or a meta-principle like "Do unto others. . . ." A virtue ethicist might talk about the virtue of benevolence. But they will probably all try to save the ever-unfortunate Larry.[35]

The frameworks do, however, vary greatly in how they treat uncertainty and complexity, and therefore in how well they answer to the needs of the digitally transforming world.

In this chapter I've begun sewing together a Frankenstein creature of loose body parts from the great philosophical theories of ethics. Its skeleton is the idea of virtue as the core of workplace behavior. For a heart I've sewn in a few pieces of feminist and Confucian ethics; a deontological guardrail, CIv2 or the principle of autonomy, will serve as a conscience. For a face, I've borrowed ideas from the existentialists. And the contractarian element will give it some muscle in business contexts. My Frankenstein monster will walk and talk, even if it's a bit ugly. But in the second and third parts of the book we'll nurture it, care for it, and engage with it to examine the important questions of digital transformation.

PART II

PERILS AND PREDATORS

Social Responsibility and Business Ethics

Virtues: Courage, Caring, Stewardship, Justice

In this world, shipmates, sin that pays its way can travel freely and without a passport; whereas Virtue, if a pauper, is stopped at all frontiers.
—Herman Melville, *Moby Dick*

Did you ever expect a corporation to have a conscience when it has no soul to be damned, and no body to kick?
—Edward, First Baron Thurlow, Lord Chancellor of England

Business leaders today must find a way to resolve the conflict between their duty to earn returns for investors and a duty to meet "social responsibility" objectives. Traditional, bureaucratic organizations, as I've said, are neutral with respect to goals; their task is to find the most effective way to meet whatever ends they're given. Since at least the 1970s, executives have been told that their only duty is to maximize returns for shareholders. Using company resources for other purposes violates this obligation. Yet company leaders feel pressure today to invest in environmental sustainability, to support the communities in which they do business, to stock the fridges with cage-free kombucha, and to satisfy the many other "stakeholders" that appear with demands.

That's tough enough; but actually the conflict goes much deeper. The duty is not just to return money to shareholders, but to *maximize* returns, which implies that companies must take advantage of any legal opportunities they find to increase profits; not doing so has an opportunity cost for investors. Leaders of digitally transforming enterprises may find many opportunities to increase profits—and some of these opportunities will involve manipulating customers and employees in ways that should make them pause. Whether and when such manipulation is acceptable is our focus in Part II: Perils and Predators.

For this chapter, our topic is that duty to maximize returns to shareholders—why it exists (or why not) and to what extent it constrains companies from acting out of social responsibility. Along with transformation-mania has come a kind of ESG-mania. ESG, standing for environmental, social, and governance, is an odd term that should disturb English teachers with its lack of parallel structure—two adjectives followed by a noun—perhaps suggesting the confusion out of which it was born. The intuition behind the "governance" part is that companies shouldn't just make periodic and halfhearted stabs at addressing environmental and social concerns, but should set up oversight processes to make sure those concerns become part of their everyday operations. The governance part also refers to controls against unethical behavior, including the use of biased AI.

Some ESG investments will increase a company's profits, especially now that MOM and POP approve (see Chapter 1). For those investments, there is no ethical question. Since this is a book about ethics, with only a few digressions into monsters and hats, we'll leave aside those environmental and social decisions company leaders make that directly benefit the shareholders. We'll focus instead on tough choices under conflicting ethical imperatives—whether and when to spend company money on social good *when it reduces the return to shareholders*.

The relationship between business and society has long been a concern of philosophers. Let's start there.

Business and Society

Samuel Johnson, the eighteenth-century British author and lexicographer, declared that "there is nothing which requires more to be illustrated by philosophy than trade does."[1] In *The Prevalence of Humbug*, Max Black tells the story of the elderly philosopher Samuel Alexander, who, when introduced to a Harvard professor, shook his ear trumpet with laughter and said, "I must be getting very deaf—I thought you said he was a professor of business ethics!"[2] Indeed, business has stood out through the centuries as a topic that is both ethically problematic and critical to address. According to the Jewish Talmud, the first question one is asked when facing judgment in the next world is, "Were you honest in business?"[3]

Rules for business conduct have long been part of legal systems. *The Code of Hammurabi*, from around 1750 BCE, covers loans, trade, fraud, wages of craftsmen, innkeeping, and boat hire. The barbarians, once they were done sacking Rome, also got down to business: one of the twelve books of the Visigothic Code, from 654 CE, is dedicated to business transactions. The Tamil *Thirukkural*, written in about the third or fourth century CE,[4] is full of leadership guidance ("A show of command in one without it—a cow in tiger's skin munching crops"), wealth ("Renounce at once wealth gained without fairness even if it brings only good") and even a fine Agile principle ("When possible it is good to act—when not seek possibility and act"). It even has some bonus advice for us clueless executives: "The fool entering wise company—like going to bed with one's backside unwashed."[5]

Among the Ancient Greeks, Hesiod believed that wealth was a sign of its owner's excellence and "glory."[6] He praised work and censured idleness:

> Both gods and men are angry with a man who lives idle . . . let it be your care to order your work properly, that in the right season your barns may be full of victual. Through work men grow rich in flocks and substance, and working they are much better loved by the immortals. Work is no disgrace: it is idleness which is a disgrace.[7]

Within a few hundred years, though, Athenians stopped being so sure that work was loved by the immortals. Aristotle believed work was bad because it ruined the bodies and minds of workers and left them little time for being good citizens: "No man can practice virtue who is living the life of a mechanic or laborer,"[8] he says. And commerce, to him, was "unnatural" because it used craft to deprive people of what they needed to pursue their natural goals.

Confucius thought much the same. He put merchants at the bottom of his hierarchy of occupations because he considered them parasitic—they did nothing but trade in the goods of more productive classes like farmers and artisans.[9] The Buddha approved of wealth creation as long as it was done in a way that accorded with "right livelihood," one of the elements of the Noble Eightfold Path. Wealth should not be earned through killing, complicity in the suffering of other beings (selling weapons, poison, alcohol, or meat), or through lying, stealing, or deceit. Otherwise, go for it.

Medieval scholastic philosophers and theologians were surprisingly positive. Duns Scotus considered merchants essential for public well-being, calling them "builders of public happiness."[10] The challenge for the scholastics, Thomas Aquinas in particular, was to make sure there was justice between buyers and sellers.[11] Since the purpose of commerce was to benefit society as a whole, he conceived the idea of a "just" price, a price that accurately represented the value of the thing being sold.[12] Trade was a relationship between individuals[13] (big businesses didn't exist yet), so both businesses and customers had duties of fairness to one another.

The Muslim scholar Ibn Khaldun (1332–1406) took yet a different angle. In *Muqaddimah* he wrote that sellers were understood to be trying to earn a profit by maximizing the difference between their purchasing and selling prices.

Because both the seller and buyer were taking risks, commerce was essentially a kind of gambling. Therefore, a certain amount of "cunning" or "trickery" was acceptable, just as it would be in a gambling game.[14]

Adam Smith, the father of capitalist economics, was actually a professor of moral philosophy and the author of *The Theory of Moral Sentiments* (1759). Even in *The Wealth of Nations*, his bible of free-market thinking, his perspective was that of a moralist. He worried that "all for ourselves, and nothing for other people, seems, in every age of the world, to have been the vile maxim of the masters of mankind."[15] Like most of his contemporaries, Smith believed that self-interest had to be limited by ethical considerations.[16] Smith's happy news, though, was that the invisible hand of the market would take care of it; since it would naturally correct for moral imbalances, the imperceptible paw of the economy was a *solution* to the ethical problems caused by people acting in self-interest.

You can see a theme emerging: a tension between business conducted in self-interest and business as beneficial for society as a whole.

Moral Agency

Authors who sleep through their ethics classes risk leaving out important points. I should have asked: Does it even make sense to talk about the ethics of a business? In ethics terminology, is a corporation a moral agent? People are moral agents—they make ethical decisions for which we can hold them responsible. Animals are not (except cats—we know they're evil). Later we'll come to the question of whether artificial intelligences can be moral agents.

A red herring, but a tasty one, is the fact that in many legal systems a corporation is considered a legal "person." Legal systems have adopted the personhood convention because corporations can do things like enter into contracts and own property, just as people can. But treating corporations as persons raises confusing questions about whether corporations have rights like other persons, like the right to watch *The Great British Baking Show*, drink mango mojitos, or receive phone calls from telemarketers at dinnertime.

In any case, corporate legal personhood doesn't really tell us whether a corporation is morally like a person. Corporations don't have feelings; they don't need to eat or drink; they don't have parents or schools to teach them values; they aren't going to heaven or hell; and they certainly don't possess reason, at least none that I've worked for. They're not people, even if they're persons. So what do we mean when we talk about the ethical responsibilities of a corporation?

The *individualist* position is that we don't mean anything, because a business is just a collection of individuals, each responsible for their own behavior. The company itself—a legal fiction or an abstraction—is not a moral actor. The philosopher Manuel Velasquez argued that we can only assign moral responsibility when an agent forms an intention to perform an act and then performs it with their body.[17] Businesses have neither bodies nor intentions. Intentions are only formed when individuals seek their own happiness, but corporations, even when they survive an audit, cannot be happy or unhappy. Velasquez claims that treating corporations as moral agents is actually dangerous. If we want to deter corporate wrongdoing, he says, we must stop the *people* in the corporation from doing bad things by holding them personally accountable.[18]

The *collectivist* position is that the company itself—separate from the individuals who make it up—*is* a moral actor and has ethical responsibilities. Philosophers like Peter French argue that intentions can be inferred from a corporation's official policies, decision-making procedures, and lines of authority. Since corporations maintain a continuous identity through time, even as particular employees change, they have a "decision structure" *independent* of their employees that forms intentions and executes on them.

Social Responsibilities

If corporations are moral agents, do they have social responsibilities? Do they have an obligation to "give back" to society?

Wait, wait. Companies can't just spend shareholder money on things that don't earn profits, right?

That's the question. The idea that they can't mostly developed in the 1970s. Until then, businesses were thought to play a social role.

What happened in the 1970s?

The economist Milton Friedman is what happened.

Milton Friedman and the Chicago school of economists did not believe businesses have social responsibilities—or, more precisely, they had just one, as the title of Friedman's influential essay has it: "The Social Responsibility of a Business Is to Increase Its Profits." Friedman argued that the executives of a business are hired by the owners—the shareholders—to advance the owners' interests; any other behavior, like charitable donations or investment in social impact initiatives, is irresponsible.[19] This, as we know, is a deontological argument: an argument from duty.

Friedman's message is best understood in the context of his book *Capitalism and Freedom*, where he presents a consequentialist argument as well as the deontological one. Market mechanisms, he says, allow people to cooperate while still retaining their freedom.[20] In a market economy, participants consume what they wish, produce what they wish, and invest capital as they wish. Investors invest for returns; companies provide returns; and investors can then choose to invest their returns for social good, if they desire. That's freedom.

On the other hand, if managers decide to spend the investors' money on "doing good" for society, they are effectively imposing a tax on owners and deciding by themselves how to spend that tax money. It's inimical to freedom, similar to a socialist economy where the government decides what to produce and what to spend. That is a bad consequence.

> Few trends could so thoroughly undermine the very foundations of our free society as the acceptance by corporate officials of a social responsibility other than to make as much money for their stockholders as possible. This is a fundamentally subversive doctrine. If businessmen do have a social responsibility other than making maximum profits for stockholders, how are they to know what it is? Can self-selected private individuals decide what the social interest is? Can they decide how great a burden they are justified in placing on themselves or their stockholders to serve that social interest?[21]

In the worst case, executives might use the firm's resources to benefit themselves. A notorious example was Occidental Petroleum Corporation's donation of $90 million to set up the Armand Hammer Museum of Art and Cultural Center to display Hammer's personal art collection—when Hammer was CEO of Occidental.[22]

Friedman's doctrine is not amoral or antimoral. He's taking an ethical stance by saying that it *is* a social responsibility to increase profits. The managers of a business have an *obligation* to invest only in things that increase the owners' returns.

Since Friedman's doctrine has thoroughly dominated the thinking of businesses since the 1970s and is the source of conflicting ethical imperatives for digital decision makers, we need to examine Friedman's arguments closely in this chapter. I'll present some arguments against Friedman's doctrine, but recognizing that many readers will disagree, I'll follow with a few arguments that—even though Friedman would disagree—corporate social responsibility is largely consistent with his doctrine.

Critiquing Friedman's Argument

Who Says?

The idea that firms are responsible to their owners is compelling given our everyday understanding of property ownership. If I own a toy, the toy exists for my pleasure, and mine only. If I want to play with it, I can; if I want to smash it to bits, I can do that too. But is owning a business the same sort of ownership?

Throughout history, businesses were considered to have obligations beyond maximizing returns to their owners. Executives of large corporations saw themselves as stewards of great economic institutions that served customers, creditors, employees, suppliers, and the broader society.[23] Robert Reich, a former US Secretary of Labor, wrote in his 2014 article "The Rebirth of Stakeholder Capitalism?"

> Most CEOs assumed they were responsible for all their stakeholders. "The job of management," proclaimed Frank Abrams, chairman of Standard Oil of New Jersey, in 1951, "is to maintain an equitable and working balance among the claims of the various directly interested groups . . . stockholders, employees, customers, and the public at large." Johnson & Johnson publicly stated that its "first responsibility" was to patients, doctors, and nurses, and not to investors.[24]

Some economists in the 1970s believed that this "balancing" approach, known as managerialism, had failed, and blamed it for the poor state of the economy at the time. That was probably unfair. Managerialist assumptions, after all, had successfully guided the western world through development and industrialization. The economic situation of the 1970s resulted from a number of intersecting geopolitical and sociological factors, including the Arab oil embargo—which quadrupled the price of fuel—and the decision to take the US off the gold standard, which triggered inflation.

According to author Ronald Duska, Friedman was mistaken in not distinguishing between "(1) the *motive* of individuals, who are generally motivated by profit to participate in business, and (2) the socially sanctioned *purpose* of business, or the reason why societies allow businesses to exist, which is to provide goods and services to people."[25] History is more on Duska's side than on Friedman's. With the rise of industrial capitalism, businesses needed to operate at a much larger scale and scope and to serve a broader swath of geographies. Because individuals couldn't do that so easily, governments passed laws like

England's Limited Liability Act of 1865 to make it easier for people to join together in commercial organizations.

The legislation was intended to benefit society. Companies could deal better than individuals with uncertainty and could more efficiently manage the web of contracts necessary to operate at large scale. They could exploit synergies between people's talents and reduce risk for everyone involved. Since a business would be continuous over time even as the employees within it changed, customers could have confidence it would satisfy any liabilities it incurred.

Because corporations had so many benefits for society, investors were offered the protection of limited liability and excused from obligations beyond their investments. The *purpose* of a company was to produce goods and services valued by the community at the scale and complexity required in the industrial economy. Investors were *motivated* to invest through those legal protections.

Ownership of the Firm

Friedman assumed that shareholders own the firm. Some theorists argue that actually a shareholder only owns a security with certain privileges, or a contract with the company called a "share."[26] For common stock, these include the right to receive dividends, trade the stock with other investors, vote in electing a board of directors and other major corporate decisions, and share in the liquidation value of the company. That is the extent of their rights—they don't otherwise "own" the company like you own your bobblehead collection.

According to Lynn Stout, a corporate law scholar at Cornell, the idea that executives are agents for the shareholders is based on "patently inaccurate assumptions" about corporate law. Legally, directors are not subject to shareholder control. Outside of bankruptcy, shareholders do not have a right to every bit of profit left over after other stakeholders are paid.[27]

"To the contrary," Stout says, "the corporation as a legal entity is its own residual claimant, with legal title to its profits; shareholders are only legally entitled to whatever dividends the board of directors might, in its business judgment, declare."[28] Technically, that is, a company is a legal entity that owns itself.[29] Boards have discretion to increase employee salaries and benefits, treat suppliers more generously, retain earnings to give creditors a larger "equity cushion," or decline to pursue aggressive tax-avoidance strategies.[30]

Entrepreneurial Point of View

A business begins with an entrepreneur's idea. The entrepreneur then acquires capital and other resources in exchange for certain rights. Investors provide only one of the factors of production. Investors change over time; the company is continuous from the entrepreneur's vision to its dissolution. If the company "belongs to" anyone, it's the entrepreneur. The investors just tag along while the entrepreneur locates the pot of gold at the end of the rainbow. In today's entrepreneurial economy, this seems like a natural way to view the relationship. According to John Mackey, CEO of Whole Foods,

> It is the entrepreneurs who create a company, who bring all the factors of production together and coordinate it into viable business. It is the entrepreneurs who set the company strategy and who negotiate the terms of trade with all of the voluntarily cooperating stakeholders—including the investors. At Whole Foods we "hired" our original investors. They didn't hire us.[31]

Freedom Revisited

The authors of "Stakeholder Theory: A Libertarian Defense," surprisingly, present a libertarian argument against Friedman, though Friedman's position itself is libertarian.* The hallmark of libertarian theory, the authors say, is free consent and agreement. People have the right to enter into agreements, even if some of those agreements limit their freedom by imposing obligations.

Entrepreneurs contract with suppliers, employees, investors, customers, and others to build a company. The result is a web of obligations among those parties. "Value is created," they say, "because stakeholders can jointly satisfy their needs and desires by making voluntary agreements with each other."[32] Given these agreements, formal and informal, a company has obligations to other stakeholders beyond just the shareholders. This is essentially a contractarian argument.

Going further, they argue that libertarians—like everyone else—are personally responsible for how their property is used, a responsibility that extends to their agents, including the managers of companies they invest in. Since managers operate under uncertainty, they must consider the needs of all stakeholders to make sure that they don't misuse shareholders' property to harm others or violate their right to freedom.[33]

---

* Although he called himself a "liberal."

Private, Closely-Held Companies

Friedman's arguments seem to be directed at executives of public companies, where shares are widely held and the owners' desires therefore cannot be known. Friedman is instructing executives to assume that the owners want increases in share price, and therefore increases in profits. But in a private company with few owners, executives can simply discuss with the owners what their intentions are. In that case, the owners are, individually, morally responsible for setting out ethical obligations for the business. Aside from that, the situation is the same as with public companies: executives may have obligations in addition to those given by the owners.

The Consequentialist Argument

A consequentialist argument must consider the overall impact on society, not just on the "freedom" of investors. Friedman's view was too limited; he ignored the psychological realities and perverse incentives the shareholder theory would create. According to the *Economist*, the shareholder approach has become "a license for bad conduct, including skimping on investment, exorbitant pay, high leverage, silly takeovers, accounting shenanigans and a craze for share buy-backs, which are running at $600 billion a year in America."[34]

There is a crucial ambiguity in Friedman's doctrine—should managers maximize the shareholders' returns in the short term or in the long term? His theory has generally been interpreted to favor short-term returns, because it is increasingly short-term institutional investors that hold shares in companies—the average holding period for stocks listed on US exchanges has shrunk from eight years in 1960 to around four months today.[35] The effect has been a bias toward the "freedom" of hedge funds rather than the benefit of individual investors.

The short-term focus has intensified as companies have tied executive pay to increases in profits or share price. In 1980, 33% of executives were compensated with stock options; by 1995, once Friedman's ideas had sunk in, it was 70%. A new CEO focused on the short term might slash costs by firing staff, reducing customer support, or eliminating research and development. In a survey, 80% of corporate finance officers said they would cut expenses like marketing and product development to make quarterly earnings targets, even if they believed it would hurt the company's long-term performance.[36]

A short-term focus reduces entrepreneurial activity[37] within a company, since the returns for innovation typically take time to appear. One study found that, keeping company size and industry constant, private US companies invest nearly twice as much as public companies: 7% of total assets versus just 4%.[38] Layoffs may undermine the company's ability to innovate and grow, as do dividends for shareholders that aren't reinvested in the business. In a digital economy where competition is based on continuous reinvention, this can be fatal.

Making money for shareholders is inherently uninspiring to workers, which matters considerably in a digital economy where leaders lead by motivating employees rather than task-mastering for productivity. It can also make it harder to hire top talent.

David Graeber argues that the prevailing economic system in the US since the 1970s is no longer actually capitalism, or at least not the kind of capitalism that Adam Smith or even Milton Friedman conceived of. By managing so as to increase stock prices, the executives of large organizations have essentially been in the business of managing financial securities. According to Graeber, in the 1970s the financial sector and executive management fused.[39] Instead of being about buying and selling *things*, business is now about buying and selling investment opportunities in companies.

Social Responsibility Under Friedman's Doctrine?

I know some of your readers are adamant that the purpose of a company is to return money to the owners. Do you really think you've convinced them?

No. And I haven't really shown yet that the alternatives make sense. Let me give some reasons why even if you believe in Friedman's logic, you can still accept some ESG spending even if it reduces investor returns.

Negative and Positive Duties

There's a useful distinction in ethics between *negative* and *positive* obligations, and within the latter between positive obligations that are *contingent* and those that are *pure*. A negative duty is a duty *not* to do something, like "Do not kick a robot dog." A positive duty is something you *should* do, like returning your library books.

Friedman clearly acknowledges that businesses have negative duties. Consider these two statements. The first is from *Capitalism and Freedom*:

> There is one and only one social responsibility of business—to use its resources and engage in activities designed to increase its profits **so long**

as it stays within the rules of the game, which is to say, engages in open and free competition, without deception or fraud.[40] [my emphasis]

And from "A Friedman Doctrine: The Social Responsibility of a Business Is to Increase It's Profits":

[A corporate executive] has direct responsibility to his employers. That responsibility is to conduct the business in accordance with their desires, which generally will be to make as much money as possible **while conforming to their basic rules of the society, both those embodied in law and those embodied in ethical custom**.[41] [my emphasis]

In the first quote Friedman cites several negative duties of a firm. In the second, he makes it clear that he is talking not only about law but also about ethics.* So Friedman's objection is not to negative social obligations, even those that go beyond legal responsibilities.

Positive Duties

Even Friedman would have to agree that a corporation has positive responsibilities like paying its suppliers, paying taxes, and compensating tort victims. Here we can draw on the useful distinction between positive duties that are *pure* and those that are *contingent*.

Contingent positive duties are those that arise because of some "trigger"—a situation you desire or a condition you've accepted. Victor Frankenstein—because he has chosen the role of father or creator—has a duty to care for his creature and provide him an ethical education. *Pure* positive duties are duties that everyone has, without any trigger: perhaps a duty of benevolence (to save a person they find drowning, perhaps) or a duty to give charity.[42] We'll focus on contingent duties first and then return to pure ones.

Companies have contingent positive duties for the same reason that they are considered legal persons: they can enter into contracts, which create obligations. Friedman clearly doesn't dispute the existence of contingent positive obligations, because it is central to his argument that executives take on obligations as fiduciaries for the owners.

---

* A small technicality, perhaps: In the first quote Friedman is talking about the responsibilities of a business (a collectivist statement) while in the second he is talking about the responsibilities of executives (an individualist statement). But customers transact with the business, not with the executives of the business.

The question for this chapter is whether there are also requirements to benefit society that arise as contingent obligations in the course of doing business. If so, even Friedman would have to grant that these are valid obligations. Shareholders have a right to residual profits only *after* a company has met its obligations.

I can think of a few ways that companies might incur such obligations. They might come, for example, if in return for a tax reduction, the company agrees with a local government to employ a certain number of unemployed people or build a certain amount of affordable housing. The company then has an obligation to employ the people or build the housing; the agreement has triggered a contingent positive social obligation.

Corporate branding is often referred to as a "promise" to consumers. The McDonald's brand assures consumers that every time they order fries under the Golden Arches, the fries will be crispy. The obligation to meet a brand promise might not be a legal obligation but it seems to fall under "ethical custom"—again, I don't see why Friedman would disagree with that, since an unfulfilled brand promise interferes with consumers' freedom to make informed choices of products to purchase.

Perhaps companies incur obligations from their mission statements, which are a sort of promise to employees and the public. The mission of Du Pont, "To create shareholder and societal value while reducing the environmental footprint along the value chains in which we operate" seems to imply social responsibilities.[43] Whole Foods should satisfy their mission of "helping support the health, well-being, and healing of both people—customers, Team Members, and business organizations in general—and the planet."[44] Since Hyatt's mission is "To provide authentic hospitality by making a difference in the lives of the people we touch every day," one could legitimately ask them what they are doing to make a difference in people's lives every day.[45]

Contingent Obligations and Contractarianism

Contractarian logic supports my claim that—even if you subscribe to Friedman's doctrine—companies may have a broad set of contingent social obligations. Rather than speak of "stakeholders" that need to be satisfied, we can think of the company as managing a set of promises and expectations that may be implicit as well as explicit.

We can also formalize Duska's point that the *purpose* of business entities is determined by society. According to contractarianism, businesses must act as if they had struck a deal "that would be acceptable to free, informed parties acting from positions of equal moral authority."[46] Imagine a group of hypothetical bargainers coming together to negotiate whether businesses will be allowed to exist with the advantages of limited liability for their investors. Those bargainers would try to maximize the benefits to society (specialization, stabilization of output and distribution, liability resources, increased wages) and minimize the drawbacks (pollution, depletion of natural resources, destruction of personal accountability, worker alienation).[47] The terms of the contract would not just include returns to shareholders but also make trade-offs on those positive and negative effects.

Wearing my consumer cap: When I transact with an online retailer, the explicit terms of our agreement are that I pay $20 and the retailer agrees to send me a copy of *Grimm's Fairy Tales* with illustrations of Rumpelstiltskin's tale. But it is reasonable to think there are also unstated agreements involved, for example, that the retailer agrees to protect the personal data I furnish during the transaction. The transaction would generate a contingent positive obligation for the company to secure its information technology systems.

I also transact with the company on the assumption that they are meeting certain basic social obligations—not to be employing slave labor, setting little babies on fire, or laundering money. Today it seems clearer that consumers expect that their transaction will not cause net greenhouse gas emissions. Perhaps consumers, with the rising importance of ESG, have come to expect that the companies they transact with will remedy any negative externalities of their business, which leads to the next source of contingent obligations . . .

Contingent Obligations and Externalities

Contingent obligations might arise as byproducts of a company's operations. In producing its products the company might release greenhouse gases. If it moves its headquarters to a depressed city, rents might increase, pricing out residents. If it sources goods from a country with poor law enforcement, it might be giving criminal gangs an opportunity to control supply. All of these side effects, or *negative externalities*, are costs borne by society, not by the company. Perhaps there is a duty to compensate society for these costs.

If a company is generating greenhouse gases, my purchase transaction is not just an exchange of $100 for a case of *sagne 'ncannulate* noodles. It's an exchange of $100 plus the greenhouse gas's cost to society in exchange for the noodles. If the company's presence in my community is increasing homelessness, I'm exchanging $100 and society is bearing the additional cost of homelessness. Since those externalities are not priced into the transaction, I may have an implicit understanding that the company will do something to balance them.

Friedman's doctrine forbids executives from spending on social initiatives at their own whim, initiatives that are an *arbitrary use of investor dollars*. But investments to balance externalities are not arbitrary in that way; they directly follow from the activities of the company. Even if you believe that companies are not *obliged* to compensate the public for externalities, doing so would be *permitted* under Friedman's doctrine, if it becomes ethical custom.

Friedman might even accept this argument. He talks about externalities as "neighborhood effects" in *Capitalism and Freedom* and acknowledges that governments must do something about them. But since Friedman is usually suspicious of government involvement, he might even prefer that companies deal with their own externalities.

Pure Positive Duties

So you're saying that Friedman wouldn't have a problem with what you're calling negative social duties or certain types of contingent positive duties.

Yes, and that there are plenty of possible sources of contingent duties. A Friedman fan who suspects there are social duties can just choose which they believe are real obligations.

You still haven't said anything about pure positive duties, the ones that all companies have, just because. And that seems like the hard category.

Yes, but I think there's some wiggle room there too for Friedman fans.

The real thrust of Friedman's argument is against pure positive obligations—responsibilities other than profit making that aren't incurred through something a business does or agrees to. He would deny that companies have obligations of benevolence or giving charity, for example. This isn't necessarily controversial; even stakeholder theorists might agree that there are no *obligations* to spend resources on social good, but Friedman goes further by arguing that businesses are not *permitted* to do so.

Since Friedman's argument is based on investor freedom, there may be a way to bring the two sides together: *adequate disclosure*. If a company is transparent about its plans to spend money on social benefit programs rather than returning it to investors, then investors have the choice—that is, the freedom—to invest in a different company. Today, rating agencies help provide this transparency. Or a company can incorporate as a B-Corp, or Public Benefit Corporation.

The Problem with Stakeholder Views

Opponents of Friedman's doctrine hold that companies have obligations to other "stakeholders" besides investors—customers, employees, and communities, for example. This view has its own difficulties. After all, Friedman's doctrine was a reaction to the problems of a managerialist "balancing" approach. Balancing the interests of stakeholders is too vague a requirement. It doesn't help leaders know whether to engage in corporate giving and philanthropy, where to open or close factories, whether to reject hostile takeovers, whether to make products safer than required, and what sorts of environmental controls to establish.[48]

It's also hard for leaders to know the extent of the obligation to each of these stakeholders—when has the company spent "enough" in satisfying a particular group? Employees will always want higher salaries and more benefits. Communities will want more support. Governments will want more taxes. Where does the obligation end?

For digital transformation, there is an additional difficulty: since balancing decisions have to be made centrally by the leaders, they create a bottleneck when companies try to cope with rapid change, new technologies, and increased competition.[49] Employees can't easily be empowered to make decisions themselves.

Scoping Stakeholder Responsibilities

Stakeholder theories have to explain how, more exactly, to make trade-offs between stakeholders. Ethicists and management theorists have proposed some ideas.

Given a company's unique capabilities, it might be in a position to spend a small amount to accomplish a social benefit that is worth a great deal more, and it should do so. Thomas Dunfee argues that companies with special abilities to help in catastrophes are obligated to do so. A healthcare company operating in Africa, he says, can't just look away when the AIDS crisis is ravaging the continent.[50]

Friedman would not buy that one.

No. But it does limit the obligation to one where the company's special capabilities are relevant.

Similarly, T. M. Scanlon, a former Harvard philosophy professor, claims that companies have a duty of benevolence to "rescue" anyone they encounter, the same way that a person who encounters someone drowning is obligated to help them.[51] He argues that if an individual can prevent someone's dire plight while making a small sacrifice, then they are obligated to do so. So is a company.[52]

In the 1970s, Merck discovered that a drug it was developing to treat parasites in livestock could also be used to treat river blindness in people. Unfortunately, the people at risk for river blindness were generally too poor to pay for the drug. Together with nongovernmental organizations, Merck decided to distribute the drug for free.[53] A consequentialist argument for this decision would be that the disadvantage to shareholders is small, since Merck already had the drug, but the positive contribution to society is tremendous, so the net consequences are strongly positive.

The naturalist and philosopher Aldo Leopold suggests that we should include the planet among the stakeholders. In his view, an ethic, ecologically, is "a limitation on freedom of action in the struggle for existence."

> All ethics so far evolved rest upon a single premise: that the individual is a member of a community of interdependent parts. His instincts prompt him to compete for his place in that community, but his ethics prompt him also to co-operate (perhaps in order that there may be a place to compete for). The land ethic simply enlarges the boundaries of the community to include soils, waters, plants, and animals, or collectively: the land.[54]

So, in summary? Can you boil this down? What's your point on the Friedman doctrine?

I don't think it should necessarily stop businesses from socially responsible spending. But that doesn't mean they can just spend freely on pet projects of the executives. There should be a unifying logic that's specific to the company, an executive ethical "vision" that provides context and transparency.

Adaptive Business Ethics and Social Responsibility

Because bureaucratic enterprises largely took up Friedman's doctrine in the 1970s, it's become conventional wisdom that the purpose of a business is to maximize shareholder returns. With that as a given, managers are in a bind when they are told that their companies must demonstrate social responsibility. But a more careful analysis of Friedman's arguments shows that there are nuances. His reasoning doesn't really show that all decisions must be made to maximize shareholder returns; there is room for social responsibility. The challenge is to figure out what the social responsibilities are and how much of them is required. That requires clear guidance and communication from the company's leaders, both to employees and investors.

Numbers and Persons
Virtues: Integrity, Courage, Respect

I was once told that on Corfu there's a superstition that when you see a praying mantis, it either brings good luck or bad luck, depending on what happens.

—Ian Stewart, *Do Dice Play God?*

"Man," I cried, "how ignorant art thou in thy pride of wisdom!"

—Mary Shelley, *Frankenstein*

We've released a Frankenstein monster and we need to be better parents to it. I'm talking about the notion of a "data-driven" company. The need to become data-driven is something executives in every company seem to agree on and an opportunity for an IT department to showcase its value to the rest of an enterprise.

Businesses no longer enter the bobblehead market because it is "big"—they enter the market because there are 4.2 million people who want bobbleheads and 23,421 celebrities for whom bobbleheads have not yet been created, while existing bobblehead producers have penetrated only 14.8% of the market. (Please don't rely on those numbers—I made them up before my first Nespresso). Perhaps it's more accurate to say they begin producing bobbleheads because numbers like those have been reported in bold fonts on PowerPoint slides with the company's standard formatting and recited in a meeting by a serious-looking presenter.

In 2020 the National Development and Reform Commission (NDRC) of China declared data to be a "primary factor of production," along with the traditional ones—capital, labor, land, and entrepreneurship.*[1] The timing is terrible: most of the authors of classic economic texts—Karl Marx, that's you—are dead and can't update their books.

---

* Factors of production are defined as inputs to the production of goods and services that don't appear in the final product (that is, they get combined with the raw materials that do appear in the final product).

In the meantime, businesses have realized that they've been collecting data for years but didn't know it! That's because it was hidden in separate databases, each zealously guarded by the counterintelligence unit of a different department. By extracting the data from the department's control and combining it with other data according to a yet-to-be-discovered alchemical formula, the business could turn it into gold.

Imagine the potential: with this new data asset they'd not only know who bought which bobblehead, but what those people ate for breakfast on the day of purchase and their shoe size! There would surely be some way to monetize such an asset to increase shareholder returns. "Data is the answer, for which organizations have to come up with the questions," says Jerry Muller in *The Tyranny of Metrics*.[2] Venture capitalists and IT departments are pouring money into finding questions.

Our obsession with data extends deeply into our personal lives as well. Smartwatches make a game out of "improving" health metrics. People have gone as far as quantifying details of their lives in what's been called "lifelogging"—as if tweeting their Wordle results wasn't boring and personal enough. On his blog *Measured Me*,[3] Konstantin Augemberg quantified nearly every aspect of his life. His datasets included sixty-six daily measurements of twenty-one variables each, including "mental energy," "charisma," "self-esteem," calories consumed and expended, six variables for the weather, and a measure of how "chaotic" a particular morning, afternoon, or evening was.

The Frankenstein problem: for leaders of digital transformation, data seems to provide a way to retain the bureaucratic elements of control that we fear losing. Data-drivenness is not a business strategy, but a value system. As bureaucratic structure declines, data-drivenness is taking its place as a way to sustain bureaucratic values.

The Utopian Idea

Data-drivenness is as loosely defined as "digital transformation" itself. It seems to include everything from using data to make management decisions to increasing sales by more aggressively targeting customers and increasing the stickiness of game worlds by selling players magical formulas they can use to turn leprechauns into Death Stars. The vagueness of the term is a clue that we are not dealing with a well-defined set of practices, but rather a more general value system.

The dream of data-drivenness is the dream of a world where business decisions are rigorous, where the "right" thing to do is apparent from analysis, and where the uncertainty of the future is eliminated because we can see the future reflected in the data from the past. It's a world where managers don't need to exercise judgment to make difficult decisions; they simply need to be skilled and industrious in interpreting the data they increasingly have at hand.

We've become a teeny bit obsessed with data. It's the lens through which we see our customers, our employees, our market position, our futures, and our successes. We ask the gods for a large harvest of it and then hope we can sell it in the markets for a good price. As Muller says, "The spreadsheet is a tool, but it is also a worldview—reality by the numbers."[4] The idea that someday we'll make all our decisions with perfect assurance because we've analyzed the data is a Utopian one and an article of faith in the digital world.

One thing we've learned from bureaucratic organizations is that we should be suspicious of Utopian ideas.

What Gets Measured Gets Measured

Everyone knows that what gets measured gets managed. Or is it what gets managed gets measured? In any case, you can't manage something unless you measure it, or vice versa. Do you remember who said this? Trick question and a paradox: probably no one said it, though it's repeated often enough. Some say it was management guru Peter Drucker, some the scientist Lord Kelvin, or the quality sage W. Edwards Deming, or maybe Yoda.

Peter Drucker definitely talked about the importance of measurement, but according to the Drucker Institute, he never said the measure-manage thing. In fact, Drucker told an executive he was advising: "It is the relationship with people, the development of mutual confidence, the identification of people, the creation of a community. This is something only you can do. . . . It cannot be measured or easily defined. But it is not only a key function. It is one only you can perform."[5]

The nineteenth-century physicist Lord Kelvin, the guy with the temperature scale that goes all the way down to absolute zero, beat Drucker to it anyway, saying that "If you cannot measure it, you cannot improve it."[6] Actually, he didn't quite say that—apparently Lord Kelvin never said anything so pithy in his life. What he said was:

> I often say that when you can measure what you are speaking about, and express it in numbers, you know something about it; but when you cannot measure it, when you cannot express it in numbers, your knowledge is of a meagre and unsatisfactory kind; it may be the beginning of knowledge, but you have scarcely, in your thoughts, advanced to the stage of science, whatever the matter may be.[7]

The pithier version of the measure-manage quote is quite correctly attributed to the quality sage W. Edwards Deming. The problem is that if you include the words at the beginning and end of Deming's sentence, he actually wrote the opposite: "It is wrong to suppose that if you can't measure it you can't manage it—a costly myth."[8]

Deming wasn't the only one to find something wrong with measure-manage. In 1956, V. F. Ridgeway of Cornell University's management school published a paper, "Dysfunctional Consequences of Performance Measurements." Simon Caulkin, a journalist, summarized Ridgeway's paper this way: "What gets measured gets managed—even when it's pointless to measure and manage it, and even if it harms the purpose of the organisation to do so."[9]

Not only is it unclear who said the measure-manage thing, but it doesn't make much sense, largely for the reasons Drucker gave. Management is about people. Not everything that matters is measurable.* Even when it is, it still might not be effective or practical to measure. Managing to numbers often results in gaming and dysfunction. But we want to believe that what gets measured gets managed, because it promises an objective way of making decisions that are by their nature subjective.

Data in the Enterprise—Decision-Making

Traditional, bureaucratic organizations are reassuringly certain about how things should be done: rules are to be followed, more senior levels of management are to be obeyed, processes are well defined, and the ultimate goals of the organization have already been set. Stir in a tablespoon of Friedman doctrine, and we can even be sure of what success looks like: shareholder value creation. We can trace that value creation through numeric measurements of the firm's activities.

In transforming to a digital organization, much of this certainty and comfort goes away. As a manager you're no longer a passive cog in a calculating machine, but a true decision maker who must face the existential dread of choosing without complete justification. A manager of people in all their complexity, responsible for leading them with only the legacy powers you were granted by Michael Porter and other management theorists. Every decision you make is an act of creation. You're committed.

Data can seem like a good way out.

---

* Yes, I know Douglas Hubbard wrote the opposite in *How to Measure Anything: Finding the Value of Intangibles in Business*.[10] But all he showed is that you can measure a proxy for what you care about, and that proxy will share some of the characteristics that matter. Or that if—big if— you can define it precisely, then you can measure it—which verges on the tautological.

There's nothing new or wrong with using data in making decisions. In fact, it's critical. Companies have always managed with their financial statements in mind; the monthly and quarterly "close" rituals have always brought managers together to recite from Excel and pray for ROIs. Cost accounting data has given managers insight into their unit economics. Market research data informs product design. I don't mean to offend anyone by suggesting that their pet data isn't adorable.

What's new is the religious belief that data answers all questions, that what gets measured gets ministered. The moral notion that everything an individual contributes must be traceable to an impact on the data. A worldview that says that when you have a question you should consult a spreadsheet, rather than, say, the entrails of a sheep.

We're a bit sarcastic today, it seems.
I'm anticipating a lot of disagreement on this point from people I know.

Where do these ideas come from? Partly from geeky management joy at having access today to so much data. Partly it comes from the Friedmanian idea of accountability to shareholders: every decision must be judged on its contribution to profits and share price. Partly from legal pressures—the keenly felt danger of lawsuits that makes us prefer solid numbers to back up our decisions. It comes from the natural fear of having to make difficult decisions under uncertainty. Even though the fine print tells us that yesterday's data does not necessarily predict tomorrow's, we will eagerly base decisions on it.

It's also our attempt to hold on to bureaucratic mechanisms while we transform: we still want to control autonomous, empowered teams and employees (impossible by definition). Holding them accountable for numeric targets seems to give us a way.

The Numbers Made Me Do It

It is misleading to imply that data "drives" decisions. Data doesn't tell us what to do. Human judgment is always involved, even if that judgment has been rendered into an algorithm that operates autonomously. Data is inert, it just is what it is—always an *input* into a decision process. *Data*: according to our IoT sensors, the water level has risen one meter. *Judgment*: we'd better do something about it because we don't know how to swim.

From the fact that customers who buy flashlights usually buy batteries as well, we cannot logically infer that we should market batteries to customers who buy flashlights. It is human judgment that tells an algorithm that when it sees that type of correlation, it should offer the related product. Maybe my employee Rumpelstiltskin has missed his gold-spinning targets by 20%—does that mean I should fire him? Thirty-seven percent of our customers say their email inboxes are too empty and they feel lonely. Does that mean we launch a new email newsletter? The data is neutral; managerial judgment decides how to activate it.

We say that we fired Rumpelstiltskin "because" he missed his target by 20%. While the number has some explanatory value, there remains the question of whether missing the target by 20% should result in being fired. The number does not relieve the manager of responsibility for the decision. But just as bureaucracy displaces responsibility by putting it on rules rather than individual decision makers, data obsession can displace responsibility by putting it on numbers.

But isn't data just a way managers legitimately explain their decisions?
It can be. If the data is used to support the decision. But watch—you'll see that decisions are often attributed to the data itself, not the human. I'm just getting warmed up.

Data obsession can manifest itself in delayed decision-making, as managers seek more data to erase uncertainty and personal risk. This delay has a cost to the organization (though there's a cognitive bias that effort spent reducing risk is always justifiable and valuable). And if the data doesn't quite justify the decision, then the analysis is stretched beyond statistical rigor to have "something" to base the decision on. It is "suggestive" or just "the best information we have."

Numbers End Life on Earth

The Frankenstein story got a unique twist in the 1920 play *R.U.R.* (*Rossum's Universal Robots*) by Karel Čapek—the play that introduced the word "robot." Like Victor Frankenstein, Rossum figures out how to create artificial life.* It's an intellectual exercise: "For him the question was just to prove that God is unnecessary. So he resolved to create a human being just like us, down to the last hair."[11]

His son, Rossum the younger, decides to begin manufacturing robots at scale—and at an ever-increasing scale as market demand grows. He is inspired

---

* Rossum's robots are different from today's—like Frankenstein's creature, Rossum's are actually alive, though created artificially.

to do so as he realizes that robots are "better" than humans—more efficient, less distracted by emotional concerns. "My dear Miss Glory," the factory manager says, "Robots are not people. They are mechanically more perfect than we are, they have an astounding intellectual capacity, but they have no soul." That's a good thing—souls get in the way of achieving results. Souls are hard to quantify, too.

The executives of R.U.R. try to avoid taking responsibility for the inevitable catastrophe when the robots decide to take over the world.

> BUSMAN: My, you are naïve! No doubt you think that the plant director controls production? Not at all. Demand controls production. The whole world wanted its Robots.[12]

Robots demanded equals robots produced, as if R.U.R. executives weren't involved. It's math. If anyone is guilty, it's the invisible hand of the market, or arithmetic. But actually, the plant director *does* control production.

The name "Rossum," by the way, is derived from the Slavic word for reason, rozum.[13] Enlightenment logic infuses the play—robots promise a rationalist Utopia where people no longer have to work. They are a bureaucrat's dream—a way to bring efficiency to everything from housework to manufacturing, through beings who don't bring their biases or feelings to work—because they have no feelings.

Bureaucracy of Numbers

Both bureaucracy and number obsession abstract away the details of a concrete situation so that it can be dealt with more simply—bureaucracy identifies the critical elements to which a rule can be applied, and number fixation derives a summary or aggregate metric that can be used in place of individuals.

"The most characteristic feature of metric fixation is the aspiration to replace judgment based on experience with standardized measurement," says Muller.[14] That's bureaucracy in a nutshell: replacing judgment with objective, rule-based decision-making. Employees on the front lines of an organization have practical, informal, implicit knowledge that they can apply in their everyday activities—analogous to the "practical wisdom" of virtue ethics. That implicit knowledge can appear to be imprecise or uncertain, but it's based on the employee's experience and their direct accountability for results.

Abstract knowledge is more useful to those at a distance from the action. It removes messy details and allows managers to reason at a higher level. There's nothing wrong with this—mathematics and science depend on abstraction too. Managers have "bounded rationality"—they are constrained in how much information they have the time and ability to deal with. A new CEO who wants to quickly set a new direction begins by "getting the data" as a shortcut to understanding the organization.[15]

Problems only arise when abstracted knowledge is used to make decisions that require concrete and practical knowledge. In *Seeing Like a State*, James Scott shows how decisions made in the abstract often miss crucial details. Abstractions used by central planners have created soulless cities like Brasilia and Chandigarh, resulted in famines during Soviet collectivization, and destroyed forests in Germany by replanting them in straight rows and columns without essential underbrush. The consequences of metric obsession can be similar to those of central planning in the Soviet system.[16] Scott believes that the abstract use of data also makes it hard to deal with uncertainty—our central concern in the digital world:

> Throughout the book I make the case for the indispensable role of practical knowledge, informal processes, and improvisation in the face of unpredictability. . . . my point is that formal schemes of order are untenable without some elements of the practical knowledge that they tend to dismiss.[17]

Bureaucracy disturbs us because its generalized rules often don't seem relevant to the details of a particular situation. Metric fixation runs the same risk. Robert McNamara, secretary of defense during the Vietnam War, analyzed his data to its apparent conclusion: the US was winning the war. He based this on the count of "body bags"—a gruesome metric for how many soldiers had been killed. Unfortunately, counting body bags missed some critical details: strategy, morale, determination, and so on. McNamara's error (as he admitted himself) was a "materialist bias"—a tendency to focus on concrete, physical things that are easily measured.[18]

Metrics support traditional hierarchies. In a bureaucratic organization's three-class system—senior managers, operational managers, and workers—the division between classes is upheld by the practice of sending data upward at increasing levels of abstraction. The more senior the manager, the more their decisions are based on summarized data. The data, in turn, lets them control those below them[19] in the hierarchy through targets and quantitative performance assessment.

The abstracted data held by senior management is supposed to help them formulate strategies. But the problem, as Matthew Stewart says in *The*

Management Myth, is that you can't derive particular actions from abstract data: knowing that you want to increase profits does not tell you what actions you need to take to do so.[20] In the digital world, especially given our focus on continuous innovation, we recognize that strategies emerge through a complex set of interactions between those with abstract data and those with practical knowledge.

That's why we find leaders of firms struggling to "monetize" their newly excavated data assets. Knowing at a high level that monetizing the asset will bring profits does not help in figuring out how. It is only through the creativity that comes from practical understanding that the abstraction connects with reality.

Targets "Drive" Behavior

Consumer fedora: I recently rented a car from a company I won't name because they later set things right. When I declined insurance for damage to the car, saying that it was covered by my credit card, the agent reminded me that the credit card wouldn't cover damage to the car from acts of God, like hailstorms. In fact, she said, there was a hailstorm—with golf-ball-size hail—predicted for the very next day, so I'd better reconsider.

There was no hailstorm predicted for the following day, and none appeared. Want to bet she was operating under an incentive to get customers to take the extra insurance coverage? Her behavior was not just a matter of greed, I believe. It was more a matter of focus. She was encouraged to care about a single metric—and, consequently, not encouraged to think about anything else, including whether deception was okay. She was doing what the company seemed to want, given the success measures they had chosen.

Consider the scandal at Wells Fargo. In an effort to "deepen" customer relationships, leaders had chosen the amount of cross-selling as a way to measure the depth of customer relationships. Salespeople responded by opening accounts for people who didn't want them. It's a great example of a metric-induced displacement of goals, analogous to the displacement that takes place in a bureaucracy. Wells Fargo employees missed the point of the metric—deepening relationships with customers—and, in fact, subverted it through their actions.

If their metric became separated from its business purpose, even more was it separated from any ethical context. Leaders were never forced to address the critical ethical question, because all they did was choose an innocuous metric. For employees there was no ethical issue—remember that in a bureaucracy, ends are set externally and employees act neutrally to accomplish it. They found the best way, and they saw that it was good. The metric had taken "good" out of the realm of the ethical and made it an operational matter.

Why couldn't they have had ethical guardrails in addition to the numeric targets? Like "maximize cross-selling but without deceiving customers"? Or just a strong company code of conduct?

In Chapter 7 I'll come back to codes of conduct. But I think you're forgetting the whole point of numeric targets.

Managers use numeric targets to *focus* employee behavior. In *Measure What Matters: How Google, Bono, and the Gates Foundation Rock the World with OKRs*, John Doerr and Larry Page's book on OKRs (objectives and key results), the authors are very clear about their goal: "Then come the four OKR 'superpowers': *focus*, align, track, and stretch" (my italics).[21] "The one thing an [OKR] system should provide par excellence is *focus*. This can only happen if we keep the number of objectives small."[22]

I agree; focus is an advantage of target metrics. But the focus is on things that are not the ethical guardrails.

Numbers create a distance between decision makers and the people affected by their decisions. To refer to "customers" in the aggregate is not to refer to particular people but to a variable in the domain of the business. In *Virtue at Work*, Geoff Moore, Professor of Business Ethics at Durham University, says that using numerical targets diverts the attention of even the people who set the targets from ethical considerations:

> They [numbers] serve to separate the thought from the deed and, in doing so, they result in decisions being made in relation to abstract entities as opposed to the real Others that those who carry out these decisions must confront. And, conversely, they enable the latter to absolve themselves of responsibility for their actions by virtue of the fact that the decisions that prompted their actions were not their own. Thus, we can see that, by separating decision-making from implementation, the moral impulse is for all intents and purposes by-passed, the substitution of technical for moral responsibility.[23]

In *R.U.R.*, executives' decisions were based on a number representing demand; in McNamara's case, political leaders' decisions were based on the count of body bags. The ethical issues were not computed.

Data in the Market—Personalization

An enduring myth of the digital age is that it's an era of personalization.

Putting on my consumer kufi: When I read the news online every day, I find myself overwhelmed with ads for hearing aids mixed with my news. I do not need a hearing aid. I'm guessing that some algorithm has noticed that I'm in an age group—or some other demographic group—of people who often have hearing problems. Is this *personalization*? Or is this the opposite—putting me into a group that has a reasonable probability of hearing problems?

What we call personalization is more about group membership—specifically, groups that we can target to generate revenue. A better name for it is simply "targeting." When the company makes the data-driven decision to enter the bobblehead market because there are 4.2 million possible customers, Large Larry may be one of those customers. Nothing else about Larry is relevant aside from his membership in this group; the point of making a data-driven decision is that that number, the 4.2 million, and Larry's inclusion in that number, tells the decision maker everything they need to know about Large Larry.

Consumer kalpak: Personalization is about finding an intersection of groups that I belong to, or the data cluster I seem to be nearest, not about the complex, conscious being that I believe myself to be. It's not just that companies need to become better at personalization by finding me at the intersection of more categories. No matter how precise the categories are and how many of them are used, they still don't capture what it is to be me. And what it is to be me changes from moment to moment; good luck to the personalization engine that wants to pin me down. You know how difficult that would be—come on, have you ever read a quirkier book on digital transformation?

You know for sure, wearing your consumer songkok, that personalization is not what it claims to be, for the simple reason that the companies you deal with actively try to suppress what makes you different from others. Digital transactions and customer service can be very smooth—as long as you follow the "happy path." But when you have a problem or present an exception, it has become harder to solve it. A voice response system walks you through menu after menu of options, none of which fit. You have to guess which key you can push to "speak to a customer service rep" to get a personalized solution. The recorded message tells you over and over that you should use the website instead—even though you know it can't do what you need.

This is the opposite of "personalization."

Data in the Enterprise—People

The same abstraction process that slots consumers into target groups puts employees into categories that can be targeted by HR. Employees may be ranked to determine their eligibility for bonuses and promotion or for termination. When Rumpelstiltskin missed his gold-spinning target, he found himself in a group targeted for termination, even though he might have been contributing greatly to team morale, might have saved a miller's daughter from execution, and might have invented a world-changing machine that converts straw into gold for the company to sell. His gold target might also have been too aggressive. Rumpelstiltskin is a person, though his HR record isn't.

Depersonalization shows up in our language. Central governments don't refer to "nature," but to "natural resources."[24] Resources are things that we can use; a means to our ends. Similarly, employees are referred to as "human resources," that is, people we can use. When it's time to plan next year's hiring, a manager will say "I need three resources for spinning straw and two for bringing the gold to the king." If the straw-into-gold department can't keep up with demand, it means they don't have enough resources. The implication—a plainly bureaucratic implication—is that the people are interchangeable parts, and it's the quantity of employees you feed into the machine that matters.

Though digital businesses value innovation, metric fixation puts risk on employees who innovate. They may miss short-term targets since the benefits of an innovation are only realized over the long term. The benefits of an innovation may not yet even be included in the employee's targets. Traditional managers don't suppress innovation just because they're risk averse, but also because it takes time away from production, as measured by the targets.

Metric fixation—and bureaucratic rules—are prevalent in environments where employees aren't trusted to use their judgment.

Important public service announcement from the author: There is no such thing as "trust but verify." It sounded cute when President Reagan said it in connection with verifying that Russia had reduced its nuclear stockpile. But one verifies because of a lack of trust. It's sane to monitor outcomes and work backward to diagnose problems and fix them. But data will never be a way to both trust employees and make sure they are performing adequately. Thank you for listening.

Productivity

Productivity is the crucial measure for traditional enterprises. The bureaucratic model, after all, has its roots in factory work and the idea of buying an employee's time. Productivity makes less sense as a measure for knowledge work. You can't measure a software developer's performance by the number of lines of code they write or evaluate an advertising director on the number of creative ideas in their ads. But if you can't measure productivity, what can you measure? How do you know if an employee is actually delivering what you expect in exchange for their paycheck?

These questions are uncomfortable for managers who have grown up in the era of traditional enterprises. Sometimes, they continue to apply productivity metrics even for knowledge work, a pressing issue now that more employees are working from home. In an August 14, 2022, article in the *New York Times*, "The Rise of the Worker Productivity Score," Jodi Kantor and Arya Sundaram showed just how committed companies are to productivity metrics. According to a venture capitalist they interviewed, investments in "performance management" (employee surveillance) technologies have increased eightfold in the last five years.[25]

Productivity scoring systems, the article reports, are used to monitor even radiologists, architects, academic administrators, nursing home workers, lawyers . . . and hospice chaplains who care for the dying? While the chaplains may view the essence of their jobs as helping patients with deep, searching questions like how they will face death, their employer measures them in "productivity points" where visiting a dying patient earns 1.0 point, attending a funeral earns 1.75 points, and making a phone call to grieving relatives is worth 0.25 points.

> But dying defied planning. Patients broke down, canceled appointments, drew final breaths. This left the clergy scrambling and in a perpetual dilemma. "Do I see the patients who earn the points or do I see the patients who really need to be seen?"[26]

For simple, repeated, factory-like work, productivity is a sensible measure (although standards should be humane, of course). But it's pure desperation for managers to use productivity measures for roles that are about judgment, human connection, innovation, and the many other functions of a knowledge and service economy in a digital age.

Misusing Data

Obsessive data-drivenness can lead employees and managers to misuse data, especially if they are not data experts. If your company demands that you provide data to justify your decisions, you find some—whether or not it is high-quality or your inferences from it are statistically valid. Here are a few common misuses.

Gaming

British colonists in India were concerned about the number of cobras they encountered. Their solution was to offer a bounty for cobra skins. The idea was popular, but strangely, the British found that the number of cobras was actually *increasing*. Enterprising Indians had begun breeding cobras so that they could collect the bounty. When the British realized it and ended the program, the breeders released their worthless snakes into the wild, making the problem even worse.[27] The moral of the story is clear: don't colonize India. But perhaps there's another important point: setting targets can backfire as people find ways to game the metrics.

The French government in the early nineteenth century established a door-and-window tax, on the theory that the number of doors and windows was proportional to a house's size, and easier to measure. Consequence: homes were redesigned to have as few openings as possible. Windows were boarded up. The government didn't get its tax money—and the health of the population was impaired.[28]

When surgeons are paid based on outcomes, they cherry-pick, or "cream"— they refuse to accept any difficult cases that will lower their success rates. Also, as Muller states, when statistical techniques were used to measure policing effectiveness,

> a whistle-blower from the London police force told a parliamentary committee that massaging statistics had become "an ingrained part of policing culture": serious crimes such as robbery were downgraded to "theft snatch," and rapes were often underreported so as to hit performance targets.[29]

Stretching

What if the data you need just isn't there? You find data that's *sort of* related. After all, it's "all you have to go on." If your target market is women over sixty and all you have is data from men over fifty, you can call it "suggestive." You can also ignore the fact that your data is from a limited sample or that the margin of error is huge.

Oversimplification

People with limited statistical abilities love averages. They'll brush their teeth 2.07 times a day and attend 0.8 weddings each year and have 1.8 babies. If you give them a bunch of numbers, they'll automatically compute the average. But even when a metric must be summarized, medians, modes, variances, standard deviations, distributions, and all the other tools of descriptive statistics may provide more useful information than averages. The appropriate tool depends on the data's characteristics and how it will be used.

It can be dangerous to oversimplify complex raw data through a single summary statistic, especially if others don't have access to the original data to propose competing explanations.[30] Decentralized software development teams have detailed information that is lost when a more centralized authority calculates their "velocity"; still more information is lost as data is further summarized into HR costs and returns on investment.

Post-hoc Reasoning

"Our team decreased the time we took to respond to customer support issues by 7%." That's great!—maybe. Was that an important goal, or did you just choose to report it because it looked good? Should the $1 million you spent have resulted in an improvement more like 15%? Did you get the 7% improvement by discouraging customers from notifying you of difficult problems? Did you choose the one time period where there was a successful outcome?

Backward-looking analyses like these pretend to be scientific but are often poorly reasoned. Scientists use a control group, decide in advance what they are testing, report all results, make their data available for analyses that contradict their interpretations, and make sure that their experiments can be repeated by others.

Spurious Correlations

As I'm sure you're aware, it's important to avoid eating cheese before going to bed because of its correlation with fatal bedsheet tangling accidents. In his book *Spurious Correlations*, Tyler Vigen reports this relationship and jokes "Sweet dreams aren't made of cheese. Who am I to diss a Brie?"[31] His attempts at humor are correlated with the soundness of the points he makes. As if there weren't enough other reasons why people try to convince me to eat less fatty red meat, a correlation between beef consumption and deaths caused by lightning has now been found.

Noise

Some data is signal and some is noise. Today, one of our best public speakers, who always had a high average customer satisfaction (CSAT) score, unexpectedly received a lower score. What should we do about it? What went wrong? Have they lost their touch?

Or is it just noise? Perhaps the presentation was right before lunch and the audience was eager to have it over with. I know I would be. Perhaps the audience didn't like the way the conference was being conducted, and the anger spilled over into ratings. Perhaps they were distracted to see a leprechaun staring at them from outside a window. A series of presentations with low CSAT scores is one thing; a single instance something else.

But you have to do something about the drop in CSAT scores, right?
No.

Numbers and Digital Transformation: Data Virtues

Back in our business bycocket: The faith that data will bring rigor and control to all business decisions is an easy way out for leaders of digital transformation. It seems to offer us a way to keep one toe in the bureaucratic world of predictability, control, and planning while we try to find our digital footing. Decentralizing authority allows employees to use their practical knowledge and their proximity to customers to innovate and make decisions. When we abstract away that practical knowledge into summary metrics and targets, we forego that advantage. And, unfortunately, abstraction can direct everyone's attention away from ethical issues, as in the case of Wells Fargo.

The best way to act ethically in a data-intensive environment is not by making rules, but by cultivating the virtuous use of data. Becoming data-driven is not a strategy. It is rather a set of virtues that employees and managers must bring to the workplace. In Chapter 11 I'll propose a set of virtues for digital transformation, but three of them stand out when it comes to the use of data: integrity (rigor in making inferences from data), courage (taking responsibility rather than blaming the numbers), and respect (for people as individuals rather than increments to a metric).

Bullshit
Virtues: Authenticity, Care, Courage, Respect

It is no more than a moral prejudice that truth is worth more than mere appearance; it is even the worst proved assumption there is in the world.
—Nietzsche, *Beyond Good and Evil*

Mundus vult decipi: the world wants to be deceived. The truth is too complex and frightening; the taste for the truth is an acquired taste that few acquire.

—Martin Buber, *I and Thou*

"The important thing about the world today is that there is so much bullshit," says the philosopher Harry Frankfurt, and he's right. Bullshit, in Frankfurt's definition, is a kind of phoniness, different from lying and other deceptive behaviors, and it is something distinctive and central to today's society. As I will explain, bullshit is a serious danger to companies that are transforming digitally; it is a form of communication that hides and evades, using the impersonal language of bureaucracy to avoid speaking authentically and sincerely.

Inauthentic and depersonalized language come in many forms, from euphemism to outright deception and verbal trickery. Today, it represents a heavy investment in insincerity. Its result is a sustained, high level of babble and chatter in the communications that customers and employees have to process every day. Because listeners become good at tuning it out, costs are higher for companies that want to rise above the noise and deliver authentic messages. Worse, insincerity works against our desire to build meaningful relationships with customers, a topic we'll return to in Part III.

Overcoming bullshit is especially hard because we've come to think of it as normal. We pay marketing people to produce it in industrial quantities, and when we open our mouths to speak to our employees, customers, industry analysts, news reporters, and shareholders, bullshit flows out. And we often don't notice it. As leaders of digital transformation, we'd do best to unlearn the patterns of inauthentic communication that we've been absorbing throughout our careers.

Lying and Deception

To simplify the philosophical jargon, we'll say that *lying* means making a statement that you know to be false, in a way that warrants that it is true.[1] *Deception* is causing someone to have a false belief. Lying necessarily involves language, while deception does not. In fact, you can deceive someone by *not* speaking when they hold a belief you know to be false. In cybersecurity, a honeypot is a technique used to deceive malicious hackers into thinking they've compromised your network. It too deceives without language.

Although lying involves making a false statement, the false statement might not deceive anyone. The listener might not believe you. Deception, on the other hand, always implies success—if you've deceived someone, then you've succeeded in deceiving them.

The second part of the definition of lying, that you warrant the statement to be true, is important. There are contexts where a false statement isn't a lie— for example, if you are an actor portraying a fictional character, or if someone asks "How are you?" and you respond "Fine" even though you aren't. In context, the hearer doesn't expect your statement to be true—or, at least, accepts there might be some falsehood to it.

For some reason, people seem to think that lying is morally worse than other forms of deception—they'll use all sorts of verbal trickery to avoid technically telling a lie, even though their intention is to deceive.[2] Perhaps they think it relieves them of responsibility for the deception—if they haven't lied and yet the hearer was deceived, it must be the hearer's fault. Or maybe they're just thinking legalistically instead of morally.

A story is told about Saint Athanasius, an Alexandrian pope and revered saint in several Christian sects, rowing on a river when his persecutors came rowing in the opposite direction. "Where is the traitor Athanasius?" "Not far away," the Saint replied, and rowed past them unsuspected.[3] Since Athanasius made a true statement, he did not lie, yet he deceived. It doesn't seem to make his response any more ethical, although in the circumstances, he had no obligation to give an illuminating answer.

What's Wrong With Lying And Deception?

Most of us are pretty sure lying is bad, but why exactly? And why do we lie so much if we think it's bad?

Kant thought there was an absolute prohibition against lying. For most of us, though, a rule against lying would have to admit lots of exceptions. Are "little white lies" or "fibs" okay? If someone is about to die and they ask how their favorite sumo wrestler did in today's match, is it okay to lie so that they don't end their life unhappily? If your aunt gives you an ugly sweater for your birthday and you already have enough ugly sweaters, should you say you love it?

Many critics have seized on an odd example Kant gives. In his example, you are hiding a friend in your house. A murderer comes to the door and asks if you know where they are. Kant says you must answer the question honestly.[*] If you were a citizen in World War II–era Netherlands, hiding Jews in your attic, and the Nazis came banging on the door looking for them, Kant's position— that you must tell the truth—seems bizarre.

If you believe, contra Kant, that you *should* sometimes lie, or at least that it's sometimes okay, there are a few ways to justify your belief. One is a consequentialist argument: lying is fine when it leads to more overall goodness. How you calculate total goodness is important: if selling you the used car whose brakes aren't working means that I win a sales contest and get a free trip to Disneyland and a personal lunch with Goofy and Pooh, perhaps the benefit to me outweighs your loss, so the net benefit to society is positive.

Philosophical explanations of why deception is wrong generally invoke the principle of autonomy, or Kant's CIv2. When you deceive someone, you deprive them of the ability to make the decisions they should make based on their goals. Or you manipulate them into making a decision based solely on your own ends and not on theirs.

Some ethicists argue that lying for the good of others is entirely consistent with respecting their autonomy, and is a very *good* way to treat them as ends in themselves.[4] In *Lying and Deception*, Thomas Carson makes the case that lying is often ethically *preferable*; complete, unrestrained candor that expresses every petty annoyance and nasty thought that enters one's mind is not a virtue. Openness, candor, and self-disclosure must be negotiated in personal relationships.[5]

Virtue ethics allows for the use of practical wisdom to decide when and how to apply the virtue of honesty; honesty should be calibrated by care for the person you're talking to. Honesty as a virtue is a disposition to avoid deception in all of its forms, while telling the truth as a rule can lead to legalistic word shaping to avoid technically telling a lie.

A duty not to deceive can easily conflict with other moral duties. In my story about Mary in the introduction, I chose to deceive Mary because of a duty to obey a superior in the organization and because of a promise I had made. In

---

[*] Actually, Kant's arguments are more subtle; he is using this not as an example of the absoluteness of the prohibition on lying, but in the context of a discussion on justice.

the case of the Nazi at the door, the duty to tell the truth might conflict with a duty not to harm others.[6] As a way to deal with conflicts like these, the philosopher W. D. Ross said that the duty not to lie is a "prima facie duty"—to be observed if there is no stronger prima facie duty that must be observed.[7]

Lying and Deception in Business

In the 1980s, Beech-Nut advertised a drink that contained no juice of any kind as 100% apple juice. They were fined $2 million and two executives went to prison. Today, Red Bull advertises its drink with the slogan "Red Bull gives you wings." It does not actually give you wings or any other new body parts. They eventually had to change it to "wiiings," but isn't there a difference between the cases? It seems to have something to do with an intent to deceive, present in the first case but not in the second. Or, to take it out of the realm of intention—as I said earlier, it is debated whether companies have intentions—Red Bull would say that a reasonable person would not be misled by their ad.

Perhaps advertisements are not really warranted to be true—everyone understands that "they need to be taken with a grain of salt," so lying in advertisements is not morally wrong. Advertising ethics are worth a separate discussion and we'll come back to them in Chapter 8.

Are businesses ever justified in lying or deceiving? The examples I gave above where lying seemed to be justified—the ugly sweater or the favorite Sumo wrestler losing—were justified by care or compassion for the person being deceived. But businesses don't feel care or compassion. One area that's been proposed is negotiation: since misstating one's negotiating position is so common, perhaps statements made during a negotiation are also not really warranted to be true.[8] The sternly redundant "This is my last and final offer" is not really a commitment to make no further offers.

Today's Mail Arrives

On with my consumer capotain: I have before me an envelope I received yesterday. The return address is for "Records Division" and the envelope says "Important Document Enclosed" and in red, "Second Notice: Time Sensitive." Inside is a piece of paper laid out to mimic a tax form, with "2022" in the IRS font in the upper right hand corner and a form number, "T-2," in the upper left. The text says "2022 Benefit Information for Massachusetts Citizens Only. As a resident of Massachusetts, you are entitled to more benefits not provided by government funds." And then, the punch line: "You now have access to a 2022 state-regulated life insurance program which will pay 100% of all final expenses up to $35,000." That's the first clue that this is actually a commercial offering, not a government notice.

I get these kinds of mailings often. They are from companies that deliberately want to mislead me into opening an envelope I wouldn't otherwise open, to read an advertisement I wouldn't otherwise read. It is true that there are technically no lies on or in the envelope. That matters legally, I suppose. Does it really matter ethically when the intent is clearly to deceive? It's strange to think that some of the companies that are lying to me are the ones that are trying hard to "build a relationship" with me.

Another example of "focusing" on a metric, like you said in the last chapter. They're trying to increase the number of people who open the envelope.
Yes. Some marketing employee is trying to hit their annual targets.

For another example of corporate deception without lying, consider "shrinkflation," the art of subtly manipulating packaging or product design so that consumers don't notice that they're getting less but paying the same price. In an echo of the "numbers made me do it" reasoning I noted in the last chapter, Krishnakumar Davey, from the market research company IRI, says that manufacturers are shrinkflating out of necessity. "Manufacturers are facing huge costs," he explains, referring to the price of ingredients, labor, and shipping.[9] True; but they are deciding to do something that may be unethical.

Haleon, the manufacturer of the cough syrup Robitussin, changed its formula so that more of the syrup was required for each dose. Their spokesperson's comment was "While we continually innovate our formulations to meet the evolving needs of consumers, the quality and integrity of our products is always paramount."[10] Which brings us to the theme of this chapter—bullshit.

Bullshit

In lying, you deliberately state something false that you want people to believe as true. In bullshit, author Harry G. Frankfurt says, you make a statement whose truth you really just don't care about. Bullshit is performative: you want people to believe that you are a certain kind of person, the kind of person who would say the kind of thing you're saying. The essence of bullshit is not that it's false (though it may be) but that it is phony.[11]

"Your call is important to us." The company doesn't really care whether that's true or not, and they don't expect you to care either. A better measure of your call's importance, actually, is how long the company makes you wait before answering it. It's not a lie, exactly—maybe in some sense your call is important to them. They are really just trying to persuade you that they are a certain kind of company, a company that values its customers.

The flight attendant says, "Your safety is our number one priority." Is it? I suspect the company's investors believe earning a profit is the priority. If the airline's executives subscribe to Friedman's shareholder doctrine, you can be sure that your safety is not their number one priority. For the flight attendant, the number one priority is probably making sure they repeat the message as they're supposed to without screwing it up or, maybe, getting through the announcement to be able to sit down and take a break. But the airline wants you to think that they are the kind of company that cares about the safety of its customers.

I love to pick on airline speech because it's an easy target, but in fact bullshit is all around us. It is a notable aspect of today's economy. The TV station keeps claiming that they have "breaking news" and then talking about yesterday's weather or someone's opinion. They talk about "exclusive" stories—without telling me what's excluded. The term "exclusive" is also used by those direct mail marketers who want me to open their envelopes. Whether or not the news is "breaking" or an offer is "exclusive" is not the point. The TV station wants to present their news program as exciting and important and unique; the direct marketer wants me to believe that they are personalizing their offer to me.

Lying, Frankfurt says, "is an act with a sharp focus. It is designed to insert a particular falsehood at a specific point in a set or system of beliefs, in order to avoid the consequences of having that point occupied by the truth."[12] Bullshit lacks that sharp focus. It is a kind of deception that implies with vague words. It may be true or it may be false, but it's a picture out of focus, indistinct but with nice colors.

The term "bullshit" itself is apt, Frankfurt says, because

> when we characterize talk as hot air, we mean that what comes out of the speaker's mouth is only that. It is mere vapor. His speech is empty, without substance or content. Just as hot air is speech that has been emptied of all informative content, so excrement is matter from which everything nutritive has been removed.[13]

He could easily be talking about today's "marketing speak." There's a kind of generic gung-ho babble that could apply to any product equally well. Delta's website tells us "We're not just an airline. We're 75,000+ people passionate about how travel brings us together, encourages appreciation and creates a better world for us. . . . As a purpose-driven brand, we connect people to opportunities while expanding the understanding of our planet and the people within it."[14]

Actually, they are just an airline. I bet Leprechaun Airways employees are just as passionate about how travel brings us together, just as tired after serving a few hundred passengers their meals—and just as concerned with matching their prices to market demand. Bobbleheads Unlimited surely also "expands the understanding of our planet and the people within it" through their analysis of facial features and shared realization that life is like bobbling heads. Strozzapreti Specialists Inc. undoubtedly "expands the understanding of our planet and the people within it" because we can best understand people through their foods, and pasta is what all cultures have in common.

The noise of bullshit envelops us so thoroughly that we rarely pause to be astounded by it. In the supermarket I find a product labeled "Gourmet Lemonade." When I check its ingredients I find that it's made from lemons and water—like every other lemonade. In a coffee shop I spot a "Luxury Minced Pie" pastry. Luxury?

To return to our favorite theme, bullshit is a feature of bureaucracy. Frankfurt's example is "spit-and-polish and red tape do not genuinely contribute, it is presumed, to the 'real' purposes of military personnel or government officials. They are bullshit, intended to convince the public of their earnestness in fulfilling their public duty."[15] Inauthentic language is an important tool of traditional bureaucracy both because it erases the speaker—keeping them "faceless"—and speaks to its audience as abstractions rather than as individuals.

Bullshit is another kind of depersonalization, a communication where a company isn't really trying to communicate, in the sense of transferring thoughts between real people. Perhaps bullshitters are reciting a legal formula, checking a checkbox, doing their jobs. Airlines aren't talking to you; they're talking to passengers in the abstract. The pandemic of bullshit degrades our expectation of sincerity. M. F. K. Fisher, on a break from food writing, says in "As the Lingo Languishes" that the "distortion of values, this insidious numbing of what we once knew without question as true or false, can be blamed, in part, on the language we hear and read every day and night."[16]

Brand advertising, for the record, is a species of bullshit. Its goal is to associate positive feelings and desirable brand attributes with the advertiser. It doesn't really matter whether the statements it makes are true or false. They're simply associations:

It was the Golden Age of Russia, and the Czar reigned supreme. Europe, Asia: all the empire was his. Regal coaches carried him in elegance, but with his Cossaks he rode like thunder. Hunting wild boar in the northern forests, hosting feasts for a thousand guests in the Great Palace, no man could match the Czar's thirst for life. And his drink? The toast of St. Petersburg. Genuine Vodka. (Brand name omitted) January 21, 1980.[17]

It's an ingenious nonsequitur that takes us from his "thirst for life" to what he drinks. How can a czar ride like thunder? None of this has anything to do with vodka, which is essentially tasteless. The ad says things but it's not trying to communicate those things. The goal is to make people think of the vodka company as a certain kind of company, a company that makes treats for czars, presumably. Or at least as a vodka that will make its drinkers feel like they share something with a thirst for life and vodka.

It sounds kind of poetic to me. Why, exactly, is it wrong?

It's not especially good poetry, for one thing. But that's not an ethical issue. John Keats's "Ode on a Grecian Urn" is not trying to sell you Greek pottery. Robert Frost's "The Road Not Taken" is not a commercial for a travel agency. Sales and poetry have different intentions.

Are you telling your readers they shouldn't do brand advertising?

Nah. I'm not sure it hurts anyone. I've got bigger fish to fricassee. Really, I'm just trying to make the point that bullshit so thoroughly surrounds us that we've ceased to notice it.

My breakfast cereal's box says that their cereal is "made with love." It's not made with love, it's made with machines. But that isn't really relevant, is it? Like the Charles Dickens character:

> Mr. Pecksniff was in the frequent habit of using any word that occurred to him as having a good sound and rounding a sentence well, without much care for its meaning. And he did this so boldly and in such an imposing manner that he would sometimes stagger the wisest people with his eloquence and make them gasp again.[18]

I've given a number of examples of bullshit because I want to make sure leaders of digital transformation see how prevalent it is in our business environment today and how natural it is to us to produce it. Yet it conflicts with our digital goals of building authentic relationships with customers and motivating employees to care about and take ownership of their work's results.

Humbug and All Its Forms

A related kind of speech is "humbug." Max Black, in his book *The Prevalence of Humbug*, defines it as "deceptive misrepresentation, short of lying, especially by pretentious word or deed, of somebody's own thoughts, feelings, or attitudes." Black offers as synonyms: balderdash, claptrap, hokum, drivel, buncombe, imposture, and quackery.[19]

The difference between bullshit and humbug, Frankfurt says, is that humbug is designed to deceive—its falsehood is not inadvertent—while bullshit is not concerned with truth or falsity.[20] Perhaps you remember the scarecrow's exclamation in *The Wizard of Oz*, upon the revelation that—spoiler alert—Oz is just a man hiding behind a curtain manipulating special effects machines. Oz says,

> "I'm supposed to be a Great Wizard."
> "And aren't you?" [Dorothy] asked.
> "Not a bit of it, my dear; I'm just a common man."
> "You're more than that," said the Scarecrow, in a grieved tone; "you're a humbug."

The self-proclaimed master of humbug was P. T. Barnum. "The titles of 'humbug,' and the 'prince of humbugs,' were first applied to me by myself," he is proud to claim.[21]

In 1835, Barnum "exhibited" Joice Heth, a 161-year-old slave—Barnum claimed—who had been George Washington's nanny. She told compelling tales of Washington's boyhood, and she looked pretty old. Brilliantly, Barnum also placed a letter in a newspaper under a pseudonym claiming that Joice Heth was a fake—that she actually was not a real person but an automaton made of whalebone.[22] The dispute that followed, unsurprisingly, increased the size of his audience.

He later toured with an "actual" mermaid—well, actually a bizarre fabrication, "a fish's body and tail with the breasts of an orangutan and the head of a baboon." The impression it made was mostly good:

> The public appeared to be satisfied, but as some persons always will take things literally, and make no allowance for poetic license even in mermaids, an occasional visitor, after having seen the large transparency in

front of the hall, representing a beautiful creature half woman and half fish, about eight feet in length, would be slightly surprised in finding that the reality was a black-looking specimen of dried monkey and fish that a boy a few years old could easily run away with under his arm.[23]

Barnum didn't see anything wrong in this; after all, he also provided some exhibits that truly were what they claimed to be. The problem, he seemed to think, was the few unpoetic customers who objected. His humbug was in the service of fun, and therefore justified.

Barnum had a good point; he was deceiving people for their own entertainment, and he was in the entertainment business. Arguably, much of his humbug came in a context where he might not have been warranting its truth. What's wrong, then, with humbug? Black's complaints against it are only in part ethical ones: he also says that it is pretentious, affected, insincere, and deceptive.

Often there is also a detectable whiff of self-satisfaction and self-complacency: humbug goes well with a smirk. A common symptom is clever-me-ism, as in Jack Horner's case. In this respect, it resembles *cant*, which Dr. Johnson memorably defined as "a whining pretension to goodness, in formal and affected terms."[24]

The digital world demands sincerity and authenticity; bullshit and humbug undermine those attributes. Building a closer relationship with customers and motivating employees to take ownership of meaningful goals are inconsistent with pretentious and affected communication.

Depersonalized Language

Personalization, as I said, is a form of depersonalization. That depersonalization rises to the surface in the language businesses use, in the form of what I'll call audience-less speech and in double-talk, euphemism, bomphiologia, and puffery. These common patterns of inauthentic speech degrade the relationship between companies and their publics, and interfere with the customer-centricity we value in a digitally transformed organization.

Audience-less Language

I'm fascinated by the language airlines use when they speak to us. "I'll be more than happy to assist." *More* than happy? What—ecstatic? Instead of telling me something, airline staff ask me to "please be advised that." "This will serve as your last and final boarding call for flight 666 with service to Hades International." Both my last *and* my final call? Does it *go* to Hades or *have service* to Hades? And why is it *serving* as my last call, rather than *being* my last call? "Please proceed to gate H6." *Go* is a perfectly good word. "I *do* want to welcome you," my flight attendant says. "We *do* thank you for your continued loyalty." I *do* wonder how that word *do* floats into sentences. And, please, what are "in-lap children," and can they be cured?

A personal favorite: "Historically those bags will have to be checked." *We're* not going to make you check them, history will, though we're the ones who decided how much overhead baggage space to construct. And if you dare to check them ahistorically you'll have to answer to the bobbleheads.

What's going on here? It doesn't sound like the airline is talking to *me*. This is not how you communicate with a person. It's more like they're talking to customers in the abstract. Or complying with a legal requirement ("This will serve as your . . . legal summons to your gate").

In March 2022, India accidentally launched a missile at their archenemy Pakistan. Reuters quoted an Indian minister's comment: "It is learnt that the missile landed in an area of Pakistan. While the incident is deeply regrettable, it is also a matter of relief that there has been no loss of life due to the accident."[25] A translation into realtalk: "We accidentally fired a missile at Pakistan. We're sorry, and relieved it didn't kill anyone." It's a beautiful example of using the passive voice to avoid admitting responsibility. It doesn't even say "we learned." There is no subject at all, no actor. No one did anything, which makes sense, given how hard bureaucracies try to be "faceless."

Obfuscation

Honesty is not the same as true speech, which can be used for many questionable purposes, including deliberate obfuscation.[26]

Bomphiolgia, our vocabulary word for the day, is the rhetorical technique of bragging too much. The sixteenth-century English rhetorician Richard Sherry uses the equivalent term *verborum bombus* in *A Treatise of Schemes & Tropes* to mean: "when small & triflyng thynges are set out wyth great gasying wordes." Shakespeare's Falstaff is a great bomphiologist: "I would to God my name were not so terrible to the enemy as it is."[27] Bomphiologia is used to great effect in hip hop and dancehall reggae: consider MC Hammer's "You Can't Touch This," Shaggy's "Mr. Boombastic" ("I'm Boombastic, tell me fantastic . . . she says I'm Mr. Romantic"), and Big Daddy Kane with "I won't say I'm the baddest or portray that role, but I'm in the top two, and my father's getting old," from "Cause I Can Do It Right."

Have you noticed that all businesses are "the leading" business of something or the "number one provider" of something? "Electrolux is a leading global appliance company that has shaped living for the better for more than 100 years."[28] They certainly say so wyth great and gasying wordes—they've shaped living, which otherwise would be formless mush. State Farm promises "We will continue to be the leader in the insurance industry and we will become a leader in the financial services arena."[29] I like that careful distinction between "the" leader and "a" leader. This book, I'm sure you've noticed, is *the* leader in books about ethics in digital transformation that mention the gingerbread man, and will undoubtedly become *a* leader in IT pasta nonfiction literature.

A related concept, *puffery*, is the use of complicated words to make statements sound more important—an apt description of most business communications. *The Book of Strange and Curious Legal Oddities* tells the story of a district attorney who "never uses one word when two or three will do just as well." When prosecuting Jacob Henderson, an alleged electronics thief, he used the word "burglariously" three times. On appeal, the defense called as an expert witness an English teacher who testified that "consistent with accepted rules of English grammar, the indictment did not charge Jacob Henderson with anything." Instead, it accused the electronics of breaking, entering, and stealing themselves. The judges agreed.[30]

Euphemisms are sometimes used to say something disturbing in a gentler way, often out of care for the hearer—for example, saying that someone "passed away" rather than that they died. I mentioned earlier that morals at one time came to refer specifically to sexual behavior; unsurprisingly, euphemisms have played a large part in that area of agile behavior. Elizabethans didn't have sex with each other, which would probably have led them straight to the sizzling place below. Instead, they would jape, or sard, or fucke, or swive, or occupy.[31]

More often euphemisms are used to avoid responsibility. How about this: "the entry is in the early stages of finalization," which seems to mean it's not finished.[32] While "It's not finished" would be an admission of guilt, "in the early stage of finalization" blurs the situation just enough so that it's not clear there's any guilt to be admitted.

Euphemism and its cousin *doublespeak* have donated heavily to political campaigns and military dialogue. "Servicing the target" means bombing. In 1979, the nuclear power industry referred to an explosion as an "energetic disassembly," fire as "rapid oxidation," and reactor accidents, oddly, as both "abnormal evolution" and "normal aberration."[33]

A common occasion for euphemisms in business is employment termination, probably because no one feels good about it. There's a notable difference in the way management and employees talk about firing and layoffs. Managers may say "We're letting you go," "We're terminating your position," or "Your position is redundant." Employees say things like "He was shit-canned," "He got whacked," or "He got walked to the door."[34] In the workplace novel *Then We Came to the End*, employees refer to it as "walking Spanish,"[35] by which they mean being walked to the door while being held up by the scruff of the neck.

Termination can also be career transition, involuntary separation, early retirement opportunity, personnel realignment, surplus reduction in personnel, staff reengineering, workforce imbalance correction, corporate outplacing, adjustment to shifts in demand, rebalancing human capital, smart sizing, driving a fitness plan, implementing a special forces philosophy, or "We decided to go in a different direction."[36]

Hidden in the language of termination is the pattern I mentioned in the last chapter: managers trying to push responsibility onto the numbers rather than owning up to a decision they made themselves. "Imbalance correction," "adjustment to shifts in demand," "smart sizing"—these are all ways of saying "The numbers forced me to do it."

These euphemisms could be a virtuous attempt at being sensitive to the feelings of the terminee. It could be an attempt to deflect responsibility ("I didn't do anything. You just somehow became redundant"). It could be puffery or great gasying words that managers feel is required of them in a business setting. I see it as depersonalizing the listener. It's not about you—it's about an abstract group that you happen to be a member of.

As a new category of euphemism, I'll propose *misdirection*. In October 2022, Dunkin' (formerly Dunkin' Donuts) announced changes to its loyalty rewards program with the message "Because our members deserve more!" The change was that members needed twice as many points before they could redeem them for drinks, and free birthday drinks would no longer be provided. According to the *Washington Post*, which titled its article "What Idiot Do You Think I Am? Customers Chafe As Rewards Programs Are Pared Back," "regular customers were not amused."[37]

Noise

Another category of verbal deceitfulness that I think is new to the discussion is the noise that we see on social media. You know, where one employee tweets something meaningless and then another tweets something like "Great tweet! I agree!" and then someone else tweets "+1" so that the tweet stays at the top of everyone's feed. It's echo-chamber posting, reposting, and meaningless replies to direct more attention to a post.

Additional noise is made by *humblebragging*. "I'm humbled to have been named the sexiest serverless Elizabethan-hat-wearing coder in northwest Ouagadougou." Or "it's so annoying when my superexclusive health club that's so expensive only the extremely rich can join it runs out of cologne in the men's room." Let's be serious—if you were really humbled you wouldn't be tweeting about it. At least, I think that's true—I'm not really sure what it means to be "humbled" by an award. The Israeli Prime Minister Golda Meir was reported to have said, "Don't be humble—you're not that great."[38]

Humblebrag is a kind of bullshit, as its purpose seems to be to try to make people think you are a humble sort of person, despite bragging about your yodeling skills or Tyrolean hat collection. But with the volume of messages on social media, it's just noise.

Can I mention a pet peeve? It seems relevant.

Sure, go ahead.

It bothers me that when something bad happens in the world, people keep posting little messages on social media saying it's bad. I feel like saying, "Yes, we know it's bad, and your little message doesn't add anything."

Like when?

You know—there's a news story that some country is arresting journalists. And then everyone is posting messages like "Awful!" or "This is unbelievable" or something like that.

Why does that bother you?

It's just too easy. It's like you just want people to like you for having the "right" opinion.

There's a term for that kind of low-emotional-investment social media posting: "hashtag activism."[39]

I was thinking that, in your terms, it's sort of a combination of bullshit and humblebrag.

Nicely put.

Secrecy and Transparency

Then there's what is *not* said in an organization. In the stories in the introduction I called out a pattern of closed-door meetings. In *Secrecy at Work*, Christopher Grey and Jana Costas point out that secrecy is used as a matter of course in bureaucracies to delineate power relationships. Secrecy, they say, is not just a matter of concealing secret information; it's a way that people demonstrate their authority, form cliques, and initiate new employees into company culture. It helps organize power hierarchically[40]—bureaucratically—because those at the top of the hierarchy know things that no one else can know.

> It is through the mysteriousness created by secrecy that rulers, kings, and statesmen can surround themselves with a certain sacredness that is otherwise reserved for the divine men, the priests and, of course, God.[41]

Max Weber also recognized that because knowledge is power in compartmentalized bureaucracies, there's a tendency to withhold information.[42] Knowledge in Weber's world was stored in documents, which could be kept secret by burying them in a locked drawer under the Hershey's Kisses. Today, units of an organization withhold data from each other by controlling access to databases, resulting in what we know as "data siloes." They are abetted by privacy rules that require "least privilege"—a control that forces anyone who wants access to data to prove that they have a "need to know." The standards for determining a need to know are controlled by those in possession of the "secrets," giving them an easy way to restrict access.

Because there's more organizational power if everyone else knows that secrets are being kept, it's not unusual for employees to hint that they are "in on" a secret.[43] Closed-door meetings fulfill that function by advertising that something secret is going on. Even when no secrets are being shared, the trappings of secrecy cause employees to believe that important decisions are being made "behind closed doors" and that others are acting with "hidden agendas."[44]

There are also "open secrets"—things that everyone knows and no one talks about.[45] Their existence is conveyed in a language of "innuendo, ambiguities, well-placed pauses, carefully worded jokes, and so on."[46] It's language that allows for deniability. Like euphemism, bullshit, and other forms of insincere communication, secrets create a space in which morally questionable behavior can flourish. It's a form of deception that conveys an impression of tactfulness—bullshit!—while at the same time hiding questionable behavior.

Sincerity and Digital Transformation: Verbal Virtues

Organizations undergoing transformation are trying to build a closer, more intimate relationship with their customers. Speaking inauthentically gets in the way. The patterns of communication described in this chapter increase the distance between speakers and listeners rather than bringing them closer. It distances companies from their customers and managers from the employees they are trying to motivate by engaging their "caring" for the results of their work.

The focus on legalistic nitpicking and the "letter of the law" we've inherited from bureaucracy make it seem like deception is okay as long as it is not technically lying. And if it is okay, then the shareholder doctrine seems to say that we must do it, when it will increase investor returns. Somehow, deception can come to seem like responsible behavior, because it delivers on an ethical duty to the company's owners.

Digital organizations have to find the right balance between secrecy and transparency. While it might be impossible to have full transparency, it's also important to understand that secrecy supports and sustains bureaucratic power structures; there is a good reason why transparency is valued by digital organizations. Data about individuals must, of course, be protected by privacy controls. But the privacy controls should be used for precisely that purpose—to control privacy—rather than to enforce power structures within the business.

In Chapter 11, you'll find several virtues of communication among the others: authenticity (speaking as a real person), care (considering the person you're speaking to), courage (willingness to take responsibility in your communications), and respect (preserving the autonomy of the listener).

Culture

Virtues: Stewardship, Manners

Mischief-makers overtaken by punishments have for thousands of years felt in respect of their "transgressions" just as Spinoza did: "here something has unexpectedly gone wrong," not: "I ought not to have done that." They submitted to punishment as one submits to an illness or to a misfortune or to death . . .

—Nietzsche, *The Genealogy of Morals*

Punish with principle, teach meaningfully. The act of stopping evil leads to the lasting establishment of virtue.

—*The Maxims of Ptahhotep*

Enron Corporation had a banner in its lobby promoting its values: integrity, communication, respect, and excellence.[1] Employees were given a copy of Enron's sixty-five-page *Code of Ethics*, which explained these values in detail. According to the code, employees were required to conduct their affairs with "the highest ethical standards." The code specified that "relationships with the company's many publics—customers, stockholders, governments, employees, suppliers, press, and bankers—will be conducted in honesty, candor, and fairness." In defining what was meant by respect, it said, "We treat others as we would like to be treated ourselves. Ruthlessness, callousness and arrogance don't belong here."

The company and its executives were widely respected and admired. Articles in *Fortune*, *Forbes*, and *Business Week* spoke of the "Enron miracle." Enron won the Forbes America's Most Innovative Company award six years in a row beginning in 1996. *The Financial Times* named it the Energy Company of the Year in 2000. Its senior executives, Kenneth Lay, Jeff Skilling, and Andrew Fastow, appeared in cover stories,[2] and Fastow was honored with a CFO Excellence Award by *CFO Magazine*. CEO magazine named Enron's board as one of the top five in America, saying it "works hard to keep up with things." At least five Harvard Business School case studies touted the Enron model. The management guru Gary Hamel waxed enthusiastic: "Like Microsoft created DOS, Enron is creating MOS: the market operating system. And they can apply it everywhere."[3]

All this respect and admiration ended in 2001, when the company went spectacularly bankrupt. In the investigations that followed, it became clear that they had strayed far from the principles on the lobby banner and in the corporate handbook. They had been deceiving industry analysts, investors, partners, the press, regulators, and just about everyone else. They failed to disclose material information to companies they were doing deals with. "Ruthlessness, callousness, and arrogance" certainly *did* belong there—they were thoroughly institutionalized in the company's culture and incentivized through its reward systems. Enron leaders had used every type of bullying and coercion imaginable to keep their stock price increasing. In no way were they excellent—most of their businesses failed. Their board might have "worked hard to keep up with things" if it hadn't been so busy looking the other way.

I bring up Enron not to point out that it was bad. It was, but that's not news. Instead, I want to look at the relationship between ethics and company culture. What's stunning and instructive about Enron is just how distant its culture was from its stated principles. It's not just that the company went bankrupt (a financial consequence) and not that its leaders went to jail (a legal consequence). What's interesting is that its principles and rules—a traditional, bureaucratic approach to ethics—stated clearly enough in its ethics code and on its lobby banner—did not prevent bad behavior.

Historically, Enron stood at the junction of bureaucratic and digital organizational models. Enron's leaders wanted to present the company as both a low-risk, stable, oil and gas logistics company, and at the same time as a new kind of digital innovator, naturally misunderstood by those used to old ways of doing business. With the magic it harnessed by being both, it could have both high returns and low risk.

It was, in fact, a traditional bureaucracy. Its hierarchy, where top leaders cashed in and harvested perks while low-level workers were considered commodities ("Go buy me some smart people"), its forced ranking system and performance review process dominated by office politics, its independent fiefdoms, and its legalistic verbal manipulations that ignored the spirit of the rules all smack of bureaucratic thinking.

We think of codes of conduct as ethical guardrails; if nothing else, Enron shows that they are no such thing. Instead, ethical behavior is a matter of corporate culture, developed and sustained through feedback and learning, role modeling, development of virtues, and care—care about the public and about fellow employees.

Deception

Ah, the point you mentioned a few chapters ago about codes of conduct.

Yes. Enron's hit all the key points, was widely distributed, and was backed by a letter from the CEO.

I remember hearing about Enron, but it always sounded like what they did wrong was really just a technicality—getting on the wrong side of some accounting rules, maybe.

Legally, yes. The legal issues were complex. The ethical issues were simpler and plentiful: deliberate deception, coercion, conflicts of interest, and poor treatment of human beings. Let me tell you a few stories.

Enron engaged in deliberate deception, and lots of it. According to *Enron: The Smartest Guys in the Room*, while their financial situation was becoming ever more precarious, Enron still somehow managed to show steadily increasing accounting profits each quarter. "There was nothing at Enron that required more effort, more cleverness, more deceit—more everything—than hitting its quarterly earnings targets," say the authors. As Enron was running out of cash, its leaders were denying it, claiming that their energy trading business was healthy and that they were paying all their bills—neither of which was true.[4]

Their mark-to-market accounting method gave them great flexibility in deciding how to value their investments. When they had the opportunity to show good results, they exaggerated them, and when they should have shown losses, they didn't. They labeled one-time income events, like selling off an asset, as recurring revenues from operations. They delayed writing off dead deals so their quarterly numbers would look better and justified it by claiming there was no "official" letter declaring the project dead. These were more than technicalities; they were deliberate and systematic deception.

Enron created thousands of "special purpose entities," artificial companies that they could use to hide nonperforming investments. These entities were supposed to be independent, arms-length businesses, but the owners were actually Enron leaders and their relatives and friends, and the companies were under Enron's control. "To a staggering degree, Enron's 'profits' and 'cash flow' were the result of the company's own complex dealings with itself."[5]

The public face of Enron was carefully managed to keep analyst reports positive. Instead of admitting that Enron's primary business was risky speculation, executives claimed that Enron was a logistics company that was simply very good at delivering power from one point to another. They convinced analysts that they had a world-class risk management program keeping their risks low, while in fact the opposite was true.

At one point, they impressed analysts with a tour of their Enron Energy Services business unit's "war room." The war room had, in fact, been hastily set up just for the analysts' visit. The employees in the war room had been moved in from other locations and other departments of the business, and went back to their real jobs right after the analysts left. They were coached on appearing busy; one of them later said she had just been talking to friends on her phone.[6]

Enron's CFO Andrew Fastow admitted, "I knew that what I was doing was misleading. But I didn't think it was illegal. I thought: That's how the game is played."[7] There's the crux of the issue—Enron didn't accept that there were relevant moral concerns outside of the legal concerns (not that they didn't stray outside of legal bounds as well). The legalistic mode of thought—the bureaucrat's smug way of dancing around the intent of the rules—blocked out considerations of moral issues. Leaders had no reservations about deceiving the public, regulators, investors, partners, suppliers, or industry analysts as long as no one could point to a law they were violating.

A Pandemic of Scandal

Until near the end, Enron was entirely successful in the Friedmanian sense of returning money to investors, since they made sure their stock price kept increasing. Oddly enough, the deals they were making failed in the ordinary business sense, since Enron wasn't able to execute profitably on any of them. They were the first alchemists ever to succeed in turning base metals into gold and were successful as long as they could hide their secret formula.

It's not just Enron that blew up in corporate scandals. Worldcom, Tyco, Imclone, Vivendi Universal, Credit Lyonnaise, Elan, Ahold, Addecco, Lernout & Houspie, Parmalat, SK, BNI, China Aviation Oil, Bank of China, and Sagawa Kyubin also self-destructed.[8] In 2021, *CFO Magazine* abandoned its annual Excellence Awards because winners from each of the previous three years had gone to prison.[9]

According to John R. Boatright, a professor of business ethics at Loyola University, these scandals had common elements: (1) business strategy gone awry, (2) an attempt to boost short-term stock price by any means, (3) directors who failed to detect warning signs, (4) accountants who acquiesced in aggressive accounting, (5) investment bankers who structured questionable deals, and (6) lawyers who showed how to create plausible legal veneer.[10] That's a lot of factors that somehow came together in each of these incidents. Is it a coincidence, or is there some underlying cause?

The increase in corporate scandals is sometimes attributed to deficient checks and balances within organizations. Friedman's doctrine was meant to align executives with the shareholders and remove conflicts of interest. At the same time, it detached executives from their alignment with the long-term success of the company and the morality of the company's behavior. Tying executive pay to stock price created new conflicts of interest; with returns to shareholders as the only goal, executives no longer functioned as a check on the owners' desire for profits. Like Wells Fargo's reductivist cross-selling metrics, Enron's obsession with stock price directed its attention away from ethical constraints.

On the other hand, checks and balances are a bureaucratic mechanism, and one that slows a company down. A typical bureaucratic response to mistakes and bad behavior is to insert more checks and balances. The real issue at both Wells Fargo and Enron was that bad behavior was rewarded and reinforced, not that there was a lack of checkpoints.

Freakonomics, by Steven Levitt, attributes the scandals to information asymmetries, implying that particular structural market conditions allowed the scandals to take place.[11] Enron deceived the public through hidden partnerships, disguised debt, and secret manipulation of energy markets. Salomon Smith Barney's analysts wrote glowing research reports on companies they knew to be junk. Sam Wassail of ImClone and Martha Stewart traded on insider information. WorldCom and Global Crossing pumped up their stock prices by inventing fictitious revenues. In each case, experts took advantage of or created information asymmetries to conceal their actions.

No doubt the information asymmetries, absence of checks and balances, and Boatright's common factors made these scandals possible, but those were just the mechanisms by which the scandals were perpetrated. They don't quite explain why the unethical behavior occurred, given that other firms had access to the same opportunities. And in each scandal there were people who had access to the information and could have blown the whistle—but they didn't.

Corporate environments also breed a range of smaller day-to-day moral lapses. According to a United States Chamber of Commerce study, 75% of individuals steal from their employer at some time or other.[12] Studies have found that 42% of supermarket employees and 60% of restaurant employees admitted to stealing from their employer in the previous six months. The philosopher Joseph Heath, of the University of Toronto, says, "One of the peculiar features of business ethics, as compared to other domains of applied ethics, is that it deals with a domain of human affairs that is afflicted by serious criminality, and an institutional environment that is in many cases demonstrably criminogenic."[13]

What gives? Why do we see these behaviors in business? One reason might be the bureaucratic approach that separates the workplace from "real" life; that makes employees part of a rational-efficient machine that executes unquestioningly; that values achieving targets over all else. But there's more to it—why do those factors turn into crime in some cases and not in others?

Our interest in this book is ethics of workplace behavior, not workplace crime *per se*, but some academic work that's been done in analyzing corporate crime is illuminating.

The Wrong Reasons

In "Business Ethics and Moral Motivation: A Criminological Perspective," Heath[14] examines the typical "folk" explanations of corporate criminal behavior: (1) that criminals have some defect of character, (2) that they are excessively greedy, or (3) that they don't know right from wrong.[15] None of these theories survive close examination.

It seems obvious that corporate criminals have some character flaw—that they are sociopathic or that they have no conscience. Yet corporate criminals for the most part are quite ordinary. There is no particular psychological trait that they share. They know—at least in the abstract—that what they are doing is wrong.[16] The problem, Heath says, is institutional rather than individual, and blaming it on sociopathic behavior directs attention away from the more important organizational issues.[17]

In fact, most people have a tendency to behave as these criminals do. Even though people believe it's a severe offense for a drug company to sell a drug with an undisclosed harmful side effect, 79% of executive training students in a role-playing scenario chose the "highly irresponsible" option of continuing to sell the drug while taking action to prevent government regulation. The other 21% chose to continue selling the drug for as long as possible, though they didn't try to interfere with the regulatory process. So it seems that ordinary people—if you consider executive trainees to be ordinary—would commit crimes in certain situations. We can't consider them all to be sociopaths.[18]

Greed is not a good explanation either. For one thing, much corporate crime is comitted for the benefit of the firm, not the individual. In many cases it's not a desire for gain that motivates the criminal, but an aversion to loss—corporate crime is more prevalent in companies that are doing poorly than those that are doing well. Sometimes the crime takes place while gains are just somewhat short of expectations. Many white collar criminals say they felt "squeezed" in some way—they were motivated more by anxiety than greed. Craig Standland, who defrauded Cisco of $800K of equipment, said "It was just pure shame from the beginning—not being able to tell my wife that I couldn't afford that life style, all the way through getting arrested."[19] "Greed," Heath says, "is more just a name we attach to the behavior, rather than an explanation of it."[20]

The idea that criminals don't know right from wrong isn't plausible either. If you talk to the people who have committed the crimes, you find that they know quite well what the rules are. Enron's lobby banner and code of values show that they knew what ethical behavior looked like. Heath says it's a question of motivating employees to make the right choice when the moment for a decision arrives:

> There is often no real dispute about the content of our moral obligations (i.e., what we should be doing), the question is rather how to motivate people to do it. The tough questions arise in particular, concrete situations: what to do when a rival firm gains competitive advantage through deception, or when a supervisor orders sensitive documents to be destroyed, or even when ethical behavior simply conflicts with the bottom line."[21]

Once again, it's a matter of concrete situations and conflicting ethical imperatives. This is a job for the virtue of practical wisdom.

Heath wants to understand not just why some people commit white collar crimes, but also why so many don't. The legal system doesn't seem to provide a strong enough incentive, since few criminals get caught and the penalties are often not that severe. The incentives seem to favor criminal behavior.[22] Heath suggests looking at situational factors—in particular, organizational culture—that account for the instances where the usual moral scruples are suspended.

Criminal Culture

White collar crime is a learned behavior, more common in certain sectors of the economy than others. The unsavory practice of backdating stock options started in Silicon Valley and then spread to other parts of the business world: "The vectors could be traced to specific individuals who served as directors or auditors of multiple companies,"[23] Evan Osnos says in a *New Yorker* article on corporate crime. "Pockets of crime" persist over time, even though employees come and go.[24] The financial services sector is particularly vulnerable to ethical lapses. Gee, it's a mystery why:

> Greg Smith, an executive director at Goldman Sachs resigned, saying "Over the last 12 months I have seen five different managing directors

refer to their own clients as 'muppets.'. . . You don't have to be a rocket scientist to figure out that the junior analyst sitting quietly in the corner of the room hearing about 'muppets,' 'ripping eyeballs out,' and 'getting paid' doesn't exactly turn into a model citizen."[25]

According to Tom Hardin, known as "Tipper X," who traded on inside information in 2007 as a partner at the hedge fund Lanexa Global Management, "You can say, 'I'm highly ethical and would never do this.' But once you're in the environment, and you feel like everyone else is doing it, and you feel you're not hurting anybody? It's very easy to convince yourself."[26] This may answer the question of why there isn't more corporate crime: employees are influenced ethically by the culture in which they operate; it is only in certain deviant subcultures that employees learn criminal behaviors.[27]

In the digital world the impact of a deviant subculture might be even worse. Company campuses that include banking services, medical clinics, dry cleaners, daycare centers, and convenience stores can isolate employees from other moral influences.[28] The prestige of working for certain firms can also contribute. More ominously, given the direction the digital workplace is taking, to the extent to which work dominates an employee's life, or the extent to which it is inextricable from an employee's personal life, the influence of the workplace culture can be more pronounced.

Back to Digital Bureaucracy

In his book *Why They Do It*, Eugene Soltes of Harvard Business School interviewed criminals and found that there was no evidence of a growing inclination to break laws. Instead, as he told reporter Evan Osnos, he found a growing psychological distance between the criminals and their victims. "Business is done with individuals at greater length now, which reduces the feeling that managers are harming others."[29] Many of the perpetrators had never personally encountered their victims. Research has shown that in thought experiments, people are much more likely to sacrifice the life of someone they can't see than someone who is standing in front of them.[30]

Digital interactions increase the distance between corporate actors and their customers, vendors, and partners. An online customer is not a person before you, but rather the object of a transaction in your database.

Both bureaucracy and data fixation separate ethical decision makers from the people they affect. A bureaucracy is deliberately impersonal, concerned only with general rules that apply across individuals. Metric fixation focuses employees and managers on sets of customers that have affinities, aspects of customers that can be targeted through marketing campaigns, and AI models into which they have little transparency. So-called personalization, as I've said, makes the distance from individuals even greater.

Corporate bureaucracy also breeds unethical practices because it generates a steady stream of plausible—or at least plausible-sounding—excuses for misbehavior. Because of the separation of duties and the siloed org chart, responsibility is generally spread over a number of employees, with none of them fully culpable for moral lapses.[31]

As single-metric targets are passed up and down the org chart, the effect is to divide responsibilities without assigning moral accountability. One department may be assigned to increase cross-selling and its success measured by the cross-selling rate. The budget for the call center might be cut, reducing the number of operators who can help customers close the accounts that have been opened for them. The IT department may be instructed to spend time on other initiatives rather than developing system features that would make it easy to spot unwanted accounts. With all this separation between strategy, goal setting, and implementation, it's hard to say who is responsible for unethically forcing new accounts on customers.

Because employees in a rigid hierarchy operate only on the basis of local information—local to their boxes on the org chart—they can't even see the full consequences of their actions. Siloes hinder the movement of information. Secrecy, used to manage power relationships, gives managers and employees an excuse for not knowing that bad behavior was going on, and for not trying to find out.[32] Information that makes its way up the management chain doesn't include the particulars that would call out wrongdoing. If anyone, it's some middle manager who knows just a bit too much who will wind up taking the blame.[33]

A telling example of the diffusion of responsibility was the failure of the Latin Investment Corporation in Washington, DC, and the resulting loss of $6 million in savings of DC-area Hispanics. Depositors blamed lax regulation by politicians; politicians denied blame. One politician said, "Frankly, I think the responsibility belonged to several agencies, including federal agencies. . . . Thus, effectively the responsibility belonged to no one."[34]

The authors of "Moral Responsibility in the Age of Bureaucracy" claim that this is intentional. "Bureaucratic organizations," they say, "parcel out morally significant knowledge among various individuals along the same lines as organizational tasks."[35] Bureaucratic activity is supposed to be morally neutral, as we know; individuals strive to become cogs in a larger machine, doing as they're instructed. The need for belongingness cited by Whyte in *The Organization Man* prevents employees from questioning the actions of fellow workers.

Enron's ineffective code of conduct shows us another reason why bureaucracy can lead to bad behavior. It is a legalistic, compliance-oriented document, seemingly intended to shield the company from question ("Well, we told employees not to do that."). Bureaucracies easily become compliance focused; ethics becomes a matter of staying within the wording of the rules, rather than the exercise of virtues or the thoughtful application of principles. If something is not specifically forbidden by a rule, it's fine, and rules can be interpreted in a legalistic, narrow, technical way.

Manuel Velazquez, mentioned in Chapter 3 as someone who doesn't believe in corporate moral agency, insists that in some cases of wrongdoing no one should be blamed:

> But if organizations are never morally responsible for their actions, who then is morally responsible when an organization injures someone and no human individual is morally responsible for the action? . . . Barring negligent behavior on anyone's part, the obvious answer, I think, is: no one. Cases like these are cases where the concept of accident applies, not the concept of moral responsibility.[36]

Unethical behavior is an accident, then. The same could be said of ethical behavior—the company is lucky if the actions of all those involved happen to add up to good behavior.

Excusing Behavior

While there is no fundamental disagreement about right and wrong among corporate criminals, wrongdoers rationalize their behavior with excuses that make them "exceptions" to the agreed-upon rules. Heath provides a catalog of those common excuses:

Denial of injury: "No one was really hurt by my action." This excuse comes especially easily if the perpetrator doesn't know the victim, or if the injury is distributed over a large group. As I said, this excuse is easier to come by when transactions are digital. The perpetrator can easily believe that a "buyer beware" rule applies or that investors could have invested their money elsewhere.

Denial of the victim: "The victim deserved it." This excuse comes easily when there is a competitive situation involved. Or the company "owed" me those office supplies I stole; they don't pay me enough or they treat me badly.

Denial of responsibility: "I didn't do it" or "I had to do it." In any case, I'm not responsible. This is especially plausible if the individual's actions were only some of those that led to the injury, as in the case of siloed bureaucracy.

Condemnation of the condemners: "I'm the victim of a witch hunt." The perpetrator questions the motives of those who condemn their actions. The law is illegitimate; the government has political motives for accusing me.

Appeal to higher loyalties: "I did it for others, not for myself." I did it for my family. I did it for my company. I did it so that my fellow workers wouldn't lose their jobs, or so the company wouldn't go bankrupt.

Everyone else is doing it: "I had to do it because everyone else was." It's unreasonable for society to expect compliance. This excuse is heard, for example, in connection with doping in sports.

Claim to entitlement: "I was obligated for moral reasons to do what I did." The victim did something bad, so this was legitimate payback. There is also a "karmic" version of this excuse: "We do so much good compared to this small transgression."

Quick survey of all the expositors on this book. Any of these excuses sound familiar?
Yes, of course. I think I even heard the pres—
Stop! This isn't a political book.
Right.

With these excuses the offender can affirm the moral principle that everyone agrees on, but at the same time claim an exception from it. The excuses work best in a culture where excuses are easily accepted, or even encouraged. An employee's need for belongingness makes them especially susceptible to the influence of coworkers. In *The Lonely Crowd*, the sociologist David Riesman explains that in premodern societies, people were *tradition-directed*; actions outside of accepted norms resulted in shame. In early modern societies people were *inner-directed*, with an internal moral compass that was acquired in childhood; they suffered guilt when they deviated. Contemporary society has become *other-directed*, he says, with people looking to others as a source of values and for signals of approval or disapproval.[37]

The locus of ethical reinforcement within a company is the immediate workgroup. Studies have found that corporate crime typically occurs at the lower to middle management level[38] and that an individual employee's primary loyalty is to a small group in the organization with which they identify.[39] Workgroups screen data before presenting it to the rest of the company and filter incoming information. The resulting isolation is a little cultlike.

Isolation is natural in a bureaucracy. It's even encouraged; each piece of the org chart has limited, structured interactions with the rest of the company; what happens within that piece of the org chart is no one else's business. Goals are delivered to the workgroup from higher levels of management and the workgroup is expected to deliver on them; if the goals are aggressive, the workgroup may develop bad behaviors to satisfy them.

With a digital transformation the influence of the workgroup becomes even stronger. Cross-functional teams are autonomous and empowered, self-sufficient and long-lived. A necessary counterpart to a decentralized organizational structure is a shared ethical vision and an understanding of what is good behavior. That is a responsibility of leaders in the transformation.

Building the Culture at Enron

The Enron scandal shows how leaders can set a powerful and consistent ethical vision—and how it can be a bad one. Despite the official code of conduct, Enron's leaders consistently communicated the *real* values of the company.[40] The CEO, Kenneth Lay, was known to use corporate assets for his own benefit and that of his family. He took large personal loans from the company. His family members used the corporate jet freely; while the company was self-destructing, he spent $45 million to refurbish it. Until he was told to stop, he had everyone at Enron use a travel agency that was 50% owned by his sister (Lay himself owned a share of the travel agency until he was forced to divest it).

Everyone at Enron could see that its leaders were lying to the press and to industry analysts, despite the handbook's mandate for honesty, candor, and fairness. At some point Enron stopped referring to its clients as customers. Instead they began calling them "counterparties"—emphasizing that the company's obligation to them was, at most, a legal obligation.[41]

Culture forms around whatever makes employees successful. Even when Enron fired employees for misbehavior, they sometimes rehired them or put them on contracts. In one odd case, a Bankers Trust employee, Kevin Hannon, who had maliciously erased Enron's trading files, was later hired. When Tim Belden, one of Enron's traders, pleaded guilty to manipulating the California electricity markets and his actions were publicly acknowledged by Enron's leaders, he was promoted. Enron's leaders were continually signaling that misbehavior would have positive consequences.

The company's culture isolated employees from the outside world and replaced employees' moral codes with Enron's own value system. The company took care of picking up dry cleaning and prescriptions, shining shoes, and cleaning the house.[42] "People didn't just go to work for Enron. It became a part of your life, just as important as your family. More important than your family."

The annual review and forced ranking system (known as "rank and yank") was exceptionally harsh.[43] Incentives rewarded employees for closing deals but not for implementing them or keeping customers happy. Lou Pai, an Enron executive, was well known to take credit for others' achievements, ridicule other managers behind their backs, and ignore instructions he didn't like. Another executive, John Wing, would routinely tell his subordinates that they were failures, take away their titles, and make them report to someone junior.

Enron was remarkably *successful* in creating the culture it desired. Skilling didn't care if his employees didn't get along; in fact, he thought that tension was a good thing. One recruiter described the culture this way: "They roll you over and slit your throat and watch your eyes while you bleed to death. . . . You could see the green MBAs coming in, so happy-go-lucky and innocent. Within six months, they'd become assholes."[44]

Formal versus Informal Norms; Local versus Global Norms

A traditional organization tries to keep behavior within ethical boundaries by *regulating* it. Its tools are rules, codes of behavior, and governance processes like those of Enron's risk management committee. Unfortunately, codes of behavior can easily be ignored; rules can be interpreted legalistically and obeyed in letter but not in spirit; and governance processes, like Enron's, can be ineffective.

In contemporary IT, we use automated guardrails to enforce security, cost, and compliance controls. Software developers can work quickly, knowing that if they accidentally go outside the constraints, automated tests and policy enforcement will stop them. We'd like to think that ethical guardrails have the same effect. Enron's code should have at least acted as a backstop—decisions could always be "tested" against its principles. But it didn't work.

The reason ethical codes don't work as guardrails is the reason why deontological rules don't work well in the digital world. A proper software guardrail is an absolute prohibition—something that can be tested for precisely and will stop work dead if the test fails. As much as we wish, the ethical guardrails don't work that way—they don't provide unambiguous, deterministic ways to reject behaviors. It's hard to imagine Google's former principle "Don't be evil" working as a guardrail, although that was clearly its intention.

The only way to be sure a company will act ethically is to "shift left," by encouraging the virtues, removing cultural elements that permit or reinforce misbehavior, and making explicit the informal and implied contracts the company has with stakeholders. In the fast-moving digital world, governance processes that cause friction are costly and employees look for ways to circumvent them. Shifting left is the only solution—as IT organizations have already found. Informal norms are even a cheaper substitute for the traditional, slower-moving corporate governance mechanisms.[45]

Transparency and Bullshit

In the last chapter, I noted that secrecy creates space for bad behavior. It does more: it hides the reasoning behind improper actions and lets managers manipulate people by "spinning" secretly made decisions. For example, in a closed-door meeting about layoffs, managers will certainly wind up discussing "How shall we tell them?" and "How shall we communicate it to the press?" In fact, this is probably why the meeting is secret in the first place—the presumed necessity of dressing up the decision before it is communicated.

From secrecy flows euphemism and bullshit, the need to make the company seem more human, to spin a story in ways that will not fool anyone—but which will, they hope, affect the way the company is perceived. A culture of secrecy, that is to say, is likely to be a culture of bullshit. A culture of bullshit is likely to be one that communicates to employees that ethical issues are not important.

The Potential of Transformation

Digital transformation, with its broad cultural change, is an opportunity to transform ethical norms along with other aspects of culture. Indeed, some sort of ethical norms will emerge from transformation—the question is which ones, and how they will be reinforced.

The fact that culture is important in determining ethical behavior has a positive side: it suggests that by attending to cultural issues, companies can reduce or eliminate bad behavior. In the role-playing study mentioned above, researchers told some participants that a board resolution had been passed saying that the board's duty was to represent the shareholders. Seventy-nine percent of these participants chose the "highly irresponsible" course of selling the harmful drug and lobbying the government. Other participants were told that the board's duty was to represent all of its "interest groups" or "stakeholders." Among this group, only 22% chose "highly irresponsible" conduct.[46]

A stakeholder focus, in other words, seems to work better than a shareholder approach for communicating that ethical behavior is expected. It's not that shareholder theory is greedy and unethical; the problem is that it oversimplifies the real decisions that management must make. At Enron, the culture developed around managing quarterly earnings per share. Specifically, it was concerned with *accounting*, rather than true economic earnings per share. Accounting numbers are those which are disclosed to the public and which Enron could manipulate without improving the fundamental economics of the company. That manipulation served to burnish the company's public image, a species of bullshit. And it became an accepted part of the Enron culture.

Companies with one limb in the bureaucratic world tend naturally to use formal governance mechanisms like codes of ethics, company policies, and formal compliance training. They didn't work in the case of Enron or the other corporate scandals. They might be more effective if a reinforcement mechanism is built in to transfer the guidelines from paper to culture; that is, from static principles to virtuous dispositions. Amazon, for example, has sixteen leadership principles that are constantly reinforced—they are used in hiring, in feedback, in making decisions day to day. As a result, they are deeply embedded in the culture—shifted left.

Most important, according to Heath, is that managers "create an environment in which the standard techniques of neutralization used to excuse criminal and unethical behavior are not accepted."[47] The ethical behavior of employees depends on the signals they get from their immediate workgroup, the culture of the organization as a whole, and the model set by their leaders. Workplace virtues are developed through reinforcement by the company's culture.

If Heath is right, the ethics instruction provided in business schools is not all that important. Nor is my advice in this book. As Heath says, people "do not commit crimes because they lack expertise in the application of the categorical imperative or the felicific calculus." They commit crimes because their social environment allows or encourages them to talk themselves into excuses for bad behavior.[48] As for the value of this book, please be advised that you may complain in colorful language that you wasted your money. I do sincerely more than value your feedback.

Manipulation

Virtues: Care, Respect, Presence, Courage, Humility

When we encounter another individual truly as a person, not as an object for use, we become fully human.

—Martin Buber, *I and Thou*

Moral law is an invention of mankind for the disenfranchisement of the powerful in favor of the weak.

—Cormac McCarthy, *Blood Meridian*

The central ethical challenge for digitally transforming organizations is when and how to use their power to manipulate customers, employees, and other stakeholders. It's time to circle back to the point I raised at the beginning of this second part of the book, the imperative to *maximize* shareholder returns. Again, the word maximize is significant—it implies that managers cannot leave opportunities on the table if they are legal and would result in higher returns. As a company moves into the digital age, many such opportunities present themselves. And many of them involve psychological manipulation.

Enron's success—while it lasted—flowed directly from their ability to manipulate customers, partners, employees, industry analysts, the press, markets, the economy, and supply and demand for electricity. Their executives had mastered the art of controlling people by playing on their weaknesses; they had a kind of evil wizardry reminiscent of the character Saruman in *Lord of the Rings*. As much as they tried to paint themselves as a digital company, their manipulation was of the old-school sort: coercion, bullying, silos, performance reviews, relationships with crusty oil and gas players, an almost-all-old-boys network.

Digital businesses have new powers to manipulate. We can mine customer data to find the most effective ways to stimulate purchasing activity. We can target messages to the customers who will be most influenced by them. We can tweak the design of our products and marketing materials by conducting experiments on customers to see what attributes are most effective. We can insert special offers just as customers are making their purchasing decisions. Gaming companies and social media networks are mastering the wizardry of making their sites "sticky" to keep customers clicking.

These abilities are the reasons we want to transform in the first place. They deliver on the duty to increase profits and shareholder returns. In many ways, they are a matter of doing what we've always done, but doing it better. But, this being a book on ethics, we also have to consider whether there are limits to the use of these superpowers, for it is when we have power over others that we are most likely to face moral issues.

Perhaps you're surprised that I raise manipulation as the central ethical issue of digital transformation, rather than, say, biased AI, misuse of personal data, leprechaun business models, or robot dogs. I think a number of factors have been drawing our attention away from its importance. For one thing, all eyes have been on Frankenstein and the gingerbread man, issues that are easier for the media to frame for us. Metrical bureaucracy has narrowed our focus to measurable targets and distracted us from concerns about how we meet them. The inauthentic and impersonal speech and great gasying words that congest our communication channels diffuse accountability, even as its constant, suggestive murmur whispers "buy wanko soba noodles" in a seductive voice. And, most of all, we've maintained unquestioned the belief that maximizing shareholder returns is our only true objective.

In other words, all of the issues I've raised in "Perils and Predators" are masking this important issue.

Manipulation is a strong word, and we'll have to explore its nuances in this chapter. Throughout the bureaucratic era, managers have understood their job as "getting" productivity from their employees, and they've had the tools of managerial science to use in doing so. Companies have used advertising and packaging to "get" customers to purchase. In both cases, the intent is to use psychological influences to accomplish the company's objectives. I'll use the term "manipulation" broadly, to refer to all such activities to "manage" the thinking of others to accomplish our own ends, and use this chapter to explore when it might be bad and when it might be harmless.

The techniques of "professional management," the ideas taught in business schools and in the books of management gurus, set the stage for manipulative leadership. The assumption of management "science" is that there is a set of techniques, or a conceptual framework, independent of particular business domains, that can be used to engineer higher profitability without necessarily building better or cheaper products. Different from most sciences, however, it has to engineer *people*. That's where manipulation comes in. And that brings us to Frederick Taylor, the "father" of scientific management.

Frederick Taylor

Frederick Taylor is best known for his consulting work at Bethlehem Steel. Because iron prices had been low, Bethlehem had built up an inventory of 80,000 tons of ninety-pound "pigs" of iron, which they now wanted to sell as prices increased. They had a crew of seventy-five workers to load the iron onto trucks and the average worker, when Taylor entered the scene as a consultant, could load 12.5 tons a day. Taylor believed that the fundamental threat to business performance was "soldiering"—the tendency of employees to under-produce—and he was sure that with proper management, Bethlehem's workers could do better.

Taylor and his assistants approached the problem with stopwatches and managerial discipline. They determined, after some experimentation, that a worker could load 47.5 tons per day if they followed Taylor's instructions and worked hard at it. They demonstrated with one worker, Henry Noll, that it could be done. Noting that some workers could do the task better than others, Taylor helped Bethlehem Steel set up a hiring process for "first-class" pig-iron loaders. With the help of Taylor's team, the company quickly loaded the 80,000 tons and sent it to market.

That was—ahem—the way Taylor told the story. As Jill Lepore said in a *New Yorker* article, "Taylor's methods were flawed to the point of being ridiculous. He fudged his numbers. He cheated and lied. He was at best misguided and at worst a shameless fraud."[1]

Actually, there were less than 10,000 tons to be loaded, not 80,000. There were never 75 loaders, just a couple of dozen general laborers who did miscellaneous tasks that sometimes included loading pig iron. To calculate the possible loading rate, Taylor's team first rounded up an average group of laborers and found that they could load 23.8 tons in a day. He then got a crew of ten "large powerful Hungarians" and asked them to load 16.5 tons as fast as they could. Based on the rate they achieved, he calculated that they could load 71 tons per ten-hour day, which he rounded up to 75. He then applied a 40% reduction to this number, based on—nothing. He just made it up as a law of "heavy laboring" to derive his 47.5 ton number.

Unfortunately for Taylor's theory, the next day, the Hungarians refused to continue at that pace. So Taylor found a new team of burly laborers, who were able to load 32 tons per person on the first day. The next day two of them were too tired to work. Of the rest, two more lasted only half of another day. Only Henry Noll ever came close to loading 47.5 tons in a day, and he couldn't do it again.

Taylor never documented his methodology or data in a way that would allow other researchers to verify his findings—which, of course, is critical to the scientific method.[2] His hiring process for "first-class" pig iron loaders never took place as far as anyone can tell from examining job ads in local newspapers.[3]

Fortunately, Bethlehem Steel didn't apply Taylor's "findings." There is no evidence they benefited from the experiments, and they eventually asked Taylor to stop.[4] But the idea that labor could be managed "scientifically" caught on. Peter Drucker later referred to Taylor's book *The Principles of Scientific Management* as "the most powerful as well as the most lasting contribution America has made to Western thought since the Federalist Papers."[5] Herman Melville and Albert Einstein, take notice.

Taylor performed similar "studies" at other companies. Workers whose jobs had been "Taylorized" kept complaining about being exhausted,[6] but those who protested against his standards were fired.[7] In 1911, molders at a gun factory went on strike, refusing to work under Taylor's time constraints. Previously it had taken them fifty-three minutes to pour a mold to make a gun carriage. Taylor's timekeeper told them to do it in twenty-four minutes. Taylor had told the timekeeper not to worry about the stopwatch, but just to make a rough guess of how quickly it could be done.

Aside from his dishonesty, Taylor's "scientific" approach masked a serious ethical issue:

> At stake in the brutal "experiments" in pig-iron lifting was not just how much work a laborer *could* do, but how much he *should* do. This confusion of facts and values—or, more generally, the attempt to find pseudotechnical solutions to moral and political problems—is the most consequential error in Taylor's work and is the cardinal sin of management theory to the present.[8]

When Taylor explained to a congressional committee that a "first-class man" could quickly move a pile of coal by lifting shovelfuls of 21.5 pounds, a committee member exclaimed, "You've told us the effect on the pile. But how about the effect on the man?"[9]

You might recognize this as a sort of is-ought problem. Knowing that we *can* do something is different from knowing that we *ought* to do it. Management faces true questions of value, not just of mechanics. Matthew Stewart says that "scientific management was not a body of facts but a proposal about how managers should treat workers—principally, as mute, brainless bundles of animal muscles."[10]

Managers had to manipulate employees into producing because the bureaucratic enterprise assumes that workers are recalcitrant, or that they will "soldier" in Taylor's terms. Later management theory accepted that people aren't machines; Taylor's intent, the engineering of more productivity from workers, could be accomplished better through psychological influence than through his coercive methods. The goal was the same, though—increase production beyond what employees would produce if left to themselves. And manipulation could be extended beyond the walls of the company even to those not under the company's direct control, as Enron did so successfully.

When you use the word "manipulation" it seems like you're biasing the discussion. You're going to say that manipulating customers and employees is bad, obviously.

Not at all. Just like the way I use the word "bureaucracy." It's good and bad. But I want to be very honest about what we're talking about. And I want to make a solid connection with CIv2 and autonomy.

With such a broad definition, it's not really new, though. Companies have always tried to manipulate customers with their advertising. Especially brand advertising, as you said before.

Right. It's not new. Companies want to transform so they can do it better. It's a kind of continuous improvement.

In this chapter, we have two topics to cover: manipulation of employees and manipulation of customers. I'll start with employees.

Section One: Manipulating Employees

In the factory model, workers are "resources," a factor of production that managers must oversee, along with machines, to deliver output. Machines are easy to manage. They can be "manipulated" (the word comes from *manus*, the Latin word for "hand") directly; dials can be set, buttons pushed, Siri commanded. Humans, however, are independent actors, "ends in themselves" in Kantian terms. To get results where people are involved, managers have to master techniques based in psychology, sociology, organizational theory, and perhaps wizardry or the occult to "operate" the human beings.

Since a bureaucracy's goals are given, even to managers, from outside,

managers allow themselves, and are allowed, to manipulate others simply because this is the most effective way to get things done. . . . And hence relationships tend to become manipulative because the manager's role is to achieve the given ends as efficiently as possible. The manager is, on this account, at best, an amoral agent.[11]

Taylor's approach strictly separated the roles of managers and workers. In Stewart's words, Taylor believed that "laborers are bodies without minds; managers are minds without bodies."[12] When tasked with improving the process of shoveling coal, Taylor said, "The ordinary pig-iron handler is not suited to shoveling coal. He is too stupid." The assumption of stupidity was baked into his theory, which explains why coercion was necessary.

Professionalization of Management

Before the rise of managerial science, a manager was someone with expertise in the company's business, often someone with skills in the task done by the workers under them; the manager's job was to organize and administer the work. Professionalized management filled a gap in bureaucracy: bureaucratic principles require that each role in the org chart have a specific technical competency, so for management roles, it became the knowledge of management science.

The twentieth century was a time of fertile innovation in the science of management manipulation. While physical scientists were inventing radio, television, and refrigeration, management scientists invented the employee of the month award—a milestone in productivity science. Industrial psychologists found they could improve employee performance by choosing the right colors for office walls and the blandest orchestral covers of Beatles songs for the elevators. In Japan, company calisthenics worked the muscles that employees would need to sit behind desks and drink lukewarm coffee. Management theorist Elton Mayo proposed that employees resisted working hard because of a psychopathology stemming from *anomie*, a sense of futility or disconnectedness; if employers could just help them overcome those psychological blocks, they would refrain from unionizing and become more productive.[13]

Wearing my management montera, I might, in a moment of inspiration, come up with a contest to motivate employees. Whoever sells the most garak-guksu noodles this month will win a lifetime supply of Schupfnudeln! I deliberately build excitement around the contest and let the employees catch the smell of Schupfnudeln wafting from the company kitchen. This is why companies hire me as a manager.

To be clear, you've manipulated employees?

Oh yes. I used employee-of-the-month technology. I mentioned employees' names in quarterly all-hands meetings. I set up a kudos board where employees could thank other employees or recognize their successes.

As I become a more experienced manager, I'm probably learning better ways to manipulate employees. I've learned things like how to make people feel at ease at the beginning of a conversation so that they'll be more inclined to accept what I have to say. Management, I've learned, is smiling at the right time and appearing vaguely annoyed the rest of the time.

As the twentieth century progressed, business schools manufactured new buzz phrases to name ways enterprises could get better performance from their employees. Harvard Business School professor Rosabeth Moss Kanter spoke of the "integrative organization." There was the adaptive organization, the informated organization, the knowledge-intensive organization, the learning organization, the network organization, the organic organization, the hybrid organization, the poststructuralist organization, the self-designing organization, and the shamrock organization.[14] The ideas of "empowerment," "the wisdom of teams," and "autonomy" were introduced in the 1960s.

Oops—wait, some of those are buzzwords of the digital organization. Damn it!

Don't panic—we're still on the right track, as long as we make the necessary value shift. Wise and informed teams and shamrocks can exist in a traditional bureaucracy or in a digital organization, and will look similar. It's not the structure and organizational principles that matter. It's the values and virtues that managers and employees bring to growing shamrocks.

Without that value shift, even Agile software delivery and other techniques of the digital age become distorted. Is the point of Agile delivery to get more "productivity" from software developers? You'd think so, the way companies are using team velocity as a productivity metric and the way Scrum emphasizes team "commitment" to sprint objectives. These are bureaucratic leftovers, getting cold on the plate.

Manipulation Might Be Bad

The problem with manipulation is best framed in terms of the autonomy principle or CIv2—an individual's ability to act as they wish is reduced or eliminated when they are manipulated. Both principles suggest that out of respect for a person's autonomy, or respect for that person as a human with their own goals and beliefs, businesses should refrain from manipulating them solely for the business's benefit.

Alisdair MacIntyre's explanation of Kant's CIv2 is a good starting point. As he says,

> I may propose a course of action to someone either by offering him reasons for so acting or by trying to influence him in non-rational ways. If I do the former I treat him as a rational will, worthy of the same respect as is due to myself, for in offering him reasons I offer him an impersonal consideration for him to evaluate. By contrast an attempt at non-rational suasion embodies an attempt to make the agent a mere instrument of my will, without any regard for his rationality.[15]

It's a starting point, but incomplete, though "making someone the instrument of my will" does sound appropriately wizard-like. I have to admit that not every argument I make in this book is purely rational. If they were, my writing would be as dry as Kant's while not being nearly as brilliant. Rhetoric is the art of making arguments more persuasive—without necessarily making the reasoning better. When you want to convince people of something that's important to you, you summon up every bit of wizardry you can. Manipulation is natural in writing and public speaking.

When we go to a movie we expect to be manipulated. A "tearjerker" film is one that jerks tears out from our eyes—a film that manipulates us into crying. In a negotiation or in a courtroom, we use emotion to sway others, and they expect it. So, where exactly is that boundary between acceptable and unacceptable manipulation if it isn't where Kant put it, at the boundary between rational and nonrational suasion?

We can define manipulation as the attempt to influence someone in ways other than those they judge to be good.[16] Most of us accept that we make some or most of our decisions emotionally rather than rationally. To get people to contribute to a charity, it's more effective to stimulate their emotions— say, by telling them about the starving children who will be saved—rather than by giving them logical arguments. It's a kind of persuasion we generally accept, and transparent enough that we can try to discount its manipulative aspects.

Paternalistic Manipulation

You're confusing me. Are you saying that managers shouldn't do their best to get employees to perform well?

Not really. I'm saying that in the old-style enterprise managers had to think of their task as manipulating employees, because they assumed employees didn't want to do their jobs well.

That's changed?

I don't know if it was ever valid. Maybe. As I said in the introduction, I have no experience, say, in factories. But the digital enterprise is based on the idea of employees who care, employees who are personally committed to their work.

You really think all employees are committed?

No. No, you're right. It's a matter of the baseline case we choose. Assume they're recalcitrant, so motivated employees are the exception, or assume they're motivated so recalcitrance is the exception?

Let's accept that all management is manipulative in the broadest sense, in that it improves outcomes for the company by getting employees to perform better. Employees are people, so managing them to improve performance will always involve influencing them psychologically. Manipulation doesn't conflict with the principle of autonomy if a person consents to being manipulated. Students implicitly consent to being manipulated into learning by their teachers. Employees implicitly agree to further the company's interests. If managers manipulate them, arguably the manipulation is consensual.

A deontologist might want to say that manipulation is either good or bad. But since Chapter 3 we've been virtue ethicists, so the question for us is what virtues managers should bring to the task of manipulating employees. It's possible for a manager to manipulate while respecting an employee's autonomy, without deception, and for the sake of ends common to both the employee and the company. It can be done with both care for the employee and proper stewardship of the responsibilities assigned to the manager. Perhaps the ideal is some kind of paternalistic manipulation, done with care for the employee, as in the Confucian idea of extending the parent-child relationship into other social interactions.

The book *Nudge*, by Richard Thaler and Cass Sunstein, makes a case for well-intended manipulation. It argues that any time we design an object for use, we make choices that will manipulate its users—so we can and *should* manipulate them in a way that is for their own good. In their words, Thaler and Sunstein argue for "self-conscious efforts, by institutions in the private sector and also by government, to steer people's choices in directions that will improve their lives."[17]

For example, school cafeterias can be designed to make it easier for students to choose healthier food options, say by placing them on shelves that are easier to reach. Students will then be more likely to choose the healthy options, while still being able to choose unhealthy ones if they like. *Something* has to be placed on the easy-to-reach shelf—why not put the healthy option there?

When I put on my unhealthy-preference pork pie, it still feels a bit off to me. Even paternalistic manipulation involves someone else deciding what's best for me, and though they might have good intentions, they may be wrong. I'm uncomfortable with someone deciding for me what I value—they might assume that I value health above all things, while I actually value the pleasure of butter, bacon, and toasted marshmallows highly. I should be able to choose how much "health" I am willing to forego for a unit of "pleasure."

Okay, but as Thaler and Sunstein point out, I'm going to be manipulated one way or another by the placement of the snacks on the shelves. Perhaps it's better to be manipulated by someone who "cares" about me, even if they are wrong. Objection withdrawn.

Manage Like the Wind

When Confucius was asked how to govern effectively, he answered, "The excellence (or virtue) of the exemplary person (or higher ranking individual) is the wind; while that of the petty person (or low-ranking official) is the grass. As the wind blows, the grass is sure to bend."[18] Confucians speak of authority in the language of fluidity, grace, beauty, peace, wind, and grass.[19] The leader guides their subordinates to "harmoniously collaborate in a way that allows them to develop their strengths and virtues while complementing the strengths and virtues of others."[20]

The leader offers something that subordinates can accept, which preserves their autonomy and dignity.[21] "The people's submission to the good Confucian ruler is not submission to some coercive power but rather to a fixed, reliable moral authority that radiates throughout the realm."[22] A good ruler sets an example that their subjects would want to emulate.[23]

> Guide them by edicts, keep them in line with punishments, and the common people will stay out of trouble, but will have no sense of shame. Guide them by virtue, keep them in line with ritual and they will, besides having a sense of shame, reform themselves.[24]

The Weirdness of Performance Management

Now assume for a moment that employees care and are doing their best, and assume that we want to preserve their dignity. What more obvious management technique is there for us to question than the annual performance assessment ritual?

Performance assessment is supposed to be about the work, not the employee. That makes sense if employees are recalcitrant and their jobs are well defined. In that case you use the annual assessment to apply carrots and sticks to mold their behavior. If, on the other hand, an employee cares about their job, is passionate, is trying to do what's right—then the performance evaluation *is* about them personally. A negative assessment means that they're not capable, not that they aren't working hard enough. The fact that employees feel bad when they receive a negative evaluation is evidence that they *do* care.

One motivation for the annual assessment is that employees will work better if they know they'll be appraised, just as people will be more ethical if they know they'll be judged at the gates of heaven. But is that actually the best way to improve performance? What's the connection between *managing* performance and *judging* performance? If the goal of feedback is really to improve an employee's performance, it's not even obvious that the manager is the best person to provide it. The best feedback giver may be someone who has coaching skills and is exposed to the employee's behavior every day.

The manager gets the job only because the point of performance reviews is *not* just to improve performance. A manager has the organizational authority to punish and reward the employee; coaching is mixed with the exercise of power. We've conflated two concepts—the retributive value of judgment and the improvement of performance, which is a different matter. We want to get better results, not demand an eye for an eye or a spreadsheet for a spreadsheet.

Bureaucracy, I've said, has advantages, among them, fairness through impartial rules and documentation. It would certainly be unfair to fire an employee without telling them their performance is unsatisfactory and giving them a chance to improve it. But forcing all employees to sit through an annual assessment auto-da-fe even if they aren't even in danger of being burned adds cost for the company, makes employees feel bad, and constrains the company's agility.

To employees who are members of groups that have suffered discrimination, objective metrics and assessments with hard numbers are appealing. But the value of diversity and inclusion is in the differences employees bring, not the objective production metrics they share. We know that metrics can be gamed to support biases, and people can be made to feel unwelcome even if they are hitting targets.

Then how do you think performance should be assessed?
What makes you think employee performance needs to be assessed?
You're just being contrary. Surely you don't believe it isn't necessary.

I'm not sure.

But it's a way of getting managers and employees in sync. The manager can make sure the employee understands what's important. And it's not just negative—the employee gets recognition for what they've done.

Do you see what's odd about that? Managers should always make it clear what they expect and should always recognize employees' contributions. What does that have to do with annually judging their performance?

Section Two:
Manipulating the Public

The history of digital business is a history of finding better ways to use data to manipulate customers. The demand to become more data-driven is largely a push to find better ways to "oversee" customers so they deliver a company's desired financial results, a kind of manipulation wizardry that escapes the walls of the company.

Companies have plenty of avenues for manipulating consumers—ads on the walls above urinals, teasing messages on social media platforms, gushing press releases that are turned immediately into headlines by publications that can't afford to hire reporters, annoying jingles, free apps with "in-app" purchases, and cute robots in stores. Retailers have found that customers perceive prices to be lower when they have fewer syllables and end with a nine.[25] Casinos are known to track the "pain point"—the amount that a particular gambler is comfortable losing—and gently guide them away from the table just before that point is reached.

Sticky digital media systems undermine customers' self-control by taking advantage of neurological and psychological quirks.[26] Game designers even speak of "addiction" and produce reports to measure it. Reed Hastings, CEO of Netflix, has said that Netflix is competing with sleep.[27]

Humans are complex; it's not always obvious how they'll respond to a stimulus. It's a "best practice" for digital organizations to test different user experiences to see which work best. There are techniques like A/B testing to handle the complexity. A misconception about A/B testing is that it tests to see which design option users like better. It would be more correct to say that it tests which design option better accomplishes the designer's goals. It's easy: field two different versions of, say, a web page, and see which has a better result for the designer's target metric.

Design manipulates users, as we saw from *Nudge*. In fact, Cennydd Bowles, a designer and the author of *Future Ethics*, claims that design is applied ethics. "Design changes how we see the world and how we can act within it; design turns beliefs about how we should live into objects and environments people will use and inhabit."[28] Digital technology constrains user behavior through its interfaces and functions. Users can select only options they are given; their attention is drawn one way or another by the user interface; the wording on the screen frames how they conceptualize their interactions with the system; design determines whether the product is accessible to people with disabilities.

Sporting my user ushanka: Sometimes I get a pop-up message in an app offering me a product I would have to pay for. It offers two choices: "Yes, subscribe me" and "Maybe later." I'm coerced into clicking a button that says "maybe later" even if I don't want to subscribe later or ever, in this lifetime or the next. Every time I click that button I experience that bit of incremental frustration. Some unsubscribe links take me to a page where I can "adjust my preferences," as if receiving spam was my preference until now.

Users have no transparency into design decisions and why they are made; design manipulates them without their knowledge.

> But technology acts invisibly, often with dubious consent, and typically using a dialect only a few can speak. The general public has no idea what sorts of unwelcome acts are happening inside their gadgets. To paraphrase Caroline Whitbeck, ethical issues are like design briefs: there are often dozens of viable solutions, each with their own trade-offs.[29]

Like it or not, as digital leaders we're drawn into manipulating customers to accomplish the company's business goals. As we cascade the company's objectives down through the organization in the form of employees' targets, we may be setting up a cultural framework for unethical manipulation.

Power and Manipulation

I'm going to put on my consumer kolpik again for a brief moment of fuming and venting. I recently went through all the pay services that were billing me every month so I could scrap the ones I wasn't really using. Even though I had subscribed to those services online, I wasn't allowed to unsubscribe from them online. I had to call each company. Once the voice response system determined what I was calling about, it lost its eagerness to connect me with anyone. When I finally did reach a person, I had to listen while they read me a script offering me options I knew I didn't want. I know, you've been there too.

When I call a company's customer service line, the agent sometimes needs to type notes on the case or send emails. They force me to wait on the phone while they do so, even though there's nothing I can add. I can only assume that they get penalized for time they are not on the phone with a customer. It wastes my time, but they have the power to keep me on the phone despite the cost to me.

On some airlines I have to listen to an announcement during the flight touting their credit cards. I can't step outside the plane to avoid hearing it. The airline can force me to listen to it and avoid paying for a radio advertisement.

All of these are cases of companies with power over me exercising that power manipulatively. In each case, I have to assume that there is someone in the company with a metric they are trying to optimize—

You're starting to sound obsessed with this stuff. Emails and mail you don't want, phone response systems. It's really just bad customer service, isn't it?

Yes. No. It's more of an abuse of power, and a manipulative one, at that.

You've got that thing with airline speech, too.

Okay, okay, I'm the author. I get to decide what to rant about. But thanks so very much for pointing it out.

So, donning my transformation leader trilby, we as leaders have a choice— we can frustrate customers and improve our metrics, or we can try to build trusting relationships with them. The two goals seem incompatible—which will be the topic of the next chapter.

Advertising

George Orwell called advertising "the rattle of the stick in the swill bucket." The philosopher George Santayana said that the purpose of advertising is to make "the worse appear the better," which is considerably nicer than the ad photographer Lester Bookbinder's description of it as "turning crap into mediocrity."[30]

If you haven't noticed, advertising is manipulative. Marshall McLuhan said, "To get inside in order to manipulate, exploit, control is the object . . . To keep everybody in the helpless state engendered by prolonged mental rutting is the effect of many ads and much entertainment alike."[31] Perhaps an ad suggests that if you don't wear the company's Smurf-certified Phrygian cap you'll be a social outcast, or that if you do wear it, you will win over the most attractive member of the sex you prefer. Or that the company's socket wrench is somehow associated with springtime, wholesomeness, fun, or czars riding like thunder.

Some ethicists say that advertising causes people to want things that— rationally or otherwise—they shouldn't want, and is therefore a violation of autonomy. Others, like the economist F. A. Hayek, counter that our desires are rarely independent of our environments and desires caused by advertising are just as valid as desires any others.[32] In *Brave New World*, people are divided into classes and, as children, trained to want exactly the things that their class will be given. Their leaders claim that everyone is happy because all their desires are satisfied. Utilitarian or preference consequentialists might have to agree.

Although advertising is manipulative, consumers sometimes seek it out. Many of us in the US look forward to the annual Super Bowl commercials, when advertisers bring their best game to crafting manipulative advertising. In the early days of television, all commercials had to be broadcast in a single half-hour program each night, called Carosello. Carosello was the most watched television show.[33]

As a contractarian matter, someone who watches a commercial on TV has agreed to be manipulated. They know there will be commercials, and they know what commercials are for. Perhaps advertising is not even warranted to be true any more than Red Bull gives you wings; the burden is on the consumer to exercise self-control. We've agreed to these contracts because we think we can defend ourselves and because we want to receive free services.

It's a very different story when that advertising is deceptive or disguised. Disguised manipulation can happen in a context where the consumer has not agreed to be manipulated: a customer may look at a product on a retailer's website and later be shown a related ad on a social media site. The consumer's reaction may be that they want the privacy of their data safeguarded. But perhaps the question is less about privacy and more about manipulation without disclosure.

A blog called "Wal-Marting Across America" seemed to be an ordinary blog by a man and a woman traveling across the continent in an RV and staying in Walmart parking lots. It was actually created by three employees at Walmart's PR firm.[34] With all the noise in social media, we don't always know that we're being advertised at. Frighteningly, disguised manipulation is becoming easier. "Two lynchpins of contemporary evidence—speech and video—will soon be falsifiable, further distorting the persuasive landscape," Cennydd Bowles points out.[35]

Your obsession is showing again.
Noted. I don't like feeling manipulated.
I thought you said in the preface that you aren't angry.
Can we just call it extreme annoyance?
Can we just call that euphemism and bullshit?

Contractarians would probably agree that our implicit agreement with advertisers doesn't allow them to mislead us through pseudonymous blog posts. In fact, it's evidence that such an agreement exists that we weight these blog posts as we would any independent product reviews. That's why they're so effective.

Manipulation and Transformation

Manipulation, treating people as a means only, turns questions of "should I" into questions of "how can I most effectively." And this, in turn, fits neatly with the idea that bureaucracy is a value-neutral system for finding the most effective means to accomplish externally selected ends. The tools of the digital world provide powerful ways to manipulate effectively.

Once again, managers have their feet sinking into quicksand in two worlds at once. Digital transformation brings out tensions in the way companies use their power. On one hand, companies deliberately strive for market power because that is their mandate from investors; they use it to earn rents or above-normal returns. On the other hand, power poses moral risks for companies, which can use their power to manipulate consumers, thereby increasing revenues and deriving returns for investors. Managers have power over employees and look to manipulate them because that's how they manage costs and increase production to maximize returns for their investors.

But manipulation, or certain types of manipulation, might not be consistent with the world we desire, the world of flourishing or eudaemonia. Once again, the questions are rarely of good versus evil; there are competing demands that must be weighed and ethical decisions made without a guidebook.

PART III

EVOLUTION

Intimacy and Privacy
Toward a New Relationship With Customers

Invention, it must be humbly admitted, does not consist in creating out of void, but out of chaos; the materials must, in the first place, be afforded: it can give form to dark shapeless substances but cannot bring into being the substance itself.

—Mary Shelley, *Frankenstein*

All my means are sane, my motive and my object mad.

—Herman Melville, *Moby Dick*

We all want to build closer relationships with our customers, and we recognize that digital interaction is a way to do so. *Customer intimacy* is a fine-sounding goal that seems to carry great promise for society. Of course customers should be at the center of everything we do; of course we should understand and respond to their needs and desires. But do customers really want an intimate relationship with the company they bought a bobblehead toy from? What are the terms and boundaries of that relationship?

The difficulty, as with AI, is that we're mixing up a metaphor with the real thing. Customers do not actually have caring relationships online with their vendors. Real relationships involve concern on both sides, and they create ethical obligations. There may be a caring relationship when a doctor and patient interact online, but not when a customer and their toilet bowl cleaner vendor interact. The customer knows that, at best, they are valued as one of many customers who might contribute to the company's revenues or to a target metric of a digital marketer.

To pretend that there is a deeper relationship is . . . creepy. Do your customers want an intimate relationship with you, or do you just want to be intimate with them? Are you taking liberties that make them uncomfortable? Is your company a creepy guy putting his arm around the shoulders of someone he sits next to on a park bench?

The intimacy thing starts with a pasta vendor pressuring its customer to register their artisan farfalle—with yet another password—so it can send the customer marketing emails with barely visible unsubscribe links. Then there's an email asking the customer to spend time indicating whether they were satisfied with their purchase. Suddenly the pasta vendor is "personalizing" its website so it displays the customer's first name everywhere. Welcome, Rumpelstiltskin! Surprise! We know your name!

A loyalty program offers itself, then invitations to a pasta-of-the-month club, then text messages with "exclusive" new pasta recipes, downloadable episodes of *The Great Italian Pasta Show* with weepy contestants being sent off the show for pasta that's too soggy, half-priced stringozzi specials and pop-up messages with dire warnings that there are still some pastas Rumpelstiltskin hasn't yet bought. Rumpelstiltskin is invited to set his "preferences," like whether prefers to receive emails he doesn't want when he's in meetings or doing yoga, and ads from an unrelated bobblehead vendor for Mother Teresa bobbleheads because once Rumpelstiltskin contributed to a charity and is therefore in the target market.

For me, with or without my customer caubeen on, I find that companies trying to have intimate relationships with me are pushing all the buttons in Part II of this book. I feel like I'm being manipulated: when someone repeatedly uses my first name in a face-to-face conversation, I put my guard up. The "personalization" is—well, look back at Chapter 5. I can't help picturing a grinning junior digital marketer's face behind the webpage, joyful that I am contributing one one-hundred-thousandth of their goal for customer acquisition. The large hotel chain I have loyalty status with is sending me emails about how much they're looking forward to having me on my next stay. They aren't and they're going to make me wait in line to check in, like everyone else. Our "relationship" is full of bullshit.

What's especially creepy is that while I have an intimate relationship with the pasta company's website designers, another department of their company is selling the information they've learned about me. It is a little like finding my name and phone number on a bathroom stall with a note about how easy they found it to "build an intimate relationship" with me. Suddenly I'm getting contacted by a bunch of other vendors looking for a ready transaction. When I go to social media to find out what my friends are up to, there's now an ad for the same socket wrench that was handed to me by a leprechaun plumbing consultant in an odd dream I had last night. Ick.

I've wondered why there is so much angry rhetoric about privacy today, when—as I'll try to show below—privacy issues are nuanced and unclear. I'll propose a theory here: it's less about privacy and more about violations of trust in the context of this pretend intimacy. Arguments about privacy today are not theoretical arguments about data. They're arguments about betrayal of trust and manipulation. We don't want to see our personal data written on a bathroom stall. Intimacy and privacy are related.

Back in my transformation leader toque: Bureaucratic impersonality gives us the hubris to think that we're building intimate relationships with our customers because we know their names and because they are included in our subscriber count. But that same impersonality makes building an intimate relationship impossible, because you can't build an impersonal personal relationship. Screech, crash, boom, values colliding, and you wind up with a bizarre pandemic of noise and insincerity.

In this last section of the book, I'll examine how by divesting our bureaucratic assumptions and *carefully* adopting digital values, we can implement an agile, adaptive ethics—and what that agile ethics would look like. In this chapter I want to look at our relationships with customers, and propose that the way we've been thinking about that relationship is responsible for today's ethical challenges.

In the next chapter, Frankenstein and the gingerbread man make their case that we can learn from them, incrementally and humbly, about what sort of world we want to live in. Then I'll propose a list of virtues for the workplace that I think captures the essence of digital transformation. In the final chapter, I will show what role managers and leaders must play in leading ethical transformation and how they can fulfill that responsibility.

Friendship

Relationships—in this case, friendship—are the building blocks of our social lives. They are governed by more ethical norms than there are types of pasta in Italy. They impose moral obligations on both parties to the relationship. There may be variations across different cultures in what the obligations are, exactly, but a relationship as a friend is not to be taken lightly.

When a company suggests to a customer that they are on friendly terms, drawing on a shared history of interactions, offering gifts and recognition, sharing privileged information—they are drawing on an analogy with real relations of friendship. They are trying to generate the same warm feelings that come with friendship to build an attachment to their brand.

The problem is that the moral obligations of friendship don't come along with it. A transactional relationship lurks behind the facade. A company will not accept any pain out of care for the customer. It cares for the customer—as an individual—not at all, though it might care for an aggregate of customers in relation to a metric like "attrition" or "revenue per transaction," or simply "revenue."

Small Town

I've lived mostly in big cities, where anonymity is one of the biggest attractions. In New York, I didn't even know my neighbors in the other apartments on my floor. That brings a feeling of freedom—of self-reliance, of endless possibility. Of course, you sacrifice something. I've always imagined that in a small, close-knit community, there's more of an atmosphere of caring, a sort of security that flows from the attention of people who take some responsibility for your well-being.

I asked some friends who grew up in small towns what it's like. Don't they feel a lack of privacy? Doesn't it feel restricting to have everyone know when they receive a new hatbox package from their milliner? When I was in graduate school I lived in a building where lots of my fellow students lived. We knew very quickly who was making nightly visits to whom, and who might be drinking too many apple and elderflower martinis a little too consistently. They agreed that they didn't feel like they had much privacy in their town.

I asked them why, in that case, online privacy was an issue for them. They thought about it for a moment and told me that in a different sense there is privacy in a small town—privacy from outsiders. The residents are guarded in dealing with strangers. That's what it means to be a close-knit community. The people who knew all about them are a sort of extended family, people they have a relationship with.

Given that very scientific study, appropriately conducted over Manhattans and cosmopolitans, the privacy question, it seems to me, is less about people having your data and more about trusting people to make good use of what they know about you. I know this vision I've formed of a small town is probably as much of a fable as "Rumpelstiltskin," but it will do for an analogy.

You can imagine a day in the vague past where you went into a store every day or every week, got to know the proprietor, chatted with them, you knew their families and their personal tragedies, and they knew yours. When you were in desperate need of candy it somehow found its way into your shopping bag, and if you couldn't pay they'd let you run up a tab or forget to charge you for the Mr. Potato Head accessories you bought. That's a personal relationship. This is precisely what an online "intimate" relationship with a vendor is not, even if they are throwing in a plastic nose or two for free.

I sometimes make the mistake of feeling like I have a relationship with a business—especially when it comes to loyalty programs. I stupidly feel like my platinum deity status with an airline means that they care about me. But then I notice that they aren't upgrading me to first class until they make sure they can't sell the seat to someone else—even when I'm tired and at the end of a long and demanding business trip. We're not actually friends. And based on my boarding priority, I know they are promiscuous with their deity status.

Companies aren't people, even if they are persons. It's another escaped metaphor, whose gingerbread legs should be bitten off.

Personally Identifiable Information

One of the worst privacy violations in history was committed against none other than Rumpelstiltskin. If you remember the story, the princess had signed a user agreement for Rumpelstiltskin's straw-into-gold service that said she had to give him her firstborn child. But the fine print said that if she could guess his name the contract would be null and void. Lucky for the princess, she "happened" to be passing by Rumpelstiltskin's cottage one day and took advantage of the opportunity to eavesdrop. She overheard him singing "tonight, tonight, my plans I make, tomorrow, tomorrow, the baby I take. The queen will never win the game, for Rumpelstiltskin is my name," which is not much of a lyric but a better one than if he had encrypted his name. When she "guessed" his name the next day, Rumpelstiltskin was as angry as anyone whose personal data had made its way to Cambridge Analytica.

In many stories, knowing a person's name gives you power over them. When Isis found out the sun god Ra's real name, she gained enough power over him to get her son Horus a job as the king and father of all pharaohs. In the Bible, when Jacob out-wrestles an angel, it refuses to tell him its name, but instead, confusingly, changes Jacob's name. Odysseus tells the cyclops that his name is "nobody"—but when the cyclops finds out his real name, Odysseus is in big trouble with Poseidon. Some mystics believe that objects, people, and gods have a secret "true name" that describes their essence. Knowing someone's name is the key to manipulating them.

Today, it is a database record filled with PII that serves as the true name of an individual; knowing it gives a company at the very least spam power over the person, but probably the opportunity to do lots more mischief.

Privacy Isn't Always About Having Data

Let's say that you come across someone lying on the sidewalk, passed out. That very fact is sensitive personal health information about them. If their evil twin knew about it, they might realize that the person was drunk or had a health condition. Should you use this information to take action, say, by calling an ambulance? If you do, you'll be telling the ambulance service that this person has passed out—again, transmitting sensitive health information. It's a serious violation of that person's privacy. But I think you'll do it and I think society will approve.

Online, however, transmitting sensitive health information about someone you don't know is generally unacceptable. The EU's GDPR may even have prevented Facebook from offering a tool that detects suicide risk.[1] In the physical world, we're sometimes willing to make exceptions to privacy norms when the intention is clearly to benefit someone, while online we call for closer regulation.

In contrast, consider the use of personal information by casinos to predict how much a particular gambler can lose and still return to the casino. There is no violation of privacy in the information they *collect*—it's just a record of the person's transactions with them, plus some data voluntarily given by the gambler for their loyalty program. There is no unauthorized transfer of information to a third party.

And yet it feels devious and manipulative. It is the *use* of the information and the *intention* behind its use—not the information itself—that seems like the relevant ethical factor when it comes to privacy. That makes sense—*using* private information for a company's benefit is using a person as a "mere means" (CIv2) or depriving them of their autonomy by manipulating them. Just holding the data doesn't necessarily do either of these things. Calling an ambulance and transmitting sensitive PII you shouldn't have is okay because it is motivated by caring; using data you legitimately have to manipulate a gambler into spending more is bad because it is not done with care.

The legal scholar Julie E. Cohen in "How Not to Write a Privacy Law" argues that we have focused too much on the collection and storage of data—an old way of thinking about privacy—and too little on what happens to the data later. In her view, that's because we've thought about privacy in terms of property rights—who has the right to *possess* our personal data. But this misses the essential point, she says; data moves through extremely complex webs of interconnections and agreements among companies. Consumers don't have much transparency into where their data goes and how it's used.[2] Privacy laws address the wrong problem:

> Individual users asserting preferences over predefined options on modular dashboards have neither the authority nor the ability to alter the invisible, predesigned webs of technical and economic arrangements under which their data travels among multiple parties. Nor can they prevent participants in those webs from drawing inferences about them—even when the inferences substitute for the very same data that they have opted out of having collected.[3]

A Contractarian Thought

When Rumpelstiltskin buys a new spinning wheel, he's giving the retailer the knowledge that he bought that product. He's also giving them data they need to fulfill the order—his name, address, and credit card information. Implicitly, he's giving the retailer permission to use that information to send him the machine he bought.

The price Rumpelstiltskin pays in the transaction is the price he's willing to exchange for the spinning wheel. If the vendor will get additional value by selling Rumpelstiltskin's secret name, that value should be priced into the transaction and should lower the product's cost. But it's probably not, or it's not priced accurately. There's an information asymmetry—Rumpelstiltskin doesn't really know what the retailer will do with his name or how much it's worth to them. If they give or sell it to another entity, Rumpelstiltskin doesn't know what *they* will do with it. And since the information will remain with the vendor indefinitely, they might find other things to do with it later.

Rumpelstiltskin also doesn't know what his full cost will be. Will the vendor email him every day, or once a year? Will the unsubscribe link on the emails be hard to find? Will other advertisers tailor their offers based on it? Will political parties use it to put Rumpelstiltskin on lists of potential donors? Will he be placed on a no-fly list?

Rational bargainers—following the contractarian approach of imagining a hypothetical contract—would never agree to a contract where the customer agreed to let the vendor do whatever they want with the transaction data, since they have no way of knowing the cost or the value. It's possible that we as a society have reached an understanding. But the negative reaction to perceived violations of privacy today is evidence that we haven't.

But companies have me check a box saying I've agreed to their terms of service. It probably says something in there about how they use my information.

Why do you say "probably"? You haven't read them?

No, of course not. Does anyone?

If you did, you'd find that what you're agreeing to doesn't help you picture how the data might be used. After all, the vendor and its "affiliates" don't know yet either.

Agreeing to the "terms of service" is coerced; it's based on incomplete information about what you are agreeing to; it's a side note to a transaction already in progress, and refusing it is a drain on the customer's time. Terms of service are a legal formalism, not the handshake agreement.

Security

Implicit in the transaction is also an expectation of security—not only will the vendor not deliberately sell Rumpelstiltskin's name, but they will take reasonable care to protect it from being stolen by a princess. It's easy for companies to slight security because it costs money, and the consequences of undersecuring systems are indirect and seemingly random. Doing so, however, betrays that implicit contract with the customer.

It's hard to say precisely what level of security is expected, because information security is such a deeply technical discipline. We judge security mostly by its ultimate results—whether a bad actor steals the data. But that's a question of accountability, not of what protections the vendor is responsible for implementing. Nor is it fair: the company might even be taking reasonable precautions but are done in by a zero-day exploit. But the bar is high for "respectable" security these days. It is not a matter of trying to avoid bad press due to a break in. It is an ethical responsibility, triggered by an implicit contract with customers.

Acting in the Public Realm

What exactly do we mean by privacy, anyway? Richard Posner, the legal scholar and former judge, defines it as an ability to conceal information about oneself that others might use to one's disadvantage. Posner's definition focuses on the use of the information as well as its possession, as I have been doing here.

"Perhaps it's better to understand modern privacy as control and self-determination,"[4] Cennydd Bowles says. You should be able to choose what information you want to disclose, and to whom. This sounds close to the principle of autonomy. But it's hard to know what information you are disclosing, and you don't know how the information will be used.

Others define privacy as a right to choose seclusion or to decline a role in the public realm.[5] But even before digital technology took over our lives it was hard to stay out of the public realm—when you bought something in a store, you were transacting *in* the public realm, where you could be observed. You left footprints pretty much whatever you did.

I've chosen to concentrate on the use of personal information rather than its collection and storage, and on the betrayal of pretend intimacy it represents, because I'm not sure our intuitions about privacy are fully formed. Everyone wants their own data to be private—or at least under their own control—but I'm not sure they want other people's data to be private. Let me give a few examples.

Accountability, Identity, and Reputation

There is a tension between anonymity and accountability. Many of our social mechanisms work because they are self-enforcing: if someone violates a social norm, it will affect their reputation thenceforward. If someone is dishonest, they may get away with it once or twice, but eventually they'll get a reputation for dishonesty and others will refuse to transact with them. If they are racist, sexist, or just obnoxious, or if their behavior is distasteful in other ways, others may avoid them. If they pose a danger, people may raise their guard when near them. The reverse is true as well—if a person is genuine in their interactions, kind, and considerate, then they will be trusted in future interactions.

Reputation, then, is critical to accountability. In the world of Ancient Greece, good behavior led to a happy life because it earned a person honor and respect, rather than causing them shame. In *The Republic*, Plato offers the example of the Ring of Gyges. Could someone be expected to act ethically if they had a ring that would make them invisible—in other words, if they wouldn't be held accountable for anything they did? Plato believed the ring would corrupt the person.

Anonymity in the guise of privacy can be a way to avoid the consequences of bad behavior and can deny people information they need to avoid risk. It's how 9,000 Nazis and collaborators escaped prosecution by hiding in Brazil, Argentina, and Chile, and it was through violations of their privacy that some of them were brought to justice.[6] In consequentialist terms, anonymity increases the friction of transactions—we might agree to transact with a person without safeguards or without further diligence if we knew their reputation was good. On the other hand, you might want to know if the person you are lending to has a history of not repaying, or if your potential roommate has a reputation of being nasty and noisy or is a character from a Brothers Grimm fairy tale.

On the other hand, anonymity can be essential for escapees from abuse. We also love narratives of redemption—people who are given a second chance and make the most of it. A "new start" story is moving, and we would like to think that if we make a big mistake, there will be a chance to start fresh. If we are too well known in our small town, we can move to another one far away.

The inability of an individual to escape from being recognized is the stuff of dystopias. According to the German Idealist philosopher Johann Gottlieb Fichte, "The chief principle of a well-regulated police state is this: That each person shall be at all times and places . . . recognized as this or that particular person."[7] Jeremy Bentham proposed the Panopticon, a design for a prison where a single guard would be able, from a central location, to see all the prisoners at all times, so each prisoner would have to assume they were continually being watched.

There is a tension between our wish for privacy and our demand for accountability.

Witnessed Behavior

You constantly disclose information about yourself. When you go outdoors, people see you and know where you are. When you talk on your mobile phone in public, people hear what you say. They might know that you're fighting with your spouse, picking up your hat from the dry cleaner, or berating the cable company. When you buy something in a store, the person in line behind you might see what you're buying. They might have observed what other shelves you were browsing. It has always been this way.

Do you "own" your personal data? If someone has seen you eating a fluffernutter sandwich, arguably that observation belongs as much to them as to you. Gossiping about it might be wrong—but then again, that's a matter of how they *use* your data, not whether they possess it. Businesses also observe what you do—in the physical world as well as online. Are they free to do what they like with *their* observations?

You have always shed personal data like a Boston terrier. What has changed is the ease with which the information can be vacuumed up, associated with you, analyzed, and then used to sell you dog food. Your totalitarian government could be watching you on video, using facial recognition to determine it's you, noting that you were visiting an address where they know the opposition lives, and coming to arrest you. The princess, as you'll remember, "overheard" Rumpelstiltskin's name. Your data has never been private, really.

Nor would people necessarily have wanted the extreme kind of privacy we talk about online. "Privacy was once the lot of the pariah," says Bowles in *Future Ethics*.[8] One's goal was to take one's place in society, not to hide from society. The extreme version of privacy we expect online may just be an artifact of contemporary Western society.

People have always been defined by their social graphs, just as we are now online.[9] MacIntyre notes that

> in many pre-modern, traditional societies it is through his or her membership in a variety of social groups that the individual identifies himself or herself and is identified by others. I am brother, cousin and grandson, member of this household, that village, this tribe.[10]

The fact that people don't want to be known today may be a consequence of the risks of being known. Some business will put its corporate arm around them and act like a buddy, while trying hard to get them to eat enough pasta to make them look like a sumo wrestler. Their photo might get photoshopped onto an image of a leprechaun convention, making it impossible for them to get elected chairman of the Equality for Women in Fairy Tales club.

Law Enforcement

Even though I rarely watch television, I can't help occasionally seeing those police crime dramas. You know, someone commits a heinous crime and the police investigators investigate, to dramatic music and despite the investigators' own human failings. Someone has snatched a valuable chengziguan hat or switched someone else's pappardelle for a zucchini-based pasta. When the police find a suspect, they interview the neighbors. "Tell me about his habits." "Oh, you say he buys flour in huge quantities and goes for walks early in the morning and hangs around the Italian market. Wearing a hat, by any chance? Have you ever noticed him replacing floury substances with green vegetables?"

Violation of privacy! We've gotten used to this, though, and after heinous crimes we root for the police. When a bomb exploded at the Boston Marathon, I went through the day thinking "Why are the police so slow at solving this? There must be some video footage or something they can use." I'm writing just after the Brooklyn subway shooter was arrested. The police were able to locate him by reviewing videos from subway station cameras, searching through Facebook posts, and publishing the man's name and photo so people could recognize him. Pretty much every police investigation is a violation of privacy, isn't it?

When the FBI demanded that Apple unlock the data contained in terrorist cell phones, 50% of the public sided with the FBI and 45% with Apple's refusal.[11] There is apparently a big divide on the issue across society. Is it fair to say that many of us are afraid of "big brother" watching us but fine with law enforcement using the tools they happen to have available to solve crimes? And does privacy, once again, have more to do with the use to which data is put rather than the fact of its collection?

Living Publicly

People advertise themselves. Sales and marketing now permeate human relationships. To get ahead, you make sure you're well known on social media and in professional networking groups. You express timely bite-sized opinions to remind people that you're relevant. You build relationships with friends by advertising your views, challenges, and activities on social media and by responding to theirs. You make new friends the same way.

Just as companies pretend to be friends with their customers, social media encourages us to think that we are surrounded by friends and bring our expectations about how friends will treat us. Social media is not actually a place where we are surrounded by friends, we're learning.

Stuff we routinely disclose is the kind of stuff you'd think we'd want to keep private—opinions, romantic histories, problems, desires. On the other hand, the battles over privacy, strangely, seem to be about the administrative odds and ends of our lives—birthdates, Social Security numbers, websites visited. (Mine are boring. Yours?) Some personal information is posted with a very specific target audience in mind, but some of it is intended for wide distribution—for example, political arguments, expressions of disgust at current events, questions that we're looking for answers to. Even in these cases, though, there are still things we don't want people or companies to do with the information we post. More than anything, we don't want disguised manipulation.

Rubbernecking

We're curious folks. It's hard not to rubberneck when you pass the aftermath of a highway accident. In one of the more bizarre instances of questionable privacy practices, Venmo shows me a list of all the recent payment transactions made by my "friends." Venmo found out who my "friends" are by asking me to give it access to the contacts stored on my computer. My list of friends includes all sorts of people I've been out of touch with for a long time. Strangely, I now know who they are paying money to (along with the note or comment they attach to it) and who is paying them.

That includes an ex-girlfriend from way back. It's cool—I can see that she's giving money to her son so he can buy a cell phone for his birthday, and I can see the happy birthday note she included with it. I can't help it—it's hard not to scroll through these transactions and see what everyone's up to. Am I a bad person?

Probably. Let that be a lesson. Pay attention in ethics classes.

Your Privacy and Others'

When you give away information about yourself, you may well be giving away information about other people. If you upload your DNA to a database, you are uploading information about your relatives, who share most of your DNA. If you upload your contacts to a social media service, you have given away other people's data—not just their email addresses, phone numbers, and possibly information like their companies and titles—but also disclosed that they are connected with you. There was the case of a psychiatrist who found that Facebook's People You May Know algorithm was suggesting that her patients "friend" one another. The patients had uploaded their contacts to Facebook, and they had the psychiatrist as a common contact.[12]

Your personal data, confusingly, may be someone else's.

Digital Transformation and Privacy

If you observe someone doing something and you use that observation to get them to act against their own interests, we call that blackmail. If your company observes someone looking at an item online and uses that information to manipulate them into buying, thereby "monetizing" the observation, is it different from blackmail? There seem to be two factors involved: first, how manipulative or coercive are the actions of your company, and, second, whether the action you solicit is truly against the consumer's interests.

Privacy is largely a matter of trust and risk. If I actually lived in a small town, I imagine I would trust my neighbors with the knowledge of my comings and goings because I have a real—and mutual—relationship with them. Some of them are jerks, it's true. But I have to take the risk, because that's what it means to live in a caring environment. Do I similarly trust a company with my data? Ummm, do I have a real and mutual caring relationship with them?

Companies that are transforming digitally face the challenge of making privacy decisions at a moment when norms are still emerging and being negotiated. Much of the discourse today is, as Julie Cohen says, about property rights in data—who has the right to have and store personal data.[13] Governments are setting up privacy laws and compliance frameworks, and the courts are adjudicating disputes. When we view privacy as a matter of law, however, we focus on the details of compliance and legal risks, rather than as a matter of care for customers. That attitude is obvious to customers—they are forever clicking on buttons and checking checkboxes that are obviously just formalities.

But privacy is not a matter of compliance. It is a matter of your relationship to your customers. If you are trying to build a deeper relationship, one that involves trust, you can't at the same time use their data in ways that make them uncomfortable. Just as the difference between lying and deceiving is a technical difference—it's not always okay to deceive someone even if you're not technically telling a lie—the fact that a customer has agreed to terms of service or checked a checkbox allowing you to use their data only means that legally you may be in the clear.

It is too easy to pretend to yourself that you are using customer data "for their own benefit." A much better sniff test that preserves autonomy is whether customers would choose to have you use their data in x way *if you gave them the choice*. It's not whether you think it would be better for them—it's a question of respecting their autonomy as decision makers. If you are exercising the virtues—care, authenticity, respect, and the like—then you are probably doing the right things.

The themes of Part II have come together in this discussion of intimacy and privacy. Companies attempting to become "intimate" with their customers *are* trying to manipulate them. Whether the manipulation is bad depends on implicit contracts—whether it's consensual, for example—and the virtues with which it is performed. Intimacy involves moral commitments. Any violation of those commitments may legitimately trigger an outraged response from customers, particularly around privacy—where, in truth, social norms have yet to fully emerge.

All I'm saying is please don't be icky.

The Monsters Speak
Toward a Learning, Adaptive Ethics

There is something at work in my soul, which I do not understand.
—Mary Shelley, *Frankenstein*

What is manifold is often frightening because it is not neat and simple.
Men prefer to forget how many possibilities are open to them.
—Martin Buber, *I and Thou*

AI, like Frankenstein's creature, wants to be loved. The International Center for Missing and Exploited Children uses image recognition technology to scour the web and the dark web to find photos of missing children so they can refer leads to law enforcement.[1] Stanford uses it to scan eyes for signs of diabetic retinopathy, the leading cause of blindness among men over forty, before doctors can spot it and while it can still be treated.[2] Sensors around the world feed data into machine learning systems that can sense impending disasters—earthquakes, floods, new episodes of Real Housewives.

In other cases, AI is just minding its own business, being unobtrusively helpful. Manufacturers, for example, may be using machine learning to spot quality control problems as products roll off the assembly line or to identify factory equipment that needs maintenance before it breaks down (I know, that one starts to come close to *Minority Report*, where people were arrested for crimes before they committed them.) It's helping retailers get the right products on shelves before a hurricane strikes. It's working quietly to treat cancer.

We hear a lot about the scary stuff. There's something frightening about almost-humans, whether they're extra-terrestrials, toys, ghosts, zombies, or the apes in *Planet of the Apes*. The Golem of Prague was created from clay by Rabbi Judah Loew ben Bezalel to defend the Jews in the Prague ghetto but went berserk and murdered people until the rabbi deactivated him. There's a Slavic version of the story that combines the golem and the gingerbread man ideas, featuring a clay boy made by childless parents who gets out of control and eats their food. No wonder AI scares us: threats to my crispy bacon are a serious matter.

Golems, of course, are the opposite of artificial intelligence—artificial stupidity, perhaps: they do only what they're commanded to do and do it to excess. Like zombies, they have no higher-order brain functions. Perhaps that's what makes them scariest. Or maybe it's the opposite—that robots with minds are scarier. Like the robots in Karel Čapek's *R.U.R.* who suddenly realize that in a science fiction story there's no need for them to serve humans.

To use the term "intelligence" in describing robots and machine learning algorithms is to seize on a metaphor. Machine learning is really just a statistical model, sometimes only a fancy form of regression, sometimes a more complex "neural network" (which is again a metaphor). After being shown a number of examples of x and y coming together, a Fancy Regression can do a good job of predicting what y will come when it sees a new x.* The "intelligence" metaphor affects how we imagine the future: it is hard to imagine Fancy Regressions taking over the world and easy to decide that Fancy Regressions shouldn't have rights. Take away the metaphors of "intelligence," Frankensteins, and gingerbread persons, and the ethical questions become clearer. Personally, I think it's fine to kick a Fancy Regression, though it's a bit deranged.

Then again, we don't really understand how human intelligence works—we ourselves may simply be Very Very Fancy Regressions and it's possible that Fancy Regressions will become so fancy that they can do most of the things that people do—talk gibberish to babies, become loud when drunk, and play solitaire on their smartphones. Anyway, mistakenly or not, like Victor Frankenstein, we've given birth to Fancy Regressions, and we can't just be disgusted by them. We have to look after their moral education.

I've argued here that ethics in our digitally transforming world must be learned, negotiated, developed incrementally, and refined over time. The fact that we can do so is encouraging, because we can use emerging technologies such as machine learning to examine our own biases and improve ourselves. A bureaucratic view of ethics would lead us to say that we must sit down now and make rules for the (yet unknown) distant future. A virtue-focused, adaptive view, however, lets us pose hypotheses, accept feedback, and learn.

Must We Plan?

If you've ever tried to fight battles with old-school technology folks about moving to more agile ways of working, you've probably wound up in a conversation like this:

---

* I'm oversimplifying. This is just one type of ML—supervised training. I think the point is valid across the other variations of ML.

Fresh-faced agilist: We shouldn't get ourselves into analysis paralysis. Let's just move forward and adjust later as we see how things go.

Wizened sage: But we have to plan. I've always said, "plan the work, then work the plan."

Fresh-faced agilist: In the agile world we say: "make decisions at the last responsible moment."

Wizened sage: That's irresponsible. You can't just go charging ahead without a plan. What if . . . ?

It is difficult to argue against planning. It's especially difficult when the planning is done to mitigate risks, and even more so when they're dire risks like monsters strangling children. On the other hand, we know that sometimes there just isn't enough information available to make good plans; it's better to gather information, try out ideas, and then, based on what we learn, make more informed decisions.

But books, articles, movies, and talkative haircutters all seem to suggest that we had better make decisions quickly before the moral issues of artificial intelligence overwhelm us. Urgency is the message, as illustrated in this example from Bowles' *Future Ethics*:

> It can seem futile to define machine morality when we can't even agree on human morality. True, it would be easier to steer a machine away from evil if we had a consistent definition of evil. **But we can't afford to wait any longer.** If we do ever create human-level artificial intelligence, it's unlikely to stop there. Able to clone itself many times over (with or without our help), it could dedicate enormous resources to improving its own algorithms and hardware design. Artificial intelligence might breeze past us in a matter of weeks, becoming an artificial superintelligence (ASI).[3] [emphasis mine]

May I raise a small question? *Why* can't we afford to wait any longer? It's *unlikely* to stop, it *could* dedicate enormous resources, and it *might* breeze past us. Those are reasons to write science fiction novels, not reasons to make laws, cower in our cubicles, or negotiate treaties. I mean, the author says that we don't even know what we mean by good and evil. And since machines are agents for human beings, how are we to control them without understanding human morality first? True, there are some issues that demand our attention today—

bias in machine learning comes to mind—but "defining machine morality" is a rather big, poorly defined goal.

England's Office of Science and Innovation has concluded that robots may develop humanlike intelligence and be able to reproduce themselves (would someone please explain to them how babies are made?), and we'll need to discuss granting rights to robots in the next twenty to fifty years. Revealingly, they also foresee robot taxation and compulsory robot military service.[4] Coincidence?

Some books are very worried about robot rights. Is it okay to discriminate against robots in the workplace? Is it ethical to turn a robot off without its permission? Again, from Bowles:

> If a machine in this moral grey zone seems to prefer solving particular types of problems, or behaving in a particular way, we should let it. Since by its continued operation it appears to show a preference to exist, we probably shouldn't turn it off or interfere in its code, although any machine this advanced can probably modify its own programming. However, we should balance its preferences with our own: To my mind, we should even extend politeness—essentially a sliver of moral consideration—to today's technologies.[5]

I have no intention of behaving politely to a Fancy Regression, and I wouldn't know how to do it. My problem is that I can't really envision the world where these are real questions. That's not to say that it won't come, just that there are so many unknowns between here and there that I can't get a good feel for that world. Future technologies will affect *future* people. How well do we know those future people and what they want?

Scary questions follow when we imagine a "slippery slope," extrapolating from what we see today. At the rate we're going, the authors worry, artificial intelligence will soon be able to create itself, at which point there will be a "singularity" where it begins to exceed human intelligence. Robots will be able to make up meaningless marketing jargon better than we can. Eventually, the goals of AIs may conflict with our own—they may snatch up all the seats at the World Cup.

This seems like an awful lot of hypothesizing. What things look like on the other side of the singularity is a little hazy to me. It's a little like asking whether classical music will be popular inside a black hole. Which is the real danger: that AIs will become super intelligent and out-argue us at the dinner table, or that they will continue to be stupid but we will use them widely without realizing they are just golems dressed in Linux tuxedos?

Writers and speakers of this "we must do something now" cult have a vested interest. An interest, that is, in being interesting. *Deontology, consequentialism, contractarianism* don't—I think—have much to say on robot ethics. *Alarmism* is not an accepted branch of philosophical ethics. I don't know what ethical questions will arise for an artificial super intelligence because . . . well . . . it would be smarter than me.

As leaders, we face pressure to "do" something about these issues, or at least communicate deep concern. But I fear that these amorphous questions are distracting us from the pressing issues of today. There *are* questions around AI that do require our immediate attention. Those include questions of bias, privacy, misuse, and a number of security threats like poisoning ML models, inferring whether a person's data was used to train a model, and exfiltrating models. Behaving politely to robots just doesn't make the list.

I assume that "poisoning" ML doesn't involve killing it with chemical substances?
No, it has to do with deliberately messing with a model by feeding it bad data that will confuse it or change it.
People do that?
They do. And we're responsible for the behavior of our AIs, even if a hacker or an evil wizard poisons them.

We must approach AI with care and caution, because we are responsible, not the AIs themselves. But even for these immediate questions I'm suggesting that we view AI as something to methodically and openly learn from, so that we'll be in a good position to curb our robot dogs. As with all things agile, we should inspect and adapt our way through it.

Robophobia

Robots are taking away our jobs!

> By 2030 robots may wipe out eight hundred million jobs, roughly one-fifth of all jobs worldwide, according to McKinsey. By 2050, robots may replace one-third of American working-age men, Brookings Institution vice president Darrell West claims in his 2018 book *The Future of Work: Robots, AI, and Automation.*[6]

Those robots! Now they want to replace "working-age men."
They don't, actually. *Employers* want to eliminate jobs by using automation. Robots do not have volition. Employers do. Personifying robots relieves

employers of responsibility. Notice how close this framing is to racist or ethnocentric fears, sort of like "By 2030, immigrants from the country of Frankenstan will have taken a third of our jobs." It's robophobia.

Also notice the logical structure of this prediction, its use of the word "may." Yes, robots "may" take those jobs, just as the world "may" someday be run by a race of gingerbread people. Is there more here than an attempt to introduce a frightening narrative, a Frankensteinization of the question?

Get Back to You Soon...

It's Frankenstein versus the gingerbread man. Is AI a monstrous creation that will escape our control and go around strangling babies, setting fires, and planting evidence to frame innocent people? If so, we'd better start planning right away. Is it a tool that's going to help us understand our biases better and let us fix them? If so, let's get to work and skip the planning. Is it a bully like Frankenstein's creature—or, like the gingerbread man, a delicious snack?

Why are we so sure that superintelligences will even be made in our image, anyway? Maybe they will be made in the form of a cockroach, which we'd have no qualms about kicking or squashing, intelligent or not.

What we must do right now is choose the right metaphors for AI and robots, and I've done some research to help. The gingerbread man, according to my findings, is more nuanced than Frankenstein's creature; there's the farting gingerbread man, the runaway pancake, the Kolobok, not to mention Muffin Man, the Magic Pudding, John Dough, Stinky Cheese Man, the Runaway Latke, the Runaway Rice Cake (a Chinese New Year entry), and Ninjabread Man. These all, I suppose, fall into the category of edible AI.

On the other side we have Frankenstein—not Frankenstein, his creature— the golem, the robots of *R.U.R.*, and—I know this will be confusing—another gingerbread man—the bad guy in Jasper Fforde's *The Fourth Bear*, a novel in his Nursery Crimes series. This category, I guess, is the smart and/or stupid AI category. If you remember my last book, Moby Dick may also fit: he is more intelligent than whales should be. Perhaps there will be a singularity where whales learn to reproduce. Wait a minute . . . !

One reason it's difficult to predict the future is that technology influences people and people influence technology. We're bound together in an ongoing dialogue. The intelligences we wind up with will be something of an accident brought about as human invention collides with society's fears and reservations about them. Technologies like social networking software, robotics, global sur-veillance networks, and biomedical human enhancement open up possibilities, rather than fixed options from which to choose.[7] "We don't fully control tech, nor does it fully control us; instead, humans and technologies co-create the world,"[8] as Bowles puts it.

Robots Demand Their Rights

Okay, despite my objections, despite the fact that we have no idea how to politely address a robot, you still want to know how we should behave toward them. Should companies hire a diverse workforce of both humans and robots? Do robots have a right to privacy? How much should robots pay in taxes?

Alright, then: Is it okay to torture robots?

Consequentialist: Yes, of course. The net amount of happiness in the world will be higher—the robot is no less happy, and the person torturing the robot seems to be having fun. So the net amount of happiness in the world has increased. It is not only permissible to torture robots but actually *required*; a consequentialist must choose the action that results in the greatest happiness for the world.

Deontologist: I'm still looking through my rule books to see which rule applies. Ten Commandments—not a word. Kant says to treat all sentient beings the same—as ends in themselves. Is a robot a sentient being? Kant didn't say—unless it's in those books no one reads. I think it's okay, since there is no contradiction in universalizing the principle that robots should be tortured.

Virtue Ethicist: The robot torturer should use their practical wisdom and consider all the details of the situation. In the meantime, I'm cultivating a virtue I call "robot EQ," a virtue of knowing what robots feel, if they feel. If they don't feel, it's a different virtue. It depends on whether robot torturing will lead to flourishing, for us or the robots, depending on the case.

Contractarian: We can start with the terms of service from the robot's manufacturer, but there might be implicit and informal agreements we have with the robots themselves—if they're sentient and we can figure out how a rational robot-bargainer would reason. Have we reached any social contracts with an operating system or some other form of software that we can use as examples?

Bonus opinion: *Hedonistic Ethical Egoist*: Yes.

Robot Bureaucracies

Maybe the fear of AI is simply a recognition of the deficiencies of human beings. Rossum the elder, in creating the robot, was following this train of thought:

> A human being. That's something that feels joy, plays the violin, wants to go for a walk, in general requires a lot of things that—that are, in effect, superfluous. . . . Robots are not people. They are mechanically more perfect than we are, they have an astounding intellectual capacity, but they have no soul. Oh, Miss Glory, the creation of an engineer is technically more refined than the product of nature.[9]

We humans suffer from the inefficiencies that come with having a soul. The problem, according to *R.U.R.*, is that God had no grasp of modern technology.[10]

R.U.R. has little to do with robots—it's a beautiful explanation of the benefits of bureaucratic organizations, updated with Taylorism. Rossum and his engineers are not evil. They have an Enlightenment-inspired vision for a world where people no longer need to work because of the rationalized efficiency of the robot workers. If work can be done more efficiently, their thinking goes, it's better for everyone.

Ding!

The trolley is back!

No, wait—this time it is a self-driving car. Three pedestrians are arguing about who serves the best barbecue in Kansas City and, not paying attention, have suddenly jaywalked in front of the car. The car can either hit them or swerve suddenly and hit a sidewalk vendor vending Mario Batali the pasta-chef bobbleheads. What should the car do? If you could program an "ethics module" into the car, what would you have it do?

As with the trolley problem, we can work a number of variations on the self-driving car problem to test our intuitions. Maybe it's three ninety-eight-year-old klansmen crossing the street and one Nobel physicist on the sidewalk. Maybe *two* Nobel physicists on the sidewalk. Maybe it's a rabbi, a priest, and a chicken.* What if instead of killing the three pedestrians the car could swerve to crash into the wall and kill just the driver?

---

* "A priest, a rabbi, and a chicken walk into a bar.
  The bartender says, 'Nope! We don't do jokes here, get out!'
  And the chicken says, 'Come on guys, I know a place across the street.'"[11]

What would you do if you were driving the car? I'll guess. You'd have a moment of panic and do something unplanned and unpredictable, probably to your own benefit. It wouldn't be a moral choice, but a question of instinct. You might very well behave badly—if we could define badly. If you have an SUV you've already made some of these decisions, since you'll be twice as likely to kill pedestrians you hit.[12]

What makes us think that human beings are any good at ethical decision-making anyway? We worry about whether *machines* will make acceptable choices, but what standard shall we hold them to? If you create AI on the model of a human rather than a cockroach, it will be no more ethical than a human. Since the Turing test was devised in 1950, that's the way we have conceptualized AI—a machine is intelligent if it can fool you into thinking it's a human. A good AI, then, is one that can produce hate speech and deceive industry analysts about its revenues.

The car could be made to perform ethically in every case, if we told it what the right ethical behavior was (I'm assuming that we used some traditional programming to give it a "conscience" module or something like that. Authorial handwaving). The car would make a better ethical decision than you or I would. Our attempts to correct human misbehavior are rarely successful. If anything, our abilities to correct AI naughtiness are likely to be more effective—after all, at least until the singularity, we actually do control the machines.

There are two problems, though. The first is that someone would have to decide how to program the car's "conscience." Who wants that responsibility? That person would have to make a bold decision and decide who to kill at a moment when they have time to think about it and therefore have no excuses. We're happy not to make these ethical decisions, because they're hard. The fact that AI forces us to make hard decisions may be a good thing.

The second problem is that we have a strong feeling that AIs should not be making life-or-death decisions. The idea of a machine deciding that the Batali bobblehead vendor will die or that the pedestrian who prefers Gates Barbecue will live is repugnant. We feel this *even though* we can make sure that the AI always makes the "right" decision—whatever we decide right is.

Allow me to suggest that the problem is not AI. It's more our own human lack of an ethical vision. This problem on a macro scale is repeated on a smaller scale for every enterprise that is digitally transforming, and it's you, the leader of the transformation, who has to face it.

Before you call on Rumpelstiltskin in desperation, let's see if I can help clarify the issues.

Sensible Co-Creation

We should be optimistic about AI ethics. Confronting the ethical issues can only help us think through what is right and what is wrong, in areas where our intuitions are unclear and where society's standards are confusing. AI forces us to be precise about what we're looking for. That's why I say that we're engaged in a dialogue with AI to co-create the world we want to live in.

As leaders of digital transformation introducing AI into our processes, we're painfully aware that there is no rule book for responsible AI; in fact, the attempts to produce one haven't come up with anything solid that we well-intentioned leaders can use to make sure we do things right. At best, we've learned a few of the things we as people don't like. But that's not surprising—I've tried to say throughout this book that rules generally aren't the best way to guide ethical behavior.

That does not mean that anything goes, or that ethical behavior isn't needed from AI. On the contrary, AI is where some of our most dangerous ethical issues lurk, and we should be vigilant and careful in how we use it. But because the issues are unclear and emergent, we have to approach them in an agile manner: shifting left by cultivating the virtues and evolving norms that will effectively act as social contracts. We're more likely to make the right decisions if we oversee our AI with care, courage, respect for autonomy, integrity, and the other virtues than if we keep searching for the missing stone tablets with rules on what is good and what is bad.

AI is a tool, neither golem nor gingerbread man. As with other tools, it changes us as we use it. In our everyday lives, it's too easy for us to hide behind abstractions like equality and fairness; our real challenge is to understand specifically what we mean by these terms and what we want to do to solve the problems we see. It's by working incrementally with our tool, shaping its behavior and using it to explore options, using it to stimulate dialogue between humans, that we'll figure these things out. We've learned from agile and digital IT delivery that complex problems lend themselves to exactly this approach of exploration, learning, and adjustment.

Moral Agency and AI

Whoa—shouldn't we ask whether AIs are moral agents? That is, can we hold them responsible for what they do?

Given that we are not living in a science fiction novel, the easy answer is that they are not, for the same reason that robots are not taking jobs away. AI does not deploy itself—or more exactly, does not form the intention to deploy itself in order to accomplish its own goals. Today, businesses deploy AIs, usually to generate profit. It is the company, or the individuals within it, that has the relevant free will: it can decide whether to use the ML to process loans, it can change the ML, it can retrain the ML. If the AI does something we consider morally wrong, it is the company that is blameworthy. If the security robot that roams a store's aisles to eliminate theft starts to pick the pockets of customers, we will not put the robot in prison. We will blame the store or the robot manufacturer.

This suggests that a company needs to manage its risk and responsibility through a thorough testing and validation process. Morality, in a sense, is an aspect of quality and must be controlled like other aspects of quality. We can no more hold the software itself responsible for its morality than we can hold it responsible for its own bugs and security vulnerabilities. Whether the software uses procedural or AI techniques doesn't seem to change its moral status.

We'd say the same thing about any algorithm the company uses, whether it includes AI or not. The moral demands we place on companies are the same whether they're deploying an AI solution or Candy Crush. Both should be fair and unbiased. Similarly, the demands on a company for the morality of its AI are the same as the demands we place on it for its humans. A Fancy Regression that makes lending decisions and a human that makes lending decisions must both make fair, unbiased decisions. The company must train both to do so.

Another way to think about it: separate the two halves of the machine learning algorithm. The first half is training; its output is a model. Models are neither ethical nor unethical, because they are not actors. They don't *do* anything by themselves. When we talk about a company deploying ML, we are really talking about the second half, which is using that model to drive decisions and actions. The company could just as well deploy a human. That is exactly where the company's responsibility lies: they have a choice of models, human and artificial, and they are choosing to use this particular model, with its moral failings.

It's true that ML models are complex; the company doesn't know exactly what they will do in production. That doesn't change the moral calculus—it doesn't mean that the ML suddenly becomes responsible rather than the company. Same with humans. They are also complex, and no one knows for sure what they will do. A company has to hire ethical employees, train them, and monitor their behavior. With AI, they can do even more to validate its behavior through continuous testing.

But at least a person can explain their decisions.

I question that. For simple decisions they can, and often the ML can too. For complex decisions, humans may not be great at explaining what they're doing. And can you trust them? Humans might be deceiving you, or themselves.

Still, from what I understand, humans can explain themselves a lot better than MLs can.

You know, as we're talking, something else occurs to me. The problem is framed slightly wrong. We shouldn't care about explainability, so much, but about understandability. What matters is whether we can understand how it works, not whether it can tell us.

How does that change things?

It seems to me that we will never understand humans beyond a certain point, but with ML models there's no limitation. If nothing else, we can look at the ML model itself, which tells us exactly how it makes decisions. We just don't have a way to understand it yet.

I see. But you agree that explainability or whatever you want to call it is an issue.

It is. For a company to have confidence that it is deploying something ethically, and for others to be able to confirm it.

AI in Dialogue With Human Ethics: Bias

There are problems today with AI, and they are big ones. Escaped pancakes can be dangerous, and Frankenstein's monster is, in fact, strangling children. We have to catch it and have a serious talk with it. A very real concern today is bias and fairness.

Machine learning discriminates. If we use it to make lending decisions, we want it to discriminate between borrowers who are likely to repay and borrowers who aren't (I'm oversimplifying of course). If it turns out that applicants who like to eat fluffernutter sandwiches are more likely to repay, then it might be okay to prefer making loans to fluffernutter eaters.

We *don't* want it to discriminate in ways that we consider unfair to certain groups. It should *not* discriminate against potential borrowers based on their race, gender, disabilities, or various other attributes. An ML model trained solely to maximize the repayment probability might find that including race or gender or sandwich preference does, for various reasons (see below), result in the best predictions. Just to be clear—the ML, as much as we want to personify it, hasn't done anything wrong in that case. It doesn't have prejudices. It's a Fancy Regression. Don't worry—it can't reproduce like a whale.

It seems like there's a simple way to avoid bias—just don't allow race, for example, to be used as an input parameter. Why not just wipe it out of the dataset entirely? But that doesn't work, because other input variables, like ZIP Code, for example, might be correlated with race. As Michael Kearns and Aaron Roth of the University of Pennsylvania and AWS say in *The Ethical Algorithm*, "If someone knows what kind of car you drive, what kind of computer and phone you own, and a few of your favorite apps and websites, they might already be able to make a pretty accurate prediction of your gender, your race, your income, your political party, and many other more subtle things about you."[13]

So, contrary to our intuition, the algorithm *must* use race as a factor, to neutralize the bias introduced by those correlations. Even better, an algorithm that considers race can proactively compensate for systemic bias that already exists; in other words, it can apply principles of equity and fairness.

Data used for training is frequently biased, and building a model on top of that data may amplify the biases.[14] Training data includes more examples of the majority population, which will therefore contribute more toward the predictive accuracy of the model.[15] The training data may also be biased because the lender only has repayment data on the customers it actually made loans to, so the model can't incorporate the many people who would have repaid but didn't get a chance.[16] These circumstances help explain why the best model in terms of accuracy alone may show a bias.

Really, what we want is a model that maximizes loan repayments subject to conditions around bias. We want it to maximize loan repayment as long as it doesn't violate certain conditions of "fairness" or "justice."[17] Or, with a slightly different emphasis, we want the ML to optimize for probability of loan repayment *plus* several social goals.

Solving for that combination of goals forces us to be more precise about how we define fairness or justice, for it turns out that there are several possibilities. Kearns and Roth examine two of the possibilities for a lending algorithm: striving for equal outcome (statistical parity) or for equal error rates (equality of false negatives). The techniques and results for these goals are different. And, mathematically, we can't use both definitions at the same time.*

Further complicating matters, intersectionality adds problems that grow geometrically. If there are several types of bias that we're trying to avoid, and several ways they can appear in combination, we have to be careful about what we ask the algorithm to do, or it may continue to show bias in certain combinations of cases—let's say cases where an applicant is a disabled African-American woman.

---

* I won't go into the details here, but anyway, Kearns and Roth are much more qualified to tell you about them, so please read their book.

Machine learning gives us something invaluable: a way to pin down where our biases are and what actions we want to take, as a society, given the realities of a history of structural discrimination. It helps us be more precise about our goals and surfaces issues that previously were hidden. These learnings are critical if we actually want to do something about the problem rather than just talk about how concerned we are. After all, the same issues lurk in human decision-making, but the imprecision, variability, and lack of transparency in human decision-making make them harder to spot.

In *Frankenstein*, the creature tries several times to teach Victor about himself, but Victor doesn't listen. To truly develop the creature's moral sense, Victor would have to examine his own behavior. Joyce Carol Oates describes *Frankenstein* as "a remarkably acute diagnosis of the lethal nature of denial: denial of responsibility for one's actions, denial of the shadow-self locked within consciousness."[18] AI can help us overcome denial and dismiss our shadow-selves.

Social Intent

Our inability to achieve a perfect solution to bias reduction might turn us off from using machine learning. But really it should point us back to the human elements of the problem, as Kearns and Roth say:

> These stark mathematical constraints on fairness are somewhat depressing, but they also identify and reinforce the central role that people and society will always have to play in fair decision-making, regardless of the extent to which algorithms and machine learning are adopted.[19]

Freedom from bias is not just a negative duty ("Don't be biased"). Eliminating the effects of bias—promoting equity—is a positive obligation. It's something we have to invest in. It requires difficult decisions. If we discover these difficult decision points by building and testing artificial intelligences, that's a good thing.

We can't tell ML what conditions it has to satisfy on fairness and justice unless we have a provisional definition of those concepts. But philosophers have been disagreeing on those things at least since they escaped from Socrates tugging at their sleeves and found some time to think. We shouldn't expect the bulb to suddenly illuminate and inspiration to strike us with the answer. What we need is a learn-and-adjust loop, a feedback cycle, a way to get better at devising standards of fairness and adapting to changes in society's conception of equity.

To summarize, we are Frankenstein (the doctor, not the monster). The golems are patiently waiting for us to tell them what we want them to do.

Deontology and Principles

Various principles have been proposed for artificial intelligence, including beneficence, nonmaleficence, autonomy, justice, and explicability.[20] Google has published ethical standards for AI: providing social benefit, avoiding creating or reinforcing unfair bias, enforcing safety, maintaining accountability, maintaining privacy design, promoting scientific excellence, and limiting potentially harmful or abusive applications such as weapons or technologies that violate principles of international law and human rights.[21]

But if you accept that—at least for now—AIs are not autonomous moral agents, these are really principles for companies that are using AI, not for AIs themselves. Which raises the question: Why don't these principles apply to everything companies do, rather than just to their AI efforts? Shouldn't companies always maintain accountability, maintain privacy design, and provide social benefit? And for the principles that don't apply to everything every company does, like promoting scientific excellence, why do they apply to AI? Why would Fancy Regressions have special rules that Slightly Less-Fancy Regressions don't have? Why don't the human beings in a company have the same obligations of explainability and promoting scientific excellence?

It seems like these principles, as good as they are, should be subsumed into a more general ethics of workplace and company behavior, flexible enough to fill in the gaps between the principles.

AI and Transformation

The bureaucratic model provides a certain kind of comfort, since your goals ("Keep those shareholders happy!") and constraints ("Don't lie too much!") are, for the most part, given. Your leadership "vision" is a vision of implementation (even though we call it strategy), the mechanics of what will allow you to bring joy to shareholders in the given societal and competitive situation. That's hard enough. But in a nonbureaucratic world, your vision must be broader. You must have and communicate an ethical vision as well. I'll come back to that in the closing chapter.

As leaders, we would like to have a rule book for what is acceptable and what is unacceptable in AI. But we don't—all we have are worries, fears, and—especially—a history of failures, things we know we don't want to happen again. Since rules aren't available, making ethical use of AI again comes down to cultivating and applying the right virtues: justice, integrity, authenticity, courage, and others. They must be applied in an adaptable, interactive, iterative way, where we learn about our own biases and about what the real issues are, and then make choices based on the virtues. We can't simplify by saying that shareholder returns are the only thing that matter. Nor can we vaguely say nice-sounding words (hashtag activism) about how eliminating bias is our goal—we have to be specific enough to turn the intention into action.

The challenge for organizations that are transforming may be stated like this: you will have to understand what societal goals must be incorporated into your AI (equity, fairness, privacy protections, and so on) and make sure they get implemented, even though you don't fully understand how your AI will act (in the sense of being able to predict its actions) and you don't fully know society's norms (since they are emerging). You can think of these societal factors as the terms of an implicit contract between your company and society, the terms of which will change over time.

You're in a difficult place, but there is reason to be optimistic. Frankenstein's creature is an excellent teacher.

Working Virtuously
The Virtues for Digital Transformation

For this is your business, to act well the character assigned you; to choose it is another's.

> —Epictetus, *The Enchyridion*

Faced with what is right, to leave it undone shows a lack of courage.
To see what is right, and not to do it, is want of courage or of principle.
Our greatest glory is not in never falling, but in rising every time we fall.
Hold faithfulness and sincerity as first principles.

> —Confucius, *The Analects*

You know what worries me a little?

What's that?

You know how in The Art of Business Value, *you wind up at the end of the book just saying that business value is just whatever a company defines it as?*

Well, sort of. That wasn't really the point—

Some readers read it that way and didn't like it. I'm worried that this book might come across the same. I understand what you're saying—that rules are the wrong way to think about ethics. But some readers might think you're not really telling them how to be ethical, just side-stepping the question.

Would it help if I was more specific on what I mean by the virtues?

Go ahead. Let's see.

In Aristophanes's *The Clouds*, Strepsiades asks Socrates to help in his business affairs by teaching him to become "bold, glib of tongue, audacious, impudent, shameless, a fabricator of falsehoods, inventive of words, a practiced knave in lawsuits, a law-tablet, a thorough rattle, a fox, a sharper, a slippery knave, a dissembler, a slippery fellow, an impostor, a gallows-bird, a blackguard, a twister, a troublesome fellow, a licker-up of hashes."[1] Though I'm not sure what all of these mean—and I am pretty curious about the licker-up of hashes—I am quite certain that these are not the virtues I would promote for the workplace.

What, then, are the virtues of the digital workplace and how can employees demonstrate them? There are many candidate virtues: we could begin with Aristotle's list, or Benjamin Franklin's, or Shannon Vallor's, or ask for Shrek's. Happily, as the author I get to make up my own. In this chapter I'll present the ones that seem most important for a digitally transforming organization. They are all debatable; perhaps Ben Franklin had it right and chastity is more important than I'm giving it credit for.

At Amazon, it's traditional to add "unless you know better ones" to lists of principles. Humility suggests that I do the same here.

Once I've explained my choice of workplace virtues, I'll talk about what it means to manage in an environment where these are the critical virtues. The role of a manager—particularly the role of the leader of a digital transformation—looks very different from what we're used to.

My list of virtues is: impeccability, presence, authenticity, manners, care, courage, humility, intellectual integrity, curiosity, stewardship, inclusivity, justice, respect, practical wisdom—unless you know better ones.

Here's how I define each of them and why they fit.

Virtues

The Master Virtue: Impeccability

In *A Seat at the Table* I wrote about a virtue of "impeccability."[2] Think of it as a workplace equivalent to Confucius's overarching virtue of *ren*, the "good person." Impeccability is the aggregate of the workplace virtues combined with a high personal standard that involves constantly asking oneself, "Am I acting impeccably?" It's a virtue of continuous learning and improvement, a self-reflecting "conscience" or "superego," applied beyond just situations where there's a clear choice between good and bad. It's a virtue of adaptability and agility.

As I said earlier, the Greek word we translate as "virtue" can also be translated as "excellence." Impeccability is the excellence of excellence, so to speak. In the workplace, it is a striving for one's employer's interests, continuously learning so as to become a better employee and a better person. A workplace is a human society, like the Greek polis, and the virtue of impeccability is what holds it all together: employees and managers with this virtue harness excellence to advance the interests of the joint undertaking they are part of. An impeccable employee is excellent on behalf of their employer and supports their coworkers in being excellent.

Presence

Presence is the digital workplace virtue of showing up; that is, bringing oneself to work. In a traditional, bureaucratic organization an employee must show up as a clean slate, all personal characteristics erased. In a digital workplace, employees show up as human beings, bringing diversity and human attributes. A digital employee cares about their work, interacts inclusively with their colleagues, and contributes to the shared enterprise.

An important point of clarification: bringing yourself to work does not mean that you must disclose your sexual orientation or have conversations about race with your coworkers. I'm not saying that employees need to *disclose* or *represent* their personal lives. That's up to them. The crucial point is to act authentically, with your whole self, rather than impersonally, as the bureaucratic enterprise would have it.

Employees contribute themselves to the organization. Research in 2015 by McKinsey showed that companies in the top quartile for gender and racial diversity were 35% more likely to produce higher-than-average financial returns.[3] Diversity supports the continuous innovation that is characteristic of digital organizations.[4] People in diverse work teams feel freer to express different ideas, while those in homogeneous teams overemphasize commonality.[5] An employee who isn't "present" denies their company the benefit of that diversity.

Employees co-create the enterprise; they influence the workplace and the direction the business will take. A digital organization is no longer executing on a predetermined set of ends, as in a bureaucracy, but is rather a complex adaptive system that continuously evolves with the contributions of employees. An employee is no longer simply a passive recipient of the organization's given goals, culture, and values.

An employee with the virtue of presence "belongs." Bureaucratic belonging is a "faceless" sort of belonging, achieved by conforming to the group, trimming away what makes an individual employee unique. Bureaucratic conformity can be used for evil as well as good: think about the Ku Klux Klan, with its anonymizing robes and hoods.* Conformity fits well with the factory model; the cogs in a machine must align perfectly for it to work.

In a digital organization, an employee belongs by virtue of being accepted as they are; unique, accountable. They sacrifice the comfort of bureaucratic conformity for the friction of working together despite differences. They find unity in accomplishing joint objectives while maintaining and negotiating differences.

---

* Capirotes.

Virtue ethicists see a person's life as a narrative; the good life, or eudaemonia, is found in that story and how it holds together. We inhabit different roles as we proceed through our narratives, and our work role occupies a large part of the narrative. Work is not separated from the rest of life, from the rest of this narrative quest, as it is supposed to be in a bureaucracy. The impersonal work of bureaucracy has become the personal work of the digital world.

Authenticity

While the virtue of presence is a virtue of showing up as an individual, authenticity is the virtue of acting and communicating as that individual. It is the virtue of presenting one's true self in communications, of speaking and writing sincerely and with a genuine desire to communicate. It is an antidote to bullshit and opposed to the bureaucratic values of conformity and neutrality. It requires suppressing all great gasying wordes.

Authenticity is acting in accordance with one's values. In *Virtue at Work*, Moore uses the term *integrity* for this virtue: "To have integrity is to refuse to be, to have educated oneself so that one is no longer able to be, one kind of person in one social context, while quite another in other contexts."[6] MacIntyre frets that people in different life roles adopt different "selves"—"But now in the modern corporate organisation character has become more like a mask or a suit of clothing; an agent may have to possess more than one."[7] Authenticity is wearing the same clothes every day.

I associate authenticity with Amazon's leadership principle "Have Backbone: Disagree and Commit."[8] It requires that you use your intelligence, passion, and expertise to make sure that your company does not go down any wrong paths. If you disagree with a proposed course of action, you must argue for your position. Authenticity in this sense is closely related to the virtue of courage, and requires practical wisdom to know when and how to fight and when to "commit" and accept decisions.

Authenticity is an important virtue for managers. Managers remain moral actors while in their role; they can't add undue formality or arbitrarily exert their authority. They can't hide behind numbers or rules; they own their decisions. In short, they have to be human beings interacting with other human beings, including the human beings who work for them.

Manners

Okay, this one is weird. I told you I wasn't going to be talking about etiquette, but I find myself strangely forced to do so. Presence and authenticity raise a worrying question: Given that some people are jerks, do we really want them to bring themselves to work?

If we value diversity in all its senses, we are going to have people in the workplace with opinions we can't stand, people who bring anger, bias, and low emotional intelligence to the workplace. Jerks outnumber even leprechauns at work. Michael Lewis, in *Liar's Poker*, describes employees on the Salomon Brothers trading floor:

> Some of the men who spoke to us were truly awful human beings. They sacked others to promote themselves. They harassed women. They humiliated trainees. They flourished (though whether they succeeded because they were bad people, whether there was something about the business that naturally favored them over the virtuous are separate questions.) Goodness was not taken into account on the trading floor.[9]

Presumably, these were authentic ways of acting for the traders. Does the principle of "bring yourself to work" mean that jerks should act like jerks?

No. There's a virtue that counteracts jerky behavior, something like a virtue of appropriateness, good behavior, propriety, adherence to form, politeness, or civility. I'll call it *manners*. As the word suggests, manners in earlier days was a larger subject than just etiquette—it was about one's "manner of acting and being in the world more generally, one's habits, tastes, and sensibilities."[10] That's why it's a fitting name for this virtue.

I'm not talking about putting the fork on the left . . . or whichever side . . . but about being sensitive in the way you speak and applying the accepted norms of the workplace. Manners is an expertise in following implicitly agreed-upon ways of working that demonstrate caring and constrain behavior. It includes the concepts of "behaving professionally" and "following codes of practice" like the Hippocratic oath.

Manners is not just a constraining virtue. One's "manner" at work includes things like a sense of humor, a generosity of spirit, an ability to defuse emotional situations and to create a comfortable, pleasant environment for others.

To Confucius, a morally superior person has a keen sense of propriety.[11] The term for ritual propriety, *lǐ* (禮), can also be translated as prescriptions for proper behavior, civility, rules of etiquette, and customs—it is broad enough to fit our needs here.[12] "In practicing ritual one does not go beyond the proper measure, nor take liberties with others, nor presume an intimacy with others."[13] Through proper behavior we communicate our respect for other people.[14]

Caring (Compassion, Concern)

A digital organization does not encourage leaving one's caring, compassion, and concern at home and acting impersonally at the office. Caring is a disposition to meet the needs of those one is collaborating with toward a common cause, and those one affects through one's work.[15]

I'm still not comfortable with this care virtue thing. It sounds squishy.

How?

I don't know. You talk about "care" and flourishing workplaces, about changing management from task mastering to inspiring—it seems to miss the whole point of business.

Which is?

I've always thought it was about competing. Winning. Working, not coming to work to play. Maybe you're right that marketing and sales are some kind of manipulation of customers, but it's kind of the point of business.

Is it?

In capitalism, it is.

I'm not an expert in economics, but I think the point of capitalism is that competition drives innovation, quality improvements, and lower prices. It doesn't necessarily require manipulation of customers. But feel free to choose your own list of virtues. I'm not saying companies should stop competing and trying to win.

But still, your time at work should be focused on profits, not caring for others.

Ah, I see where we're miscommunicating. What I'm trying to say is that these virtues of care and so on *are* about making profits, or at least about successfully accomplishing whatever we come together in the workplace to do. Not only is there no conflict, but these virtues are exactly how you get the best results in the digital world. Virtues are about excellence. The competitive market requires a workplace in which employees flourish, and where a particular ethical vision, peculiar to each company, is actually part of strategy.

Digital organizations sometimes talk about "psychological safety." This term doesn't go far enough. In a digital organization people bring their vulnerabilities and insecurities, their fears as well as their capabilities. Since the boundary between work and personal life is more porous, personal problems rise to the surface: child-raising challenges, family struggles with addiction, deaths among close relations and friends, medical decisions. As employees expose their vulnerabilities, their coworkers have the same responsibility of care toward them that they would have *outside* of the workplace.

Since inclusivity is valued, a virtuous employee works to further it; that is, to help create an environment where others' contributions are valued. They help educate others in the areas at which they are expert. That might sound obvious, but note how it differs from the bureaucratic values, which include a separation of duties and individual accountability for results. Power in a bureaucracy comes from hoarding information and skills. In a digital organization information and skills are used to steward capabilities for everyone's benefit.

A virtuous manager is concerned for their workers. It's a cliché of the bureaucratic world that a manager must make "hard" and "painful" decisions without batting an eye; caring too much for employees makes a manager unfit to do what is necessary. But *The Kural* says: "Not a taint on a king but his task—correcting the people he loves and protects."[16]

Courage

Workplace courage is the virtue of making difficult decisions; of not hiding behind data or bureaucratic rules or deferring decisions until too late. Courage is the virtue that addresses the existential fear and trembling of having to take the responsibility for one's decisions, and maybe also the fear of Big Julius, the workplace bully. A courageous employee takes responsibility for calling attention to and disrupting unethical practices and for rising to action in a complex world where there are no given right answers.

Many virtue systems have recognized the importance of courage, including those of ancient Greece and Confucianism.[17] All have seen fear as inimical to flourishing. In today's work environment common sources of fear include the fear of being fired, the fear of looking foolish, and the sorts of fear deliberately cultivated by Enron's bullying leaders.

There's also a fear that comes simply from wanting to do one's job well, yet having to make decisions for which one has no rule or experience to rely on. In a bureaucratic enterprise that situation is rare; the point of bureaucracy is repeatability and predictability. In an environment of rapid change and complexity, however, where innovation is expected and where the rule book and user manual have gone missing, the fear is more or less constant.

Courage has special significance in the data-driven organization. An employee with courage remains open to what the data will tell them and acts on the data once its implications are clear. They take personal responsibility for interpreting the data and are willing to act even when it is incomplete. Courage also requires refraining from confirmation bias—a willingness to revise one's position based on data, rather than ignoring data that contradicts it.

Humility

We all know that our own beliefs are correct. I certainly do. When we come together with a diverse group of fellow employees, it's odd to find that some of them disagree with us. Humility is an ability to accept, at least provisionally, that they might be slightly more right.

Benjamin Franklin saw that becoming humble was something he'd have to work hard at. He forbade himself from using any word or expression that "imported a fixed opinion." Instead of words like "certainly" or "undoubtedly" he resolved to use phrases like "I conceive," "I apprehend," or "I imagine."[18] If the person he was talking to made an error, Franklin "denied [himself] the pleasure of contradicting him abruptly, and of showing immediately some absurdity in his proposition."[19] Instead, he resolved, he would start by saying that in some cases the other person's opinion might be right, but in this case there "appeared" or "seemed" to be a difference.[20]

Humility is a willingness to accept feedback (preferably before it becomes formalized) and to ask questions and listen to the answers, and is therefore closely related to curiosity. Digital leaders acknowledge that solving the challenges they are given requires community action. Those high on an org chart must accept that while their purview is broad, it is not deep. They have less contact with customers than those deeper in the org chart. Many problems, solutions, and warning signals of the organization are concealed from them. Humility requires them to acknowledge that their information is incomplete and that it must be combined with the knowledge of those within their organizations.

In Ancient Greek heroic society, humility was not an important virtue; you did the right thing and were owed the respect and honor for doing so. The digital world is decidedly unheroic; we acknowledge uncertainty and accept that what we do might not turn out the way we think. We move incrementally and frequently stop to reassess our own performance.

Humility is the virtue of admitting that customers may behave differently from what you expect, that competitors may outsmart you, that your brilliant business plans may fail. It is a willingness to be surprised. It is essential for making sure innovations are effective; digital companies introduce innovations incrementally, learn from the way customers react, and adjust the innovation accordingly. You can't do that if you are sure your initial ideas are right.

Humility is therefore deeply ingrained in technologists' ways of working . . . wait, is it? It's easy for technologists to look down on those less proficient with technology, perhaps bullying them or making them feel stupid, as Socrates did to his conversation partners. We see this reflected in the distinction between "IT" and "the business," a power dynamic I've written about in previous books.

The digital world poses a danger of technocracy; those with digital expertise and an understanding of digital principles, many think, should simply run the world. As far back as 1916 Gantt—not Gantt the chart but Henry Gantt its creator—founded a society called the New Machine to advance the idea that manager-engineers should rule the world in "an aristocracy of the capable." Yes, like Socrates's idea that philosophers should be in charge. There is a danger that the tech-savvy may come to see themselves as the only true source of value in an enterprise or in society. Humility is the virtue that counteracts that tendency.

Intellectual Integrity

What I have in mind with "intellectual integrity" is a commitment to the rigorous use of the tools of the trade, a willingness to present both sides of any story, and an unwillingness to distort information or hide bad news. It is a commitment to bringing knowledge, derived from study and experience, to one's activities. It's the honest and informed use of data, the virtue of using data with openness and curiosity and making sure one's inferences from it are justified. In a digital workplace, the intelligent use of data isn't just delegated to data scientists and statisticians, but an aspect of excellence in all employees and managers.

Curiosity (Numeracy, Literacy, Education)

The virtue of curiosity is the virtue of continuously learning, being open to instruction, and having a learning mindset. It is not just about learning a particular functional skill, but about valuing learning and education in their broadest senses. Not just book-education or school-education, but a constant seeking after new knowledge.

In a bureaucracy, each employee is expected to bring precisely the education necessary to play their part in the machine. In the digital world, we value generalist skills because they contribute to an organization's agility—an employee can participate in more tasks and their responsibilities can change as needed. A broad education helps employees communicate across functional groups, which is important as groups no longer interact only through formalized rituals. A digital employee needs to sustain human relationships across the organization; skill in languages and an understanding of different cultural heritages contribute to the company's success.

Agile software delivery values "T-shaped" people: those who have a broad set of skills and also go deep in one particular area. That misses the point slightly, I think, because it focuses on "skills." An employee is not just a collection of skills any more than a customer is the intersection of the target market segments they fall into. It is an employee's ability to think and to draw on a wealth of understanding and experience that matters.

In his book *Range*, David Epstein distinguishes between "kind" problems and "wicked" problems. "In wicked domains," he says, "the rules of the game are often unclear or incomplete, there may or may not be repetitive patterns and they may not be obvious, and feedback is often delayed, inaccurate, or both."[21] In kind domains, one learns from experience; in wicked domains one must learn without experience.[22] The digital world is a wicked domain.

Solving wicked problems requires the "cognitive flexibility" that you find in people with generalist knowledge, Epstein says.[23] What works best in a wicked problem domain—and for innovation—is drawing on metaphors from other areas of experience. "Deep analogical thinking" recognizes similarities across different subject areas. It "takes the new and makes it familiar, or takes the familiar and puts it in a new light, and allows humans to reason through problems they have never seen in unfamiliar contexts."[24] The more distant an analogy, he says, the better it is for generating ideas.[25]

Epstein gives the example of the scientist Johannes Kepler:

Each time he got stuck, Kepler unleashed a fusillade of analogies. Not just light, heat, odor, currents and boatmen, but optics of lenses, balance scales, a broom, magnets, a magnetic broom, orators gazing at a crowd, and more. He interrogated each one ruthlessly, every time alighting on new questions.[26]

"Big innovation," Epstein says, "most often happens when an outsider who may be far away from the surface of the problem reframes the problem in a way that unlocks the solution."[27]

Stewardship

Stewardship is the essential *management* virtue of the digital organization. We no longer manage by applying organizational power to control a section of the org chart. Instead, the virtue of stewardship involves taking on the responsibility for advancing the ends of the organization as a whole. In a bureaucratic organization a manager "owns" a function and guards it against encroachment. "It's none of your business" or "Stay in your own lane" are reasonable responses to questioning. In the digital organization, the manager is a "steward" of a function. Their desire is to contribute to organizational results, whether it is directly through the employees they manage or through supporting another manager or organizational unit. If a non-IT manager has a great IT idea, a CIO with the virtue of stewardship does not resist it. An enterprise is a cross-functional collaboration seeking the best results.

Inclusivity

A manager must cultivate the virtue of inclusivity, for they hold the primary responsibility for using the diverse skills of the organization to achieve the company's results. A virtuous manager makes sure that everyone on their team is included (not "feels" included) in the community that is the company. They make sure the company and the employees gain the advantage of all the skills, experience, creativity, enthusiasm, etc. brought by all team members. Inclusivity is not an "additional" responsibility but a core attribute of a virtuous manager. It is stewardship through enablement, harmonization, vision, support, and impediment removal.

Justice

The bureaucratic notion of fairness in the sense of treating everyone by the same rules doesn't go deep enough for today's needs. In particular, it doesn't address equity. Treating everyone the same doesn't help balance disadvantages that some groups or individuals have for reasons external to the bureaucracy.

There is a workplace virtue—let's call it justice—that is similar to but broader than the bureaucratic ideal of fairness and includes equity and helping others achieve their full potential. It's true that a virtue of justice does not in itself provide protections for employees against unfair treatment; but then again, it is the legal system, not the ethical, that provides "protections." In an organization, our central concern is to make sure everyone flourishes.

Respect

Respect, the virtue that follows from the autonomy principle and CIv2, is the virtue of honoring the autonomy and dignity of individuals. Employees and managers should develop the virtue of seeing the human through the number. Target markets consist of individuals, not just increments toward goals. Data-drivenness should not be a distraction from human and moral issues. People are to be treated as ends in themselves rather than merely as means.

Practical Wisdom

Aristotle had this one right. The virtues described above may conflict or may need to be modified when they are applied in specific circumstances. The dilemma of digital transformation, I have said, is the need to make decisions where there are multiple, competing imperatives, especially when inherited bureaucratic values compete with new, digital ones. Practical wisdom is the virtue of weighing the facts, needs, and players in a situation and applying the virtues appropriately.

Brevity

I could propose many more workplace virtues, but the virtue of brevity suggested itself. I was inspired by *The Kural* "Those who can't speak a few faultless words love to speak many words."[28] I thought about the office bore: "If one at the end of a branch keeps climbing his life is over."[29]

Managing Virtuously

"Ask anyone to talk about a great manager they know, and, after some recognition of the individual's technical skills, the discussion will almost always take place in the language of moral obligation: respect, consideration, fairness," Stewart says.[30] Great management, in other words, is about demonstrating, applying, and inspiring employees with the virtues.

The challenge for digital managers is one of forgetting—forgetting bad things they've been taught about management, forgetting the levers of power they've been told to push and pull, and forgetting the clichés they learned from old TV shows of how bosses behave. In a bureaucratic organization, a manager's authority comes from occupying a node in the org chart vested with certain authorities. In a digital organization, where managers often must influence people outside of their hierarchies and where employees are expected to own outcomes, authority comes from an ability to influence others.

It is definitely not gained through mastery of a management science as taught in business schools.

Traditional Management Skills

Gary Hamel, one of the writers frequently cited in MBA programs, wrote that "the machinery of management—which encompasses variance analysis, capital budgeting, project management, pay-for-performance, strategic planning, and the like—amounts to one of humanity's greatest inventions."[31]*

Hamel is mixing apples and yuzu fruits. Some of the "machinery of management"—a telling term—that he mentions is truly mechanical (variance analysis, capital budgeting, project management). Those are valuable skills, useful to some employees in some circumstances, but even if we add accounting, corporate law, and other parts of the curriculum, knowing them doesn't justify any leader's authority as a senior manager or executive. They are basics, like arithmetic and dressing to come to work. What he refers to as strategic planning, pay for performance, and "the like" are a different type of skill, and might justify placement in the higher boxes on the org chart—if, in fact, they were skills.

Brian Quinn of Dartmouth says, "A good deal of corporate planning . . . is like a ritual rain dance. It has no effect on the weather that follows, but those who engage in it think that it does."[32] If a "science" of leadership existed, abstracted from particular business contexts and applicable to any managerial role, it would have to offer techniques and frameworks *that managers could use to achieve better business outcomes.* To do that, it would need predictive power— if you do x, you will get y results. There is nothing in the study of management that justifies any such power; management research can only show techniques that seem to have worked in the past in particular cases.

MacIntyre calls management theory a "moral fiction."[33]

> I am suggesting that "managerial effectiveness" functions much as Carnap and Ayer supposed "God" to function. It is the name of a fictitious, but believed-in reality, appeal to which disguises certain other realities; its effective use is expressive. There are thus two parts to the manager's claims to justified authority. One concerns the existence of a domain of morally neutral fact about which the manager is to be expert. The other concerns the law-like generalizations and their applications to particular cases derived from the study of this domain.[34]

The predictions of a science can be tested. Results are repeatable. Laws identified by one scientist can be confirmed by another. Managerial "science" is not like that at all: the result of applying a management technique is not predictable. Its "law-like generalizations" don't generalize and aren't lawlike—two companies are never in exactly the same situation. It resembles alchemy in its ability to offer excuses every time its predictions fail.

---

* Hamel, remember, was the guy who praised Enron for its "market operating system."

Popular "management guru" literature takes a small set of "successful" companies, extracts some qualities those companies share, and presents those qualities as a theory of good management. For example, in the book *Good to Great*, Jim Collins examines a group of companies that were plugging along for a while as good companies and suddenly accelerated to "greatness." Among the qualities Collins finds these companies share is "level 5 leadership," which he defines as "a paradoxical blend of humility and professional will."[35]

If I want to become a successful leader, how would I go about developing a paradoxical blend of humility and professional will? Would it really make me a great leader? What does it even mean? Would a "paradoxical blend of pasta jokes and Frankenstein references" make me a level 6 leader, even more successful than Collins's CEOs?

Valuing "success" is a way of denying the impact of uncertainty. We don't know whether the CEOs held up as role models made good decisions under uncertainty, only that their decisions led to success, by some definition of success, as many bad ones do. In our struggle to deny the impact of complex and uncertain circumstances, we attribute genius to CEOs who were successful—a kind of survivorship bias. We don't know if other CEOs made similar choices but were less successful, we don't know whether the CEO's choices were rational, and we don't know whether they could have been even more successful if they had acted differently. We'd love to find a simple formula like "have a paradoxical blend of caffeine and donuts" for transmuting bits and brawn into business success so we don't have to make difficult decisions. But the formula doesn't exist.

Managing

Managers are not value-neutral professionals who apply the techniques of management science within a bureaucratic machine to deliver efficient outcomes. The organizational distinction between people with brains and people with muscles is not a logical principle, just a historical outcome. Stewart says, "The corporate hierarchy that exists today is a work of customs, cultures, laws, and politics. It is the product of a historical process, not a logical one. Ultimately, it exists for many of the same reasons that warrior aristocracies existed in the ancient world."[36]

The characteristics of a good manager include the ability to understand and motivate people, to think critically and creatively, to handle surprises and change; and qualities like curiosity, openness to learning, integrity, trustworthiness—significantly, these are things one is more likely to learn in a liberal arts program than an MBA program. The goal of an ethical leader is not to master a science of ethical management, but to become a good person; to master the virtues that help one lead people. Business schools teach *skills*: finance, accounting, "strategy." Morality, however, is not a skill.

As Stewart says:

> Tips on organizational politics are all there in Machiavelli's descriptions of Roman and Florentine politics, not to mention Thucydides on the Peloponnesian War or William Faulkner on the American South. There is probably more to learn from studying the defects of King Lear's "management style" than there is from reading articles about Michael Eisner's shortcomings as CEO of Disney.[37]

Management is not a general-purpose discipline focused on abstract ways of achieving efficiency, but effective behavior in concrete circumstances. It is about what a manager says in the ten o'clock meeting and what their body language conveys; more about managing particular human beings with their quirks than about managing human resources with Taylor's or Mayo's techniques.

The article "Hierarchies and Dignity" suggests that a good leader is something like the conductor of an orchestra, who creates a possibility for the individual musicians that they would not otherwise have; that is, coming together in a successful performance.[38] An orchestra conductor succeeds when there are lots of different instruments in the orchestra; it is the interplay of the textures of different instruments that make for the magic of orchestral music. A manager's role is to bring out those differences in texture, yet harmonize them.

The Virtues and Transformation

The bureaucratic framing of ethics—rules, duties, and algorithms—I've argued, is not helpful to leaders of digital transformation. Instead, I've called upon virtue ethics and social contracts as the best way to think of ethics in a time of rapid change and complexity. In this chapter I presented what I consider the important virtues of the digital workplace. You'll notice that, in contrast to the stern prohibitions of deontology, these virtues are positive. A workplace where people exhibit these virtues is a place we'd want to work—and a place that can better accomplish the goals of the business. A proper view of ethics is what enables the transformation of an organization. And that leads to our final chapter, on how to lead a flourishing workplace.

Leadership and Flourishing
Toward a Vision and a Strategy

My person was hideous, and my stature gigantic: What did this mean? Who was I? What was I? Whence did I come? What was my destination?"

—Mary Shelley, *Frankenstein*

Consider, O youth, of how many pleasures you are about to be deprived— of women, of games at cottabus, of dainties, of drinking-bouts, of giggling. And yet, what is life worth to you if you be deprived of these enjoyments?

—Aristophanes, *The Clouds*

Flourishing

A transformational leader forms a vision for the future and motivates employees to realize it. Our bureaucratic bias leads us to limit that vision— even as we enter the digital age—to the concerns that business school and management literature have told us are important: discovering new business models; innovating to reach new markets; using data to make decisions, streamline operations, and increase revenues; and building agility, speed, and resilience.

But there's something missing. A transformational leader must also provide a moral vision, a vision of flourishing, a perspective on what the workplace society should be. That moral vision is a component of the company's strategy. It will drive the behavior of employees and managers and shape the relationship between the company and its customers. Establishing that moral vision is a creative act, one that distinguishes your company from its competitors, provides transparency to your investors, motivates your employees, and tells your customers who they are transacting with.

Most companies have overlooked this aspect of strategy. A bureaucratic organization, with its goals set by the Friedman doctrine, removes itself from the moral sphere; its goal is simply to execute well within the constraints of law and society. Whether that is the right approach is no longer the issue; it is simply untenable today, as we find ourselves in a Marketplace of Morals where customers and employees demand an ethical vision. Even when taking an ethical stand doesn't improve a company's position in the marketplace, even when it limits a company's returns to shareholders, it is still essential—Enron's case shows why. An ethical vision emerges one way or another—whether it is like Attila the Hun's or like Mother Teresa's—and it is a leader's job to guide it in the right direction.

Our goal is to create a flourishing workplace, which we can envision however we wish. We hesitate to talk about flourishing in the workplace because it seems unserious. Carrying forward the worldview we've taken from bureaucratic organizations, we know that work is meant to be unpleasant, especially if our sole duty is to make money for owners so they will provide a paycheck. That's why it's work. It is the opposite of play. As Aristotle said, work takes time away from being a good citizen and degrades your body and mind. You accept the degradation of your mind and body because with that paycheck, you can better enjoy your "real" life—your personal life—your life outside of work. Work is an obligation to yourself, your family, and your society.

The term *flourishing* and the suggestion that we should do it at work can seem immoral, childish, and frivolous. But once we accept that the workplace is part of our lives, not something separate, a community rather than a machine that hums away with or without our participation, it follows that we are responsible for molding it into a world we want to live in. In the digital world each of us plays an active role in creating the workplace, not a passive role serving in a rationalized, engineered-for-efficiency machine. But we can only create a flourishing workplace if we formulate a vision for what that means. A leader is someone who sets, or influences, that vision.

The Friedmanian view in its most dogmatic form—that we are working purely to earn money for owners so that we can be given a paycheck—does, in fact, suggest that the idea of a flourishing workplace is immoral, childish, and frivolous. But the opposing views that I presented in the social responsibility chapter suggest something very different. Let's entertain them for a moment:

1. The purpose of a company is to produce something valuable for society, even while investors are motivated to invest for their returns.
2. An entrepreneur creates a business venture, raises capital by contracting with investors, and assembles the necessary resources.
3. The business is a nexus of agreements, some formal and some informal, between the various parties who willingly join together to accomplish goals that are in their interests.

Now add the incredible powers of the digital world to accomplish those goals with data, with new tools of communication, with computing power. It's a very different picture, isn't it? And, I contend, it is in no way opposed to earning plenty of profits and making investors supremely happy. In fact, it's necessary today, in our Marketplace of Morals.

A business, by these assumptions, is a society in which people join together to *create*.

Work Is Not Play

Again, it's useful to look at where we are coming from to find assumptions we might have to discard.

Work has always been the thing we do that is not play, an "exertion of mind or body undergone partly or wholly with a view to some good other than the pleasure derived from the work."[1] By definition, it is unpleasant. We must be compelled to do it. Play is associated with freedom; with choosing autonomously how you want to exercise your powers. That's why in a bureaucracy the employer "buys" your time; the time is no longer your own to use freely.

One of the important enablers for the modern view of work was the invention of the clock. It was originally devised in the tenth century as a way to let monks know when it was time for their prayers.[2] When the fully mechanical clock was developed in the fourteenth century, it began to change how people thought about time. It became the basis for structuring the work day, making it possible for employers to buy measurable periods of employees' labor time. Employees could "punch in" and "punch out" to verify that they had delivered the required hours. Clocks became connected with morality by Puritan, Methodist, and evangelical preachers who instructed their congregations in the importance of "husbanding their time" as the basis for a moral life. Work was a form of self-discipline that made you a better person.

Work is more than an individual need—it is an obligation to society, participation in the production that allows society to consume. It is expected from virtually everyone; Graeber says that "we have come to believe that men and women who do not work harder than they wish at jobs they do not particularly enjoy are bad people unworthy of love, care, or assistance from their communities."[3]

You would think, then, that any way work could be reduced would be seen as positive. That is the vision of Rossum's Robots.

> Within the next ten years Rossum's Universal Robots will produce so much wheat, so much cloth, so much everything that things will no lon-

ger have any value. Everyone will be able to take as much as he needs. There'll be no more poverty. . . . People will do only what they enjoy. They will live only to perfect themselves. . . . No longer will man need to destroy his soul doing work that he hates.[4]

It's an Aristotelian Utopia—people will live "only to perfect themselves." As usual, the Utopian idea doesn't quite work out. It's an odd message if you think of work as something unpleasant you're compelled to do. The implication, in *R.U.R.*, is that we must work; something critical is missing if we don't.

Work Is Godly

The fact that work is something we're compelled to do has always seemed to need some sort of explanation.

Hesiod said that the gods kept the means of life hidden from humans because they were angry at Prometheus's theft of fire. If it wasn't hidden, then "you would easily do work enough in a day to supply you for a full year." Saint Augustine argued that we are cursed with infinite desires in a finite world and thus naturally in competition with one another.[5] You must work to win scarce resources in a competitive world.

The Protestant ethic that emerged from the Reformation treated work as a "calling" from God, and therefore a sacred responsibility. In *The Protestant Ethic and the Spirit of Capitalism*, Max Weber—that's Weber our bureaucracy expert again—argued that the Protestant attitude toward work was responsible for the development of capitalism. Since work was ordained by God, it was an obligation to be fulfilled rigorously, scrupulously, and with self-discipline. In Weber's words,

> [Protestant asceticism] also regarded wealth achieved as the fruit of labor in a calling as a blessing from God. Furthermore, and even more important, a religious value was placed on ceaseless, constant, systematic labor in a secular calling as the very highest ascetic path and at the same time the surest and most visible proof of regeneration and the genuineness of faith.[6]

Increasing the productivity of labor is doing God's work, and the best way to increase productivity, Weber believed, is through rationalized design of work systems—bureaucracy. Thomas Aquinas had also seen the division of labor, or the structuring of society according to occupation, as part of God's plan. According to the essayist Thomas Carlyle, God had deliberately created the world unfinished so that humans could finish it through labor.[7] "Consider how, even in the meanest sorts of Labour, the whole soul of man is composed into a kind of real harmony, the instant he sets himself to work!"[8] One worked to please God, and one pleased him the most in a bureaucracy.

In the Western world, we've inherited a tradition where work is valued in itself, unpleasant but necessary, regardless of what exactly it produces. The values of bureaucracy are the values of this tradition.

Myths of Work

A myth of bureaucratic organizations is that work is not part of life. At nine a.m., employees temporarily drop their personal lives (and by definition your life *is* your personal life) and become a machine at the service of a manager. At 5:00 p.m., they turn back into a person with a personal life.

That way of working has never felt quite right. People *do* bring themselves to work, despite the bureaucratic ethic. It's too difficult not to care about your fellow workers. If you didn't sleep well last night, you will not perform well today. Rumpelstiltskin may need to call the cable company. To the bureaucratic system, these are just bugs. If your tiredness makes it hard for you to concentrate, or if you converse with your coworker about how their sick child is feeling today, you are stealing time away from the productive work you owe your employer. Some amount of this is tolerated, perhaps as a cost of doing business, like shoplifting in a retail establishment, but no more.

A second myth of the bureaucratic organization is that it has always been that way, because it is the only logical or rational way to work. On the contrary, the nature of work and the role it plays in people's lives has actually changed much over the centuries, from Hesiod's view that work is beloved of the gods through the Protestant Reformation and its view of work as a "calling" from God, to the Taylorist workplace of shirking workers and task mastering managers. The bureaucratic organization is its most recent variation. It is not inevitable and it can change.

Ox Mountain

Weber ends *The Protestant Ethic* with his fear that modern capitalism is creating an abundance of "specialists without spirit, hedonists without a heart."[9] The Confucian scholar Mengzi told the parable of Ox Mountain, a place "so desolate and barren, so empty of human compassion, reciprocity, trust, empathy, and hope, that one might be forgiven for thinking that such virtues never existed."[10] It's hard not to picture Enron, with its banner in its lobby, and dead and desiccated bodies lining its halls.

That's an exaggeration, but the idea that the workplace is a special environment, cordoned off from the real world of day-to-day life, where people take on the characteristics of machines—the bureaucratic view carried to an extreme—makes one worry that it can easily become Ox Mountain. *Frankenstein* ends in the Arctic wilderness, with the creature disappearing into the snowy wastes. It's a bleak vision of creation without moral care.

We may think that the business world must be like Ox Mountain because it requires competition, ruthlessness, and compelled effort to earn money for someone else, the owner. But there is no good reason to believe that a bleak workplace is more successful than a vibrant one. Enron, the very landlords of Ox Mountain, did not succeed by any measure. A workplace can be a place of flourishing and still accomplish its goals—and accomplish them better, in fact.

I've tried to paint a picture of an Ox Mountain we want to avoid—one of its slopes in the land of bureaucratic trolls and another in the country of the digital natives. Ox Mountain Real Estate Trust has only one purpose: returning money to shareholders. It is covered with a fog of meaningless words that prevent any real communication. It categorizes customers and employees into groups like the alphas, betas, and gammas of *Brave New World*, treating each individual only based on their group membership.

Ox Mountain is a place without the virtue of care. It is neither a place we want to live in nor a place that is particularly effective even in accomplishing its own goal—earning returns for investors. We can do better.

Work Is Social Interaction and Caring

Work is something we do together. In a corporation, diverse people join to produce public goods and earn money for themselves and for the benefit of the investors who provide capital. *Making Work Human* says polarization and tribalism shadow our political and social lives even as we are more connected than ever. Yet our businesses represent the coming together of diverse people around shared values and missions. Employees come to work with different backgrounds and beliefs, but they agree to share broad goals. And as a changing world requires businesses to become more diverse, employees can potentially reach across the chasms that modern tribal life has built.[11]

When people come together in a business organization, they find themselves in a society, the workplace, where they interact with one another. What makes workplace society successful is largely what makes everyday society successful. It is the virtues of the people we interact with, the character traits and dispositions they demonstrate that we judge as good.

This coming together in a workplace society provides the belongingness that Whyte in *The Organization Man* said people were desperately looking for. In the bureaucratic organizations Whyte was writing about, the employee's corporate role replaced the employee as a person and their other roles in the world outside the workplace during the hours they were at work. Today's transformation is one where the work role is *additive* to the person's other roles, a part of the flow of their lives, and one which they co-create.

Because they are people, they also bring their caring. It's care that Weber feared might be lacking in a bureaucracy, and it's care that fails to flourish on Ox Mountain. Employees care about the goals of their organizations—work is caring work, meaningful work to them—and they care about the other people in their workplace society—and they care about the customers, the wider society for which they produce their products or services. They are working for their salary, but in their day-to-day activity at work, they are caring members of a society.

Creation and Meaning

We are all Victor Frankensteins. Work is creation. Frankenstein worked passionately, tirelessly, to create his creature. Though he was unsatisfied with the result, there is joy in creation. And that, it seems to me, is the error in the bureaucratic assumption of recalcitrant workers and soldiering. I don't know what it's like to work in a factory. I do know that in the digital world, people are often passionate about creating, about how the results of their work shape society. Not everyone has that passion, but studies have shown meaningful work as the most important factor in a job, ahead of income, job security, promotions, and hours.[12] Geoff Moore defines meaningful work as "the way we express the meaning of our lives through the activities (work) that comprise most of our waking hours."[13] That is very different from the idea that work is compelled labor during a nine-to-five break from the rest of our lives.

Studs Terkel's book *Working* is a collection of interviews with workers across a broad set of jobs. Terkel found that work "is about a search, too, for daily meaning as well as daily bread, for recognition as well as cash, for astonishment rather than torpor; in short, for a sort of life rather than a Monday through Friday sort of dying."[14] One of Terkel's interviewees, a worker in a steel mill, says, "Picasso can point to a painting. What can I point to? A writer can point to a book. Everybody should have something to point to."[15]

I'm probably not telling you anything new; these studies have been around for a while. Plenty of management and sociology books say that work must be meaningful. My point is that knowing this changes a lot; it is the change from bureaucratic ways of working to digital ways of working. The entire edifice of bureaucratic values and bureaucratic ethics crumbles once you accept that employees care about their work.

Work is work, in that it requires effort. But it can also be play. Not that employees are free to do what they want, or that everyone enjoys work. I mean that like play, it can involve pleasure in creating and pleasure in service to society. That's what justifies us in envisioning and creating a workplace of flourishing, of eudaemonia.

Joining to Create

The workplace is a place of creation, where the human desire to create is given the support of capital, machinery, data, and other factors of production to realize that desire. It is the laboratory where entrepreneurial visions are realized. *Frankenstein*, a story of entrepreneurial creation, is a fable that tells us that creation must be accompanied by a moral vision. ("The Gingerbread Man" is a fable of dessert creation, also an important topic.)

In the workplace, diverse people, with diverse motivations, experiences, and interests, come together to produce something valuable for society, and in the process earn money for themselves and for the investors who have contributed capital. They create—together. Frankenstein—not Frankenstein, but his creature—and the gingerbread man join hands and collaborate to produce socket wrenches, spinning machines, pasta, or hats, for the enjoyment of society.

This creative workplace places heavy demands on its participants. They must work toward excellence in everything they do. The primary virtue, impeccability, is a striving for perfection as a member of a creative enterprise. The virtues I've chosen require that an employee demonstrate intellectual rigor, stewardship of their responsibilities, and support for their coworkers. If we're going to join together to produce valuable products and services, let's do it right.

The relationship between the company and its customers also looks rather different in this view. If the purpose of the company is to produce something valuable to society, it makes little sense to manipulate customers to act against their interests, or to feed them insincere communications, or to violate implicit agreements we have with them. We are free to be truly customer-centric.

Ethics is not a matter of constraints on behavior, but a challenge to consider what sorts of people we want to be; that is, what virtues are important to us. Contractarianism is concerned with the terms under which we all agree, as individuals and companies, to come together to produce benefits for society, returns for investors, and better lives for employees. Ethics is not about bureaucratic trolls who crawl out from their caves to tell us we're being naughty because of a clause in section 9.2.1 (c) 4 of a document that was lost in the Napoleonic Wars.

Leading in Digital Transformation

If you are the leader of a digital transformation, I suspect that no one has told you that ethical visioning is part of your job. But it is. It is the powerful but subtle component of the transformation from traditional to digital ways of thinking. You can no longer be neutral and impersonal, as the bureaucratic ethic would have you be. A digital organization is full of people who have brought themselves to the office, and their selves have feelings, beliefs, and preferences. You must care for them, as Victor Frankenstein did not. You have customers and a public who want to preserve their dignity as autonomous human beings and are therefore sensitive to being manipulated. You can't just "do what the data says." You are compelled to make ethical decisions.

The challenge for all of us who try to lead large-scale digital transformations in our enterprises is that we're faced with conflicting imperatives. We must maximize returns for shareholders and we must satisfy social obligations. We must empower teams and we must make sure they produce reliably. We must adapt to changing circumstances and we must predict results and deliver on our predictions. We must build deep relationships with customers and we must preserve their privacy and refrain from manipulating them inappropriately. We have powerful new digital tools, and we know some of them will improve the lives of customers, but we face a shifting ethical environment and no clear guidance on what is or isn't acceptable.

We've dealt with challenges like this before, albeit in a different context. In software delivery, for example, we've learned that we can deal with complexity by maintaining a strong overall vision for where we want to go but making smaller, incremental steps to get there, using lots of feedback to stay on course. We've learned to listen carefully to customers, and today they are telling us that we need to communicate an ethical vision. It would be a mistake to think of ESG as just a matter of doing the minimum necessary for compliance. Customers want to know where we stand.

This is a book about ethics in digital transformation. But to talk about ethics in the abstract is to miss a key point: ethics, or proper behavior, only makes sense in relation to a desired target state. I can't tell you what rules to follow, because a rule book just doesn't exist. If it did, it would be incomplete and outdated in a week, and impossible to apply in the real world. Besides, as I said, I don't want to fight with Big Julius or your spiritual advisors. I'm afraid that Socrates will corner me in the market and start asking me why my ethical rules are better than anyone else's. And who am I to tell you what to do? My only qualification is that I spent many hours over my keyboard writing this book.

Ethics is not about rules handed down from the past, but about a future state we desire. We aren't limited by some kind of legacy ethical technical debt, rules that haven't been upgraded since Immanuel Kant and are no longer supported. Ethics is about transforming to an envisioned state.

Instead of worrying about robot dogs, we should focus on the most critical of ethical questions: What do we want? Or, to put it in techno-business terms, what does success look like? What are we trying to optimize?

· · ·

The Age of Enlightenment, the age that created deontology, bureaucracy, and shepherdess hats, gave way to the Romantic Era in Europe. In *The Free World*, Louis Menand explains the change:

> Romanticism rejected the end of self-understanding and replaced it with the end of self-creation. Science, reason, and universalism, the values of Enlightenment thinkers, were replaced by a new set of values: sincerity, authenticity, toleration, variety. It is from this tradition, not the Socratic tradition, that liberal pluralism derives.[16]

Now we're talking: these sound a lot like the new values of the digital organization. But Menand is quick to point out that the Romantic tradition was also the root of fascism. In our transition to digital ways of working and being, we must be sure that we retain the values of caring and humility. Manipulating customers against their best interests recalls the fascist manipulation of crowds. The potential class distinction between elite, self-satisfied, techno-savvy and agile-savvy folks and old-school techno-fearful folks is a danger. The flourishing workplace we're looking to build is one of joint support and joint learning, a community of humans engaged in mission.

That life we're shooting for—well, it's not like we know exactly what it is. It's something we will learn incrementally. As with any good agile, adaptive approach, we accept change, uncertainty, complexity—and the influence of the other people we share the world with.

That is digital transformation, stripped of its ERP systems, waterfall or agile initiatives, project or product models, its squads and tribes, its disruptive business models, and its machine learning models. It's a creative project that we execute together, giving birth to neither unmentored Frankenstein creatures nor runaway desserts, but a world—and a workplace—we'd like to live in.

Afterword

The most beautiful life that has been imagined is the life of the knight Don Quixote who created danger where he did not find it. But more beautiful still is the lived life of him who finds danger in all places. All creation stands on the edge of being; all creation is risk. He who does not risk his soul can only ape the creator.

—Martin Buber, *Daniel: Dialogues on Realization*

A stirring conclusion!
I noticed you got a little quiet there.
I just saw you were winding up for a big finish and wanted to stay out of the way.
Thanks for that.

Appendix A

Handy Chart of Virtues

Digital Transformation Virtues*

Virtue	Meaning
Impeccability	The aggregate of the workplace virtues combined with a high personal standard of continuous improvement. A "conscience" or "superego," applied beyond just situations where there's a clear choice between good and bad; adaptability and agility.
Presence	Showing up; bringing oneself to work; contributing to the enterprise.
Authenticity	Acting and communicating as a real individual; presenting one's true self; speaking and writing sincerely and with a genuine desire to communicate; suppressing great gasying wordes.
Manners	Appropriateness, good behavior, propriety, adherence to form, politeness, civility; one's "manner of acting and being in the world" more generally; one's habits, tastes, and sensibilities. And putting the fork on the left.
Care	Disposition to meet the needs of those one is collaborating with toward a common cause, and those one affects through one's work; supporting coworkers in their vulnerabilities and insecurities; inclusivity.
Courage	Making difficult decisions; not hiding behind data or bureaucratic rules or deferring decisions until too late; taking responsibility for decisions; ignoring workplace bullies; calling attention to and disrupting unethical practices and rising to action in a complex world where there are no given right answers.

Virtue	Meaning
Humility	Willingness to accept, at least provisionally, that others might be slightly more right or that they might know more.
Intellectual integrity	Commitment to the rigorous use of the tools of the trade; presenting both sides of any story; bringing knowledge, derived from study and experience, to one's activities. Unwillingness to distort information or hide bad news; honest and informed use of data; using data with openness and curiosity and making sure one's inferences from it are justified.
Curiosity	Continuously learning, being open to instruction, and having a learning mindset.
Stewardship	The essential *management* virtue: accepting responsibility for advancing the ends of the organization as a whole rather than applying organizational power to control a section of the org chart.
Inclusivity	Using the diverse skills of the organization to achieve the company's results; making sure the company and the employees gain the advantage of all the skills, experience, creativity, enthusiasm, etc. brought by all team members; stewardship through enablement, harmonization, vision, support, and impediment removal.
Justice	Similar to but broader than the bureaucratic ideal of fairness, includes equity and helping others achieve their full potential.
Respect	Honoring the autonomy and dignity of individuals; seeing the human through the number.
Practical wisdom	Making decisions where there are multiple, competing imperatives, especially when inherited bureaucratic values compete with new, digital ones; weighing the facts, needs, and players in a situation and applying the virtues appropriately.
Brevity	Test case failed.

Unless you know better ones.

Benjamin Franklin's Virtues[*]

For comparison, here is a fuller explanation of Benjamin Franklin's virtues:

Virtue	Meaning
Temperance	Eat not to dullness; drink not to elevation.
Silence	Speak not but what may benefit others or yourself; avoid trifling conversation.
Order	Let all your things have their places; let each part of your business have its time.
Resolution	Resolve to perform what you ought; perform without fail what you resolve.
Frugality	Make no expense but to do good to others or yourself; i.e., waste nothing.
Industry	Lose no time; be always employed in something useful; cut off all unnecessary actions.
Sincerity	Use no hurtful deceit; think innocently and justly; and, if you speak, speak accordingly.
Justice	Wrong none by doing injuries or omitting the benefits that are your duty.
Moderation	Avoid extremes; forbear resenting injuries so much as you think they deserve.
Cleanliness	Tolerate no uncleanliness in body, clothes, or habitation.
Tranquility	Be not disturbed at trifles, or at accidents common or unavoidable.
Chastity[†]	
Humility	Imitate Jesus and Socrates.

---

[*] See Franklin, *Franklin's Autobiography*, 34.

[†] Oddly, Franklin doesn't define chastity. According to some sources, he only had a hazy understanding of it, anyway. (See https://www.ranker.com/list/benjamin-franklin-private-life/katia-kleyman.)

Handy Chart of Excuses for Bad Behavior

Excuse	Exemplar
Denial of injury	"No one was really hurt by my action."
Denial of the victim	"The victim deserved it."
Denial of responsibility	"I didn't do it" or "I had to do it."
Condemnation of the condemners	"I'm the victim of a witch hunt."
Appeal to higher loyalties	"I did it for others, not for myself."
Everyone else is doing it	"I had to do it because everyone else is."
Claim to entitlement	"I was obligated for moral reasons to do what I did."

Index

entrepreneurial point of view, 65
executives of private companies, 66
freedom revisited, 65
libertarian argument against Friedman, 65
managerialism, 63
negative duties, 67–68
"neighborhood effects", 71
ownership of firm, 64
positive duties, 67, 68–69
problem with stakeholder views, 72
pure positive duties, 71
shareholders and shares, 64
short-term focus on shareholders' returns, 66–67
social responsibility of officials, 62
social responsibility under, 67–71
stakeholder responsibilities, 72–73
Friedman, Milton, 61–69, 71–73, 79, 110, 188

G
Gingerbread Man, The, xxviii, xxx, 194
Frankenstein vs., 160
Golem of Prague, 155–156
good person, being a, 39–40
guardrails, ethical, 120. *See also* culture

H
happiness measurement, 28
hashtag activism, 104
hierarchy, corporate, 184
honeypot, 92
human resources, 86

humblebragging, 104. *See also* inauthentic communication
humbug, 99–100. *See also* inauthentic communication
Hume's Guillotine. *See* "Hume's Law"
"Hume's Law", xxv
humility, 178–179. *See also* workplace virtues
hypothetical imperatives, 31

I
impeccability, 172. *See also* workplace virtues
imperatives, hypothetical, 31
impersonality, 8–9. *See also* bureaucratic value
vs. inclusion, 15–16
inauthentic communication, 91
audience-less language, 100
bomphiolgia, 101
brand advertising, 97–98
bullshit, 91, 95–98, 99
closed-door meetings, 104–105
corporate deception, 94–95
deception, 92–94
depersonalized language, 100
doublespeak, 102
euphemisms, 102–103
humblebragging, 104
humbug, 99–100
inauthentic language, 97
lying, 92–94, 96
noise, 103–104
obfuscation, 101–103
"open secrets", 105
puffery, 102
secrecy and transparency, 104–105

manipulation *(continued)*
    Taylor's "scientific" approach and
        ethical issue, 126
    Taylor's theory, 125
    and transformation, 138
    ways, 123–124
manners, 174–175. *See also* work-
    place virtues
market economy, 62. *See also* busi-
    ness conduct
marketing-qualified leads (MQLs), 6
market mechanisms, 62. *See also*
    business conduct
market operating system. *See* MOS
Marketplace of Morals (MOM), 15
"materialist bias", 82. *See also*
    data-drivenness
measure-manage, 77–78. *See also*
    data-drivenness
meetings, closed-door, 104–
    105. *See also* inauthentic
    communication
metaphors, xxviii, xxix
metaphysical heart of rationalism,
    10
metrical bureaucracy, 124
metric fixation, 81, 86, 114–115.
    See also data-drivenness
mission statements, 69
MOM. *See* Marketplace of Morals
moral agency, 60–61
morality, xxxi, 40
moral vision, 187
MOS (market operating system), 108
MQLs. *See* marketing-qualified
    leads

N

National Development and Reform
    Commission (NDRC), 75

NDRC. *See* National Development
    and Reform Commission
negative duties, 67–68. *See also*
    Friedman's doctrine
"neighborhood effects", 71. *See also*
    Friedman's doctrine
neutrality, 10. *See also* bureaucratic
    value
    vs. care, 17
New Machine, 179
Nicomachean Ethics, The, 41
noise, 103–104. *See also* inauthentic
    communication
Nudge, 131. *See also* manipulation
numeric targets, 84. *See also*
    data-drivenness

O

obfuscation, 101–103. *See also* inau-
    thentic communication
objectives and key results. *See* OKRs
OKRs (objectives and key results), 84
"open secrets", 105. *See also* inau-
    thentic communication
organization
    bureaucratic, 5–7, 19, 20
    digitally transforming, 123, 172
    "integrative organization", 129
    traditional, 119
our oughts and other oughts, 24–25
owned time, 11. *See also* bureau-
    cratic value
    dedicated time vs. dedicated
        efforts, 17

P

Panopticon, 149–150
Passion of Propriety (POP), 15
paternalistic manipulation, 130–
    132. *See also* manipulation

scientific management, 124–125, 126–127. *See also* Taylor, Frederick

scientism, 10

secrecy and transparency, 104–105. *See also* inauthentic communication

self-driving cars, 162–163. *See also* artificial intelligence

shareholder theory. *See* Friedman's doctrine

shift

ethical, 5

left, 41, 120, 121

slippery slope, xxvii

social ethic, 12

Socrates, xxvi, 49, 171

"soldiering", 125

stewardship, 180. *See also* workplace virtues

T

"targeting", 85. *See also* data-drivenness

targets "drive" behavior, 83–84. *See also* data-drivenness

Taylor, Frederick, 125. *See also* manipulation

is-ought problem, 126

management theory, 127

"scientific" approach and ethical issue, 126

scientific management, 124–125, 126–127

technical skills, 11–12. *See also* bureaucratic value

vs. generalist skills, 17–18

technocracy, 179

"technosocial" virtues, 41. *See also* virtue ethics

"terms of service", 147

thinking, bureaucratic, 21

three-class system, 82

traditional

enterprise, xxi. *See* bureaucratic enterprise

management skills, 182–184

organization, 119

training data, 167. *See also* artificial intelligence

transformational leader, 187. *See also* work

trolley problems, 26–27, 162

"T-shaped" people, 180

Turing test, 163

U

uncertainty, 34

of consequences, 45

plans and, xxviii

success and, 184

unethical laws, xxxii

V

values, xxxi

verbal deceitfulness, 103. *See also* inauthentic communication

verbal virtues, 105–106. *See also* inauthentic communication

virtue ethics, 40, 41–47, 93. *See also* agile (adaptive) ethics

Aristotle's virtues, 41

Buddhism, 44–45

Confucianism, 44

DevOps, 41

Eastern virtue traditions, 44

flexible through change and shifting norms, 45–47

global and interconnected, 43

"Instructions of Kagemni", 43

practical wisdom or phronēsis, 42
robots and rights, 161
"shift left", 41
"technosocial" virtues, 41
tolerant of complexity, 42–43
uncertainty of consequences, 45
Western virtue traditions, 43–44
virtues, 201. *See also* workplace
   virtues
   Benjamin Franklin's, 203
   for digital transformation, 171
   digital transformation, 201–202
   and transformation, 185
virtuous leaders, 47

W
Wells Fargo scandal, 83, 111. *See
   also* data-drivenness
Western virtue traditions, 43–44.
   See also virtue ethics
white collar crime, 113. *See also*
   culture
wisdom, practical, 42, 182. *See also*
   workplace virtues
work, 187
   bleak workplace, 191–192
   bureaucratic organization with
      Friedman doctrine, 187–188
   as collaborative effort, 192–193
   contractarianism, 194
   creation and meaning, 193–194
   creative workplace, 194
   ethics, 195–196
   flourishing, 187–189
   joining to create, 194–195
   leading in digital transformation,
      195–196
   meaningful, 193–194
   moral vision, 187
   myths of, 191

   and play, 189–190
   Protestant attitude toward work,
      190
   as sacred responsibility, 190–191
   society, 192–193
   transformational leader, 187
   Working, 193
   workplace, 188, 194
Working, 193
workplace, 188, 194. *See also* work
   bleak, 191–192
   creative, 194
   flourishing, 188
   society, 192–193
workplace virtues, 171. *See also*
   virtues
   Amazon's leadership principle,
      174
   authenticity, 174
   brevity, 182
   bureaucratic framing of ethics,
      185
   caring, 175–177
   characteristics of good manager,
      184
   corporate hierarchy, 184
   courage, 177
   curiosity, 179–180
   ethical leader, 185
   humility, 178–179
   impeccability, 172
   inclusivity, 181
   integrity, 174
   intellectual integrity, 179
   justice, 181
   "kind" and "wicked" problems,
      180
   machinery of management,
      182–183
   managerial effectiveness, 183

X,Y,Z

Bibliography

24/7 Wall Street Staff. "Misleading Marketing: Cheerios, 5-Hour Energy Drink Among Products Tagged With Outrageous Claims." 24/7 *Wall Street*. December 16, 2020. https://www.usatoday.com/story/money /2020/12 /16/39-most-outrageous-product-claims-of-all-time/115127274/.

"About Delta." Delta. Accessed December 23, 2022. https://www.delta.com /us/en/about-delta/overview.

"About Us." Progressive. Accessed December 17, 2022. https://www.progressive .com/about/.

Allan, David G. "Ben Franklin's '13 Virtues' Path to Personal Perfection." CNN. March 1, 2018. https://www.cnn.com/2018/03/01/health/13-virtues -wisdom-project/index.html.

Aristophanes. *The Clouds*. Digireads.com Publishing, 2004.

Aristotle. *Nicomachean Ethics*. Translated by Terence Irwin. 3rd ed. Indianapolis, IN: Hackett Publishing Company, 2019.

Aristotle. "Politics" in *Introduction to Aristotle*. Edited by Richard McKeon. Chicago: University of Chicago Press, 1973.

Attas, Daniel. "What's Wrong with 'Deceptive' Advertising?" *Journal of Business Ethics* 21, no. 1 (1999): 49–59.

AWS Public Sector Blog Team, "An Eye on Science: How Stanford Students Turned Classwork into Their Life's Work," AWS Public Sector Blog (October 4, 2016). https://aws.amazon.com/blogs/publicsector/ an-eye-on-science-how-stanford-students-turned-classwork-into-their- lifes-work/

Ayres, Ian. *Super Crunchers: Why Thinking-by-Numbers Is the New Way to Be Smart*. New York: Bantam, 2007.

Baskar. "Data—a New Factor of Production." BusinessLine. January 13, 2022. https://www.thehindubusinessline.com/opinion/data-a-new-factor-of -production/article64822623.ece.

Barnum, P. T. *The Life of P. T. Barnum Written by Himself*. Edited by Jeffrey Merrow. Chicago, IL: University of Illinois Press, 2014.

Bayley, Stephen. *A Dictionary of Idiocy: Stephen Bayley*. London: Gibson Square, 2012.

Belofsky, Nathan. *The Book of Strange and Curious Legal Oddities: Pizza Police, Illicit Fishbowls, and Other Anomalies of The Law That Make Us All Unsuspecting Criminals*. New York: TarcherPerigee, 2010.

Bentham, Jeremy. "An Introduction to the Principles of Morals and Legislation." Jonathan Bennett. PDF ed. Accessed December 19, 2022. https://www.earlymoderntexts.com/assets/pdfs/bentham1780.pdf.

Berenson, Robert A. "If You Can't Measure Performance, Can You Improve It?" JAMA 315, no. 7 (February 16, 2016): 645–46. https://doi.org/10.1001/jama.2016.0767.

Berlin, Isaiah. "Two Concepts of Liberty." In *The Proper Study of Mankind*. New York: Farrar, Straus, and Giroux, 1998.

"Bigfoot: Ordinance, Skamania County Washington State 'Bigfoot Ordinance.'" *Bigfoot Encounters*. Accessed December 19, 2022. http://www.bigfootencounters.com/articles/skamania-ordinance.htm.

Birch, David, and Ed Conway. *Identity Is the New Money*. London: London Publishing Partnership, 2014.

Black, Max. "The Gap Between 'Is' and 'Should.'" *The Philosophical Review* 73. no. 2 (1964): 165–181. doi:10.2307/2183334.

Black, Max. "The Prevalence of Humbug." Accessed July 18, 2022. http://www.ditext.com/black/humbug.html.

Boatright, John R. "Rent Seeking in a Market with Morality: Solving a Puzzle about Corporate Social Responsibility." *Journal of Business Ethics* 88 (2009): 541–52.

Bosché, Gabrielle. "The 7 Best And 5 Worst Mission Statements Of America's Top Brands." LinkedIn, January 2, 2019. https://www.linkedin.com/pulse/7-best-5-worst-mission-statements-americas-top-brands-bosch%C3%A9/.

Bowles, Cennydd. *Future Ethics*. East Sussex, UK: NowNext Press, 2018.

Buber, Martin. *I and Thou*. Translated by Walter Kaufmann. N.p., 1970.

"Buddhist Ethics." *Wikipedia*. Accessed July 10, 2022. https://en.wikipedia.org/w/index.php?title=Buddhist_ethics&oldid=1097348628.

Buerkli, Danny. "'What Gets Measured Gets Managed' — It's Wrong and Drucker Never Said It." Centre for Public Impact (blog). April 8, 2019. https://medium.com/centre-for-public-impact/what-gets-measured-gets-managed-its-wrong-and-drucker-never-said-it-fe95886d3df6.

"Business Ethics." *Wikipedia*. Accessed October 23, 2021. https://en.wikipedia.org/w/index.php?title=Business_ethics&oldid=1051381184.

Capaldi, Nicholas. "J. S. Mill and Business Ethics" in Heath and Kaldis.

Čapek, Karel, and Ivan Klima. *R.U.R.* Translated by Claudia Novack-Jones. New York: Penguin Classics, 2004.

Carson, Thomas L. *Lying and Deception: Theory and Practice*. Oxford: Oxford University Press, 2010.

Castiglione, Baldesar. *The Book of the Courtier*. N.p.: Baronial Press, 2016.

Caulkin, Simon. "The Rule Is Simple: Be Careful What You Measure." *The Guardian*. February 9, 2008. https://www.theguardian.com/business /2008/feb/10/businesscomment1.

Christen, Markus, Bert Gordijn, and Michele Loi. *The Ethics of Cybersecurity*. Germany: Springer, 2020.

Coeckelbergh, Mark. *AI Ethics*. Cambridge, MA: MIT Press, 2020.

Cohen, Julie E. "How Not to Write a Privacy Law: Disrupting Surveil-lance-Based Business Models Requires Government Innovation." Knight First Amendment Institute at Columbia University, March 23, 2021. https://knightcolumbia.org/content/how-not-to-write-a-privacy-law.

Coffee, John C. "'No Soul to Damn: No Body to Kick': An Unscandalized Inquiry into the Problem of Corporate Punishment." *Michigan Law Review* 79, no. 3 (1981): 386–459. https://doi.org/10.2307/1288201.

"Confucianism." *Wikipedia*. Accessed July 8, 2022. https://en.wikipedia.org /w/index.php?title=Confucianism&oldid=1097121885.

"Confucius." *Wikipedia*. Accessed July 14, 2022. https://en.wikipedia.org /w/index.php?title=Confucius&oldid=1098099451.

Confucius. "Analects." In *Delphi Collected Works of Confucius—Four Books and Five Classics of Confucianism*. Translated by James Legge. Hungary: Delphi Classics, 2016.

"Critique of Work." *Wikipedia*. Accessed July 20, 2022. https://en.wikipedia .org/w/index.php?title=Critique_of_work&oldid=1099345700.

Davisson, Amber, and Paul Booth, eds. *Controversies in Digital Ethics*. New York: Bloomsbury Academic, 2016.

Dembinski, P., C. Lager, A. Cornford, and J. Bonvin, eds. *Enron and World Finance: A Case Study in Ethics*. Basingstoke, UK: Palgrave Macmillan, 2005.

Den Uyl, Douglas J. "The Fortune of Others: Adam Smith and the Beauty of Commerce" in Heath and Kaldis.

Denning, Stephen. *The Age of Agile: How Smart Companies Are Transforming the Way Work Gets Done*. New York: AMACOM, 2018.

Denning, Steve. "Making Sense Of Shareholder Value: 'The World's Dumbest Idea.'" *Forbes*. Accessed July 23, 2022. https://www.forbes.com/sites /stevedenning/2017/07/17/making-sense-of-shareholder-value-the -worlds-dumbest-idea/.

Doerr, John, and Larry Page. *Measure What Matters: How Google, Bono, and the Gates Foundation Rock the World with OKRs*. New York: Portfolio, 2018.

Donaldson, Thomas, and Thomas W. Dunfee. *Ties That Bind: A Social Contracts Approach to Business Ethics*. Boston: Harvard Business Review Press, 1999.

Drucker, Peter F. *The Practice of Management*. New York: Harper & Brothers, 1954.

druckeradmin. "Measurement Myopia." Drucker Institute. Accessed December 18, 2022. https://www.drucker.institute/thedx/measurement -myopia/.

Drumwright, Minette E., and Patrick E. Murphy. "The Current State of Advertising Ethics: Industry and Academic Perspectives." *Journal of Advertising* 38, no. 1 (2009): 83–107.

Dunfee, Thomas W. "Corporate Governance in a Market with Morality." *Law and Contemporary Problems* 62, no. 3 (1999): 129–57. https://doi.org /10.2307/1192229.

Dunfee, Thomas W. "Do Firms with Unique Competencies for Rescuing Victims of Human Catastrophes Have Special Obligations? Corporate Responsibility and the AIDS Catastrophe in Sub-Saharan Africa." *Business Ethics Quarterly* 16, no. 2 (2006): 185–210.

Dunfee, Thomas W. "The Marketplace of Morality: First Steps toward a Theory of Moral Choice." *Business Ethics Quarterly* 8, no. 1 (1998): 127–45. https://doi.org/10.2307/3857525.

Dunfee, Thomas W. and Thomas Donaldson. "Contractarian Business Ethics: Current Status and Next Steps." *Business Ethics Quarterly* 5, no. 2 (1995): 173–86. https://doi.org/10.2307/3857352.

Duska, Ronald. "Business Ethics: Oxymoron or Good Business?" *Business Ethics Quarterly* 10, no. 1 (2000): 111–29. https://doi.org/10.2307/3857699.

Elstein, David and Qing Tian. "Confucian Business Ethics: Opportunities and Challenges," in Heath and Kaldis.

Epstein, David J. *Range: Why Generalists Triumph in a Specialized World*. New York: Riverhead Books, 2019.

Farrow, Katherine, Gilles Grolleau, and Naoufel Mzoughi. "'Let's Call a Spade a Spade, Not a Gardening Tool': How Euphemisms Shape Moral Judgement in Corporate Social Responsibility Domains." *Journal of Business Research* 131 (July 1, 2021): 254–67. https://doi.org/10.1016/j.jbusres .2021.04.002.

Ferris, Joshua. *Then We Came to the End*. Boston: Little, Brown, 2007.

Fforde, Jasper. *The Fourth Bear: A Nursery Crime*. Rep. ed. New York: Penguin Books, 2007.

Fisher, M. F. K. "As the Lingo Languishes." In *The State of the Language*. Edited by Leonard Michaels and Christopher Ricks. Berkeley: University of California Press, 1980.

Ford, Henry. *My Life and Work*. Grapevine, 2019.

Frankfurt, Harry G. *On Bullshit*. Princeton, NJ: Princeton University Press, 2009.

Franklin, Benjamin. *Franklin's Autobiography*. Edited by O. Leon Reid. N.p.: Good Press, 2021.

Freeman, R. Edward, and Robert A. Phillips. "Stakeholder Theory: A Libertarian Defense." *Business Ethics Quarterly* 12, no. 3 (2002): 331–49. https://doi.org/10.2307/3858020.

French, Peter A. "The Corporation as a Moral Person." *American Philosophical Quarterly* 16, no. 3 (1979): 207–15.

"Friedman Doctrine." In *Wikipedia*, July 26, 2021. https://en.wikipedia.org/w/index.php?title=Friedman_doctrine&oldid=1035607602.

Friedman, Milton. "A Friedman Doctrine—The Social Responsibility Of Business Is to Increase Its Profits." *New York Times* (September 13, 1970). Sec. Archives. https://www.nytimes.com/1970/09/13/archives/a-friedman-doctrine-the-social-responsibility-of-business-is-to.html.

Friedman, Milton, and Binyamin Appelbaum. *Capitalism and Freedom*. Chicago: University of Chicago Press, 2020.

Gardner, Daniel K. *Confucianism: A Very Short Introduction*. Ill. ed. Oxford: Oxford University Press, 2014.

Gelles, David. "What Jack Welch Got Wrong (Just About Everything)." LinkedIn. Accessed December 22, 2022. https://www.linkedin.com/pulse/what-jack-welch-got-wrong-just-everything-david-gelles/.

Gilbert, David. "Facebook Legally Can't Roll out Its Suicide Prevention AI in Europe." *Vice*. November 29, 2017. https://www.vice.com/en/article/j5ddn8/facebook-legally-cant-roll-out-its-suicide-prevention-ai-in-europe.

Graeber, David. *Bullshit Jobs: A Theory*. New York: Simon & Schuster, 2018.

Grey, Christopher, and Jana Costas. *Secrecy at Work: The Hidden Architecture of Organizational Life*. Stanford, CA: Stanford Business Books, 2016.

Harford, Tim. *The Data Detective: Ten Easy Rules to Make Sense of Statistics*. New York: Riverhead Books, 2021.

Harris, Sam. *The Moral Landscape: How Science Can Determine Human Values*. Rep. ed. New York: Free Press, 2010.

Harrison, Clare. "A Glossary of IT Euphemisms." *IR Magazine*. August 29, 2016. https://www.irmagazine.com/regulation/glossary-ir-euphemisms.

Hartocollis, Anemona. "U.S. News Ranked Columbia No. 2, but a Math Professor Has His Doubts." *New York Times*, March 17, 2022, sec. U.S. https://www.nytimes.com/2022/03/17/us/columbia-university-rank.html.

Harvey, Andrew, and Archana Venkatesan. *The Kural: Tiruvalluvar's Tirukkural*. Translated by Thomas Hitoshi Pruiksma. Boston: Beacon Press, 2022.

Hasnas, John. "The Normative Theories of Business Ethics: A Guide for the Perplexed." *Business Ethics Quarterly* 8, no. 1 (1998): 19–42. https://doi .org/10.2307/3857520.

Hastings, Reed. "Enron, Whose Leaders Went To." PowerPoint presentation. August 1, 2009. https://www.slideshare.net/reed2001/culture-1798664 /6-Enron_whose_leaders_went_to.

Heath, Eugene, and Byron Kaldis, eds. *Wealth, Commerce, and Philosophy: Foundational Thinkers and Business Ethics.* Chicago: University of Chicago Press, 2017.

Heath, Joseph. "Business Ethics and Moral Motivation: A Criminological Perspective." *Journal of Business Ethics* 83, no. 4 (December 2008): 595–614. https://doi.org/10.1007/s10551-007-9641-8.

Hesiod. *Hesiod & The Hesiodic Corpus: Including Theogony & Works and Days.* Translated by Hugh G. Evelyn-White. N.p.: e-artnow, 2021.

Hobbes, Thomas. "Leviathan." In *Ethics: The Essential Writings*, edited by Gordon Marino. New York: Modern Library, 2010.

"How (Not) to Write a Privacy Law." Accessed July 14, 2022. http://knight columbia.org/content/how-not-to-write-a-privacy-law.

Hubbard, Douglas. *How to Measure Anything: Finding the Value of Intangibles in Business.* 3rd edition. Hoboken, NJ: Wiley, 2014.

Huff, Darrell. *How to Lie with Statistics. Reissue* ed. New York: W. W. Norton, 2010.

Hume, David. *A Treatise of Human Nature.* Digireads.com, 2004.

Hursthouse, Rosalind, and Glen Pettigrove. "Virtue Ethics." In *The Stanford Encyclopedia of Philosophy*, edited by Edward N. Zalta, Winter 2018. https://plato.stanford.edu/archives/win2018/entries/ethics-virtue/.

"Hyatt Hotels Corporation | U.S. Green Building Council." Accessed February 18, 2023. https://www.usgbc.org/organizations/hyatt-hotels-corporation.

Internation Centre for Missing & Exploited Children. "International Centre for Missing & Exploited Children (ICMEC) Expands with AI, Biometrics, and Ad Tech." *PR Newswire.* November 27, 2018. https://www. prnewswire.com/news-releases/international-centre-for-missing--exploited-children-icmec-expands-with-ai-biometrics-and-ad-tech-300755796. html.

Jackall, Robert. *Moral Mazes: The World of Corporate Managers.* Up. ed. Oxford: Oxford University Press, 2009.

Jasanoff, Sheila. *The Ethics of Invention: Technology and the Human Future.* New York: W. W. Norton, 2016.

"Jewish Business Ethics." In *Wikipedia.* March 14, 2022. https://en.wikipedia .org/w/index.php?title=Jewish_business_ethics&oldid=1077108338.

Kagan, Shelly. *Normative Ethics*. New York: Routledge, 2018.

Kant, Immanuel. "Fundamental Principles of the Metaphysic Of Morals." Accessed December 15, 2022. https://www.gutenberg.org/files/5682 /5682-h/5682-h.htm.

Kant, Immanuel. "Fundamental Principles of the Metaphysics of Morals."In *Ethics: The Essential Writings*, edited by Gordon Marino. New York: Modern Library, 2010.

Kant, Immanuel. *Kant: Groundwork of the Metaphysics of Morals*. Translated by Mary Gregor and Jens Timmermann. 2nd ed. Cambridge: Cambridge University Press, 2012.

Kantor, Jodi, and Arya Sundaram. "The Rise of the Worker Productivity Score." *New York Times*. August 14, 2022. https://www.nytimes.com /interactive/2022/08/14/business/worker-productivity-tracking.html.

Kearns, Michael, and Aaron Roth. *The Ethical Algorithm: The Science of Socially Aware Algorithm Design*. Oxford: Oxford University Press, 2019.

Kennedy, Jessica A., Tae Wan Kim, and Alan Strudler. "Hierarchies and Dignity: A Confucian Communitarian Approach." *Business Ethics Quarterly* 26, no. 4 (2016): 479–502. doi:10.1017/beq.2016.17.

Kiel, Fred. *Return on Character: The Real Reason Leaders and Their Companies Win*. Harvard: Harvard Business Review Press, 2015.

Kim, Tae Wan, and Alan Strudler. "Workplace Civility: A Confucian Approach." *Business Ethics Quarterly* 22, no. 3 (2012): 557–77.

Klein, Christopher. "How South America Became a Nazi Haven." HISTORY. Accessed December 24, 2022. https://www.history.com/ how-south new /-america-became-a-nazi-haven.

Koehn, Daryl, and Barry Wilbratte. "A Defense of a Thomistic Concept of the Just Price." *Business Ethics Quarterly* 22, no. 3 (2012): 501–26.

"Kolobok." In *Wikipedia*, December 22, 2021. https://en.wikipedia.org/w /index.php?title=Kolobok&oldid=1061487093.

"Leadership Principles." Amazon. Accessed December 29, 2022. https:// amazon.jobs/content/en/our-workplace/leadership-principles.

Lepore, Jill. "Not So Fast." *New Yorker*. October 5, 2009. https://www.new yorker.com/magazine/2009/10/12/not-so-fast.

Leopold, Aldo. "A Sand County Almanac." In *Ethics: The Essential Writings*, edited by Gordon Marino. New York: Modern Library, 2010.

Levitt, Steven. *Freakonomics: Revised and Expanded Edition*. Rev., exp. ed. New York: William Morrow Paperbacks, 2020.

Linsley, Alice C. "Ethics Forum: Ancient Moral Codes." *Ethics Forum* (blog), December 6, 2010. http://college-ethics.blogspot.com/2010/12/ancient -moral-codes.html.

Love, Dylan. "16 Examples Of Steve Jobs Being A Huge Jerk." *Business Insider*. Accessed December 22, 2022. https://www.businessinsider.com/steve-jobs-jerk-2011-10.

Luban, David, Alan Strudler, and David Wasserman. "Moral Responsibility in the Age of Bureaucracy." *Michigan Law Review* 90, no. 8 (1992): 2348–92. https://doi.org/10.2307/1289575.

Lyons, Dan. *Lab Rats: Tech Gurus, Junk Science, and Management Fads—My Quest to Make Work Less Miserable*. New York: Hachette Books, 2018.

MacIntyre, Alasdair. *After Virtue: A Study in Moral Theory*, 3rd ed. Notre Dame, IN: University of Notre Dame Press, 2007.

Marcoux, Alexei. "The Power and the Limits of Milton Friedman's Arguments Against Corporate Social Responsibility" in Heath and Kaldis.

Marino, Gordon, ed. *Ethics: The Essential Writings*. New York: Modern Library, 2010.

McLean, Bethany, Peter Elkind, and Joe Nocera. *The Smartest Guys in the Room: The Amazing Rise and Scandalous Fall of Enron*. Rep. ed. New York: Portfolio, 2013.

McLuhan, Marshall. *The Mechanical Bride: Folklore of Industrial Man*. Illustrated edition. Berkeley, CA: Gingko Press, 2008.

Menand, Louis. *The Free World: Art and Thought in the Cold War*. New York: Farrar, Straus and Giroux, 2021.

Michaelson, Christopher. "Meaningful Work and Moral Worth." *Business & Professional Ethics Journal* 28, no. 1/4 (2009): 27–48.

Michaelson, Christopher, Michael G. Pratt, Adam M. Grant, and Craig P. Dunn. "Meaningful Work: Connecting Business Ethics and Organization Studies." *Journal of Business Ethics* 121, no. 1 (2014): 77–90.

Mill, John Stuart. *Utilitarianism (Annotated): University Edition*. Dublin, OH: Coventry House Publishing, 2017.

Miller, Michael. "Enron's Ethics Code Reads like Fiction." *Columbia Business First*. Accessed May 6, 2022. https://www.bizjournals.com/columbus/stories/2002/04/01/editorial3.html.

Moore, Geoff. *Virtue at Work: Ethics for Individuals, Managers, and Organizations*. Rep. ed. Oxford: Oxford University Press, 2017.

Moriarty, Jeffrey. "Business Ethics." In *The Stanford Encyclopedia of Philosophy*, edited by Edward N. Zalta, Fall 2021. https://plato.stanford.edu/archives/fall2021/entries/ethics-business/.

Mosley, Eric, and Derek Irvine. *Making Work Human: How Human-Centered Companies Are Changing the Future of Work and the World*. New York: McGraw-Hill Education, 2020.

Muller, Jerry Z. *The Tyranny of Metrics*. Rep. ed. Princeton, NJ: Princeton University Press, 2019.

Mumford, Lewis, and Langdon Winner. *Technics and Civilization*. Rep. ed. Chicago: University of Chicago Press, 2010.

Nadkarni, M. V. "Does Hinduism Lack Social Concern?" *Economic and Political Weekly* 42, no. 20 (2007): 1844–49.

Noddings, Nel. "Caring: A Feminine Approach to Ethics and Moral Education." In *Ethics: The Essential Writings*, edited by Gordon Marino. New York: Modern Library, 2010.

Oates, Joyce Carol. "Frankenstein's Fallen Angel." *Critical Inquiry* 10, no. 3 (1984): 543–54.

Ooker. "Did Lord Kelvin Say 'If You Can Not Measure It, You Can Not Improve It'?" Forum post. *Skeptics Stack Exchange*. September 30, 2018. https://skeptics.stackexchange.com/q/42436.

Osnos, Evan. "The Big House: Life After White-Collar Crime." *New Yorker*, August 30, 2021.

Oxford Eagle Contributors. "Doublespeak Dominates Our Language." *The Oxford Eagle*. February 24, 2017. https://www.oxfordeagle.com/2017/02/24/doublespeak-dominates-our-language/.

Peacock, Mark S. "Wealth and Commerce in Archaic Greece: Homer and Hesiod" in Heath and Kaldis.

Penn, William. *Some Fruits of Solitude: Including A Sermon Preached at the Quaker's Meeting House, in Gracechurch-Street, London, Eighth Month 12th, 1694*. N.p.: Studium Publishing, 2018.

Perrini, Francesco. *Review of The Market for Virtue. The Potential and Limits of Corporate Social Responsibility*, by David Vogel. *Academy of Management Perspectives* 21, no. 3 (2007): 107–9.

Peters, Tom, and Robert H. Waterman. *In Search of Excellence: Lessons from America's Best-Run Companies*. New York: Harper Business, 2012.

Pires, Guilherme D., and John Stanton. "Ethnic Marketing Ethics." *Journal of Business Ethics* 36, no. 1/2 (2002): 111–18.

Plato, "Euthyphro." In *Plato: The Collected Dialogues*. Edited by Edith Hamilton and Huntington Cairns. Princeton, NJ: Princeton University Press, 1989.

"Plutarch on Alexander." Livius.org. Accessed December 21, 2022. https://www.livius.org/sources/content/plutarch/plutarchs-alexanders-fortune/an-ancient-assessment-of-alexander/. An excerpt from Plutarch, *Alexander's Fortune and Virtue* (328c–329d).

"P.T. Barnum | Biography, Circus, Facts, & Quotes | Britannica." Accessed January 18, 2022. https://www.britannica.com/biography/P-T-Barnum.

"PT Barnum, The Shakespeare of Advertising." Accessed January 18, 2022. http://www.ptbarnum.org/humbugs.html.

Quantified Self. "Measured Me Archives." Accessed December 23, 2022. https://quantifiedself.com/blog/tag/measured-me/.

Quddus, Munir and Salim Rashid. "The Ethics of Commerce in Islam: Ibn Khaldun's Muqaddimah Revisited" in Heath and Kaldis.

Reich, Robert. "The Rebirth Of Stakeholder Capitalism?" *Social Europe*. August 12, 2014. https://socialeurope.eu/stakeholder-capitalism.

Reiley, Laura. "'What Idiot Do You Think I Am?' Customers Chafe As Rewards Programs Are Pared Back." *Washington Post*. October 11, 2022. https://www.washingtonpost.com/business/2022/10/11/dunkin-loyalty-points-customers/.

Reuters. "India Says It Accidentally Fired Missile into Pakistan." March 11, 2022. https://www.reuters.com/world/asia-pacific/india-says-it-accidentally-fired-missile-into-pakistan-2022-03-11/.

Ries, Eric. *The Lean Startup: How Today's Entrepreneurs Use Continuous Innovation to Create Radically Successful Businesses*. New York: Currency, 2011.

Riesman, David, Nathan Glazer, and Reuel Denney. *The Lonely Crowd: A Study of the Changing American Character*. Abr. and rev. ed. New Haven. CT: Yale University Press, 2020.

Russell, Bertrand. *Praise of Idleness: And Other Essays*. 2nd edition. New York: Routledge, 2020.

Ryan, Garrett. *Naked Statues, Fat Gladiators, and War Elephants: Frequently Asked Questions about the Ancient Greeks and Romans*. Guilford, CT: Prometheus, 2021.

Sandel, Michael J. *What Money Can't Buy: The Moral Limits of Markets*. Rep. ed. New York: Farrar, Straus and Giroux, 2012.

Sartre, Jean-Paul. "Existentialism and Human Emotion." *Ethics: The Essential Writings*, edited by Gordon Marino. New York: Modern Library, 2010.

Savitz, Eric. "The New Factors Of Production And the Rise of Data-Driven Applications." *Forbes*. Accessed July 14, 2022. https://www.forbes.com/sites/ciocentral/2011/10/31/the-new-factors-of-production-and-the-rise-of-data-driven-applications/.

Sayre-McCord, Geoffrey. *Kant's Grounding for the Metaphysics of Morals*. Chapel Hill, NC: University of North Carolina at Chapel Hill, 2002.

Schlag, Martin. "Thomas Aquinas: The Economy at the Service of Justice and the Common Good" in Heath and Kaldis.

Schopenhauer, Arthur. *Parerga and Paralipomena: Part II*. Translated by Tim Newcomb. Newcomb Livraria Press, 2022.

Schultz, Barton. "Henry Sidgwick." In *The Stanford Encyclopedia of Philosophy* (Winter 2021). Edited by Edward N. Zalta. https://plato.stanford.edu/archives/win2021/entries/sidgwick/.

Schwartz, Mark. *The (Delicate) Art of Bureaucracy*. Portland, OR: IT Revolution Press, 2020.

Schwartz, Mark. *A Seat at the Table*. Portland, OR: IT Revolution Press, 2017.

Schwartz, Mark. *War and Peace and IT*. Portland, OR: IT Revolution Press, 2019.

Scott, James C. *Seeing Like a State: How Certain Scheme to Improve the Human Condition Have Failed*. New Haven, CT: Yale University Press, 1998.

Shadnam, Masoud, and Thomas B. Lawrence. "Understanding Widespread Misconduct in Organizations: An Institutional Theory of Moral Collapse." *Business Ethics Quarterly* 21, no. 3 (2011): 379–407.

Shakespeare, William. "The Second Part of King Henry the Fourth." In *The Pelican Shakespeare. William Shakespeare: The Complete Works*. Edited by Alfred Harbage. The Viking Press, 1969.

Shelley, Mary. *Frankenstein*. Edited by J. Paul Hunter. Third Edition. New York: W. W. Norton & Company, 2021.

Smith, Adam. *The Wealth of Nations*. First published 1776. This edition published by Enhanced Media, 2016. Kindle version.

Smith, Eleanor. "Why You Bought That Ugly Sweater." *Atlantic*. November 17, 2015. https://www.theatlantic.com/magazine/archive/2015/12/why-you-bought-that-ugly-sweater/413161/.

Smith, Larry. "Shift-Left Testing." *Dr. Dobb's Journal* 26, no. 9 (September 1, 2001): 56–ff.

State Farm. "Company Overview." State Farm. Accessed February 6, 2023. https://www.statefarm.com/about-us/company-overview.

Status.net. "1500+ Best Company Vision and Mission Statements [by Industry]," November 24, 2022. https://status.net/best-company-slogans-vision-mission-statements-examples/.

Stewart, Ian. *Do Dice Play God?: The Mathematics of Uncertainty*. Ill. ed. New York: Basic Books, 2019.

Stewart, Matthew. *The Management Myth: Debunking Modern Business Philosophy*. Rep. ed. New York: W. W. Norton, 2009.

Stout, Lynn A. "The Toxic Side Effects of Shareholder Primacy." *University of Pennsylvania Law Review* 161, no. 7 (2013): 2003–23.

Strudler, Alan. "The Distinctive Wrong in Lying." *Ethical Theory and Moral Practice* 13, no. 2 (2010): 171–79.

Sutton, Bob. "A Compilation of Euphemisms for Layoffs." *Bob Sutton: Work Matters*. November 16, 2008. https://bobsutton.typepad.com/my_weblog /2008/11/a-compilation-of-euphemisms-for-layoffs.html.

Swartz, Mimi. "How Enron Blew It." *Texas Monthly*, November 1, 2001. https://www.texasmonthly.com/the-culture/how-enron-blew-it/.

Taka, Iwao, and Thomas W. Dunfee. "Japanese Moralogy as Business Ethics." *Journal of Business Ethics* 16, no. 5 (1997): 507–19.

Terkel, Studs. *Working: People Talk About What They Do All Day and How They Feel About What They Do*. New York: The New Press, 2011.

Thaler, Richard H., and Cass R. Sunstein. *Nudge: Improving Decisions About Health, Wealth, and Happiness*. Rev., exp. ed. New York: Penguin Books, 2009.

"The Gingerbread Man." Accessed November 7, 2021. https://americanlitera ture.com/childrens-stories/the-gingerbread-man.

Toeniskoetter, Clare. "Meet the Man on a Mission to Expose Sneaky Price Increases." *New York Times*. November 26, 2022, sec. Climate. https:// www.nytimes.com/2022/11/26/climate/fighting-shrinkflation-consumer -products.html.

Tom, Tootin'. *Gary the Farting Gingerbread Man: A Funny Read Aloud Rhyming Christmas Picture Book For Children and Parents*, Great Kids Stocking Stuffer for the Winter Holidays. N.p.: Independently published, 2021.

Trabert, Justin. "Flatware Placement: On the Right or Left Side of the Plate." *Artful Matters with Justin* (blog). October 24, 2016. https://www .artfulmatters.net/flatware-placment-right -left-side-history-flatware -placement-tabletop/.

Trex, Ethan. "Indiana Once Tried to Change Pi to 3.2." *Mental Floss*. March 13, 2016. https://www.mentalfloss.com/article/30214/new-math-time -indiana-tried-change-pi-32.

Tyson, Peter. *Madagascar: The Eighth Continent: Life, Death and Discovery in a Lost World*. Chesham, Bucks, United Kingdom: Bradt Travel Guides, 2013.

University, Santa Clara. "What Really Went Wrong with Enron? A Culture of Evil?" Accessed August 11, 2022. https://www.scu.edu/ethics/focus -areas/business-ethics/resources/what-really-went-wrong-with-enron/.

Vallor, Shannon. *Technology and the Virtues: A Philosophical Guide to a Future Worth Wanting*. Oxford: Oxford University Press, 2016.

Varden, Helga. "Kant and Lying to the Murderer at the Door . . . One More Time: Kant's Legal Philosophy and Lies to Murderers and Nazis." *Journal of Social Philosophy* 41, no. 4 (December 2010): 403–21. https://doi.org /10.1111/j.1467-9833.2010.01507.x.

Velasquez, Manuel. "Debunking Corporate Moral Responsibility." *Business Ethics Quarterly* 13, no. 4 (2003): 531–62.

Velasquez, Manuel. "Why Corporations Are Not Morally Responsible for Anything They Do." *Business & Professional Ethics Journal* 2, no. 3 (1983): 1–18.

Vigen, Tyler. *Spurious Correlations*. New York: Hachette Books, 2015.

Weber, Max. *Economy and Society: Outline of Interpretive Sociology*. Volume 2. Edited by G. Roth and C. Wittich. Berkeley, CA: University of California Press, 1978. Kindle Edition.

Weber, Max, Peter Baehr, and Gordon C. Wells. *The Protestant Ethic and the Spirit of Capitalism: And Other Writings*. New York: Penguin Classics, 2002.

Weld, Daniel S., and Gagan Bansal. "The Challenge of Crafting Intelligible Intelligence." *Communications of the ACM* 62, no. 6 (May 21, 2019): 70–79. https://doi.org/10.1145/3282486.

Whyte, William H. *The Organization Man: The Book That Defined a Generation*. Rev. ed. Philadelphia: University of Pennsylvania Press, 2013.

Winkler, Adam. "'Corporations Are People' Is Built on an Incredible 19th-Century Lie." *The Atlantic*. March 5, 2018. https://www.theatlantic.com /business/archive/2018/03/corporations-people-adam-winkler/554852/.

Worldcrunch. "Inside The Bizarre, Data-Driven World Of Lifeloggers." July 4, 2014. https://worldcrunch.com/culture-society/inside-the -bizarre-data-driven-world-of-lifeloggers.

Yankelovich, Daniel. *Profit with Honor: The New Stage of Market Capitalism*. New Haven, CT: Yale University Press, 2006.

NOTES

Introduction

1. Schwartz, *War and Peace and IT*, xviii.
2. Schwartz, *The (Delicate) Art of Bureaucracy*, xxxiv.
3. Berlin, "Two Concepts of Liberty," 239.
4. Plato, "Euthyphro" in *Plato: The Collected Dialogues*, 178.
5. Shelley, *Frankenstein*, 342.
6. Harvey and Venkatesan, *The Kural*, 112, ch 108 verse 1073.
7. Belofsky, *The Book of Strange and Curious Legal Oddities*, 171.
8. Belofsky, *The Book of Strange and Curious Legal Oddities*, 188.
9. Belofsky, *The Book of Strange and Curious Legal Oddities*, 67.
10. Belofsky, *The Book of Strange and Curious Legal Oddities*, 14.
11. "Bigfoot: Ordinance, Skamania County Washington State 'Bigfoot Ordinance.'"
12. Trex, "Indiana Once Tried to Change Pi to 3.2."
13. Belofsky, *The Book of Strange and Curious Legal Odditiess*, 67.
14. Belofsky, *The Book of Strange and Curious Legal Oddities*, 178, referencing Canada Criminal Code, § 430.
15. Discussion here: https://skeptics.stackexchange.com/questions/31257 /was-there-a-law-ever-passed-that-prevented-two-trains-from-proceeding -at-a-cross, retrieved 12/17/2022. See bibliography for more.
16. Schwartz, *War and Peace and IT*, ix–x.

CHAPTER 1

1. Schwartz, *War and Peace and IT*, xviii.
2. Weber, *Economy and Society*, Kindle loc. 20521.
3. Weber, *Economy and Society*, Kindle loc. 6215–6228.
4. Weber, Baehr, and Wells, *The Protestant Ethic and the Spirit of Capitalism*, 108.
5. Weber, *Economy and Society*, 20521.
6. Ford, *My Life and Work*, loc 1394–1400.
7. Ford, as quoted in Stewart, *The Management Myth*, 57.
8. Whyte, *The Organization Man*, 23.
9. Menand, *The Free World*, 349, paraphrasing Berlin's "Two Concepts of Liberty."

10. Graeber, *Bullshit Jobs*, 87.
11. Graeber, *Bullshit Jobs*, 88.
12. Graeber, *Bullshit Jobs*, 88.
13. Terkel, *Working*, 27.
14. Whyte, *The Organization Man*, 7.
15. Stewart, *The Management Myth*, 35.
16. Stewart, *The Management Myth*, 183.
17. Dunfee, "The Marketplace of Morality," 143.
18. Dunfee, "The Marketplace of Morality," 143.
19. "About Us," Progressive.
20. Yankelovich, *Profit with Honor*, 112.
21. Graeber, *Bullshit Jobs*, loc 107.
22. Graeber, *Bullshit Jobs*, loc 4001.
23. Whyte, *The Organization Man*, 39.

CHAPTER 2

1. "Plutarch on Alexander."
2. Hobbes, "Leviathan," 142.
3. Castiglione, *The Book of the Courtier*, 34.
4. Gardner, *Confucianism*, 27.
5. Hesiod, *Hesiod & the Hesiodic Corpus*," 579.
6. Trabert, "Flatware Placement."
7. Tyson, *Madagascar*, 40.
8. MacIntyre, *After Virtue*, 112, citing anthropologist Mary Douglas's statement that "Deprive the taboo rules of their original context and they at once are apt to appear as a set of arbitrary prohibitions."
9. MacIntyre, *After Virtue*, 38.
10. Kagan, *Normative Ethics*, 60.
11. Aristotle, *Nicomachean Ethics*, 14; Book I, section 10.
12. Capaldi, "J. S. Mill and Business Ethics," 305.
13. Schopenhauer, *Parerga and Paralipomena*, 179.
14. Mill, *Utilitarianism*, 19.
15. Schultz, "Henry Sidgwick."
16. Bentham, "An Introduction to the Principles of Morals and Legislation," 22.
17. Vallor, *Technology and the Virtues*, 7.
18. Kant, "Fundamental Principles of the Metaphysics of Morals," 214.
19. Schopenhauer, *Parerga and Paralipomena*, 183.
20. Harris, *The Moral Landscape*, 71.

21. Harris, *The Moral Landscape*, 71.
22. Kagan, *Normative Ethics*, 71.
23. Kant, "Fundamental Principles of the Metaphysics of Morals," 197.
24. MacIntyre, *After Virtue*, 55.
25. Kant, "Fundamental Principles of the Metaphysics of Morals," 208.
26. Kant, "Fundamental Principles of the Metaphysics of Morals," 217.
27. Sayre-McCord, *Kant's Grounding for the Metaphysics of Morals*, 5.
28. MacIntyre, *After Virtue*, 45.
29. Kant and Korsgaard ed., *Kant*, 48.
30. Kant, "Fundamental Principles of the Metaphysics of Morals," 224.
31. Donaldson and Dunfee, *Ties That Bind*, 33.
32. Vallor, *Technology and the Virtues*, 100.
33. Kagan, *Normative Ethics*, 83.
34. Vallor, *Technology and the Virtues*, 23.
35. Kagan, *Normative Ethics*, 137.
36. Kagan, *Normative Ethics*, 139.
37. Kagan, *Normative Ethics*, 108.
38. Kennedy, Kim, and Strudler, "Hierarchies and Dignity," 480.
39. Capaldi, "J. S. Mill and Business Ethics," 305.

CHAPTER 3

1. MacIntyre, *After Virtue*, 126.
2. Vallor, *Technology and the Virtues*, 36.
3. Vallor, *Technology and the Virtues*, 120.
4. Vallor, *Technology and the Virtues*, 25.
5. Vallor, *Technology and the Virtues*, 105.
6. Gardner, *Confucianism*, 16–18.
7. "Confucianism."
8. Vallor, *Technology and the Virtues*, 38.
9. Vallor, *Technology and the Virtues*, 80.
10. Vallor, *Technology and the Virtues*, 83.
11. Vallor, *Technology and the Virtues*, 40.
12. MacIntyre, *After Virtue*, 95.
13. Donaldson and Dunfee, *Ties That Bind*, viii.
14. MacIntrye, as quoted/paraphrased in Moore, *Virtue at Work*, 41.
15. Aristotle, *Nicomachean Ethics*, 26.
16. Franklin, *Franklin's Autobiography*, 34.
17. Franklin, *Franklin's Autobiography*, 35.

18. Confucius, "Analects," 4:17.
19. Love, "16 Examples Of Steve Jobs Being A Huge Jerk."
20. Gelles, "What Jack Welch Got Wrong (Just About Everything)."
21. Aristophanes, *The Clouds*, 21.
22. Graeber, *Bullshit Jobs*, 236.
23. Noddings, "Caring," 427.
24. Noddings, "Caring," 439–440.
25. Vallor, *Technology and the Virtues*, 116.
26. Noddings, "Caring," 437.
27. Elstein and Tian, "Confucian Business Ethics," 57.
28. Vallor, *Technology and the Virtues*, 103.
29. Sartre, "Existentialism and Human Emotion," 15, 328.
30. MacIntyre, *After Virtue*, 117,
31. MacIntyre, *After Virtue*, 40.
32. Donaldson and Dunfee, *Ties That Bind*, 16–17.
33. Donaldson and Dunfee, *Ties That Bind*, 167.
34. Bowles, *Future Ethics*, 190.
35. Hursthouse and Pettigrove, "Virtue Ethics."

CHAPTER 4

1. Samuel Johnson quoted in Heath and Kaldis, *Wealth, Commerce, and Philosophy*, 2.
2. Black, "The Prevalence of Humbug."
3. "Jewish Business Ethics."
4. Harvey and Venkatesan, *The Kural*, xxxii, but no one's too sure. It could have been as early as 300 BCE, according to Wikipedia.
5. Harvey and Venkatesan, *The Kural*, 88 verse 840 chapter 84.
6. Peacock, "Wealth and Commerce in Archaic Greece," 20.
7. Peacock, "Wealth and Commerce in Archaic Greece," 20.
8. Aristotle, "Politics," Politics 629–630; III.5.1278a20–21.
9. Gardner, *Confucianism*, 88.
10. Heath and Kaldis, *Wealth, Commerce, and Philosophy*, 103.
11. Heath and Kaldis, *Wealth, Commerce, and Philosophy*, 150.
12. Heath and Kaldis, *Wealth, Commerce, and Philosophy*, 105.
13. Heath and Kaldis, *Wealth, Commerce, and Philosophy*, 106.
14. Heath and Kaldis, *Wealth, Commerce, and Philosophy*, 117.
15. Smith, *The Wealth of Nations*, loc 6280.
16. Duska, "Business Ethics," 116.

17. Velasquez, "Why Corporations Are Not Morally Responsible for Anything They Do," 4.
18. Velasquez, "Why Corporations Are Not Morally Responsible for Anything They Do," 15.
19. Friedman, "A Friedman Doctrine—The Social Responsibility Of Business Is to Increase Its Profits."
20. Friedman and Appelbaum, *Capitalism and Freedom*, 17.
21. Friedman and Appelbaum, *Capitalism and Freedom*, 161.
22. Dunfee, "Do Firms with Unique Competencies for Rescuing Victims of Human Catastrophes Have Special Obligations?" 202.
23. Stout, "The Toxic Side Effects of Shareholder Primacy," 2004.
24. Reich, "The Rebirth Of Stakeholder Capitalism?"
25. Duska, "Business Ethics."
26. Stout, "The Toxic Side Effects of Shareholder Primacy," 2013 note 45.
27. Stout, "The Toxic Side Effects of Shareholder Primacy," 2013.
28. Stout, "The Toxic Side Effects of Shareholder Primacy," 2013.
29. Stout, "The Toxic Side Effects of Shareholder Primacy," 2013.
30. Stout, "The Toxic Side Effects of Shareholder Primacy," 2013.
31. Marcoux, "The Power and the Limits of Milton Friedman's Arguments Against Corporate Social Responsibility," 375: quoting an exchange between Mackey and Friedman in "Rethinking the Social Responsibility of Business" (debate featuring Milton Friedman, John Mackey, and T. J. Rodgers), *Reason*, October 2005, http://reason.com/archives/2005/10/01/rethinking-the-social-responsi.
32. Freeman and Phillips, "Stakeholder Theory," 341.
33. Freeman and Phillips, "Stakeholder Theory," 337.
34. Denning, "Making Sense Of Shareholder Value."
35. Stout, "The Toxic Side Effects of Shareholder Primacy," 2017.
36. Stout, "The Toxic Side Effects of Shareholder Primacy," 2019, citing John R. Graham et al., "Value Destruction and Financial Reporting Decisions," *Financial Analysts Journal*, vol. 62 no. 6, 31.
37. Denning, *The Age of Agile*, 193.
38. Denning, "Making Sense Of Shareholder Value."
39. Graeber, *Bullshit Jobs*, 190.
40. Friedman and Appelbaum, *Capitalism and Freedom*, 160.
41. Friedman, "A Friedman Doctrine."
42. Kagan, *Normative Ethics*, 135.
43. Status.net, "1500+ Best Company Vision and Mission Statements [by Industry]."

44. Bosché, "(1) The 7 Best And 5 Worst Mission Statements Of America's Top Brands | LinkedIn."
45. "Hyatt Hotels Corporation | U.S. Green Building Council."
46. Hasnas, "The Normative Theories of Business Ethics," 32.
47. Dunfee and Donaldson, "Contractarian Business Ethics," 177.
48. Dunfee, "Corporate Governance in a Market with Morality," 132.
49. Denning, "Making Sense Of Shareholder Value."
50. Dunfee, "Do Firms with Unique Competencies for Rescuing Victims of Human Catastrophes Have Special Obligations?" 185.
51. Dunfee, "Do Firms with Unique Competencies for Rescuing Victims of Human Catastrophes Have Special Obligations?" 197, citing Scanlon, *What We Owe to Each Other*, Cambridge, Mass.: The Belknap Press of Harvard University Press, 1998, 224.
52. Dunfee, "Do Firms with Unique Competencies for Rescuing Victims of Human Catastrophes Have Special Obligations?" 197.
53. Moriarty, "Business Ethics."
54. Leopold, "A Sand County Almanac," 489.

CHAPTER 5

1. Baskar, "Data—A New Factor of Production."
2. Muller, *The Tyranny of Metrics*, 47.
3. Augemburg seems to have taken down the measurements, but a version of his site is available in his archives: Augemburg, "Quantified Self," in "Measured Me Archives." See also: Worldcrunch, "Inside The Bizarre, Data-Driven World Of Lifeloggers."
4. Muller, *The Tyranny of Metrics*, 17.
5. druckeradmin, "Measurement Myopia."
6. Muller, *The Tyranny of Metrics*, 107.
7. Ooker, "Did Lord Kelvin Say 'If You Can Not Measure It, You Can Not Improve It'?"
8. Berenson, "If You Can't Measure Performance, Can You Improve It?"
9. Buerkli, "'What Gets Measured Gets Managed' — It's Wrong and Drucker Never Said It"; Caulkin, "The Rule is Simple: Be Careful What You Measure."
10. Hubbard, *How to Measure Anything*.
11. Čapek, *R.U.R.*, 7.
12. Čapek, *R.U.R.*, 59.

13. According to https://www.veche.net/lexicon/novegradian/entries/
%D1%80%D0%BE%D0%B7%D1%83%D0%BC%D0%B5.
14. Muller, *The Tyranny of Metrics*, 45.
15. Muller, *The Tyranny of Metrics*, 61.
16. Scott, *Seeing Like a State*, 6–7.
17. Scott, *Seeing Like a State*, 6–7.
18. Muller, *The Tyranny of Metrics*, 36.
19. Stewart, *The Management Myth*, 183.
20. Stewart, *The Management Myth*, 209.
21. Doerr and Page, *Measure What Matters*, 16.
22. Doerr and Page, *Measure What Matters*, 56.
23. Moore, *Virtue at Work*, 25.
24. Scott, *Seeing Like a State*, 13.
25. Kantor and Sundaram, "The Rise of the Worker Productivity Score."
26. Kantor and Sundaram, "The Rise of the Worker Productivity Score."
27. Bowles, *Future Ethics*, 7.
28. Scott, *Seeing Like a State*, 47.
29. Muller, *The Tyranny of Metrics*, 128.
30. Scott, *Seeing Like a State*, 21.
31. Vigen, *Spurious Correlations*, 4.

CHAPTER 6

1. Carson, *Lying and Deception*, 3.
2. Carson, *Lying and Deception*, 16.
3. Strudler, "The Distinctive Wrong in Lying," 171, citing Peter Geach, *The Virtues*, Cambridge University Press: Cambridge, 1977, 114.
4. Carson, *Lying and Deception*, 81.
5. Carson, *Lying and Deception*, 265.
6. Carson, *Lying and Deception*, 85.
7. Christen, Gordijn, and Loi, *The Ethics of Cybersecurity*, 76.
8. Carson, *Lying and Deception*, 191.
9. Toeniskoetter, "Meet the Man on a Mission to Expose Sneaky Price Increases."
10. Toeniskoetter, "Meet the Man on a Mission to Expose Sneaky Price Increases."
11. Frankfurt, *On Bullshit*, 47.
12. Frankfurt, *On Bullshit*, 51.
13. Frankfurt, *On Bullshit*, 43.

14. "About Delta."
15. Frankfurt, *On Bullshit*, 39.
16. Fisher, "As the Lingo Languishes," 270.
17. Black, *The Prevalence of Humbug*, 126.
18. Black, *The Prevalence of Humbug*, 125, cites this example, from *Martin Chuzzlewit* by Charles Dickens, as an example of humbug, but I think it fits Frankfurt's definition of bullshit better.
19. Black, *The Prevalence of Humbug*, 119.
20. Frankfurt, *On Bullshit*, 6.
21. Barnum, *The Life of P. T. Barnum Written by Himself*, 225.
22. Barnum, *The Life of P. T. Barnum Written by Himself*, 157.
23. Barnum, *The Life of P. T. Barnum Written by Himself*, 238.
24. Black, *The Prevalence of Humbug*, 120.
25. Reuters, "India Says It Accidentally Fired Missile into Pakistan."
26. Vallor, *Technology and the Virtues*, 122.
27. Shakespeare, "The Second Part of King Henry the Fourth," 05, 712.
28. 24/7 Wall Street Staff, "Misleading Marketing."
29. State Farm, "Company Overview."
30. Belofsky, *The Book of Strange and Curious Legal Oddities*, 202.
31. Bayley, *A Dictionary of Idiocy*, loc 706.
32. Bayley, *A Dictionary of Idiocy*, loc 224.
33. Oxford Eagle Contributors, "Doublespeak Dominates Our Language."
34. Sutton, "A Compilation of Euphemisms for Layoffs."
35. Ferris, *Then We Came to the End*, 35.
36. Various sources, including Harrison, "A Glossary of IR Euphemisms."
37. Reiley, "'What Idiot Do You Think I Am?' Customers Chafe As Rewards Programs Are Pared Back." According to Dunkin', "Dunkin' President Scott Murphy wrote in a statement to *The Washington Post* that the rewards changes allow customers to redeem a wider array of food and drink and to accrue points for a full meal."
38. Bayley, *A Dictionary of Idiocy*, loc 1600.
39. Vallor, *Technology and the Virtues*, 137.
40. Grey and Costas, *Secrecy at Work*, 66.
41. Grey and Costas, *Secrecy at Work*, 24.
42. Weber, *Economy and Society*, Kindle loc. 20821.
43. Grey and Costas, *Secrecy at Work*, 29.
44. Grey and Costas, *Secrecy at Work*, 45.
45. Grey and Costas, *Secrecy at Work*, 37.
46. Grey and Costas, *Secrecy at Work*, 30.

CHAPTER 7

1. Miller, "Enron's Ethics Code Reads like Fiction."
2. Dembinski, Lager, Cornford, and Bonvin, *Enron and World Finance*, 193.
3. Hamel as cited in McLean, Elkind, and Nocera, *Enron*, 238.
4. Much of the Enron story in this chapter comes from McLean, Elkind, and Nocera, *Enron*. I've noted a few exceptions.
5. McLean, Elkind, and Nocera, *Enron: The Smartest Guys in the Room*, 151.
6. McLean, Elkind, and Nocera, *Enron: The Smartest Guys in the Room*, 194.
7. McLean, Elkind, and Nocera, *Enron: The Smartest Guys in the Room*, 430.
8. Dembinski, Lager, Cornford, and Bonvin, *Enron and World Finance*, 200.
9. Osnos, "The Big House," 18.
10. Dembinski, Lager, Cornford, and Bonvin, *Enron and World Finance*, 227.
11. Levitt, *Freakonomics*, 65.
12. Heath, "Business Ethics and Moral Motivation," 595.
13. Heath, "Business Ethics and Moral Motivation," 595.
14. Heath, "Business Ethics and Moral Motivation," 596.
15. Heath, "Business Ethics and Moral Motivation," 596, citing Cressey, *Other People's Money*.
16. Heath, "Business Ethics and Moral Motivation," 598.
17. Heath, "Business Ethics and Moral Motivation," 599.
18. Heath, "Business Ethics and Moral Motivation," 598.
19. Osnos, "The Big House," 19.
20. Heath, "Business Ethics and Moral Motivation," 600.
21. Heath, "Business Ethics and Moral Motivation," 602.
22. Heath, "Business Ethics and Moral Motivation," 597.
23. Osnos, "The Big House," 20.
24. Heath, "Business Ethics and Moral Motivation," 601.
25. Osnos, "The Big House," 20.
26. Osnos, "The Big House," 21.
27. Heath, "Business Ethics and Moral Motivation," 610.
28. Heath, "Business Ethics and Moral Motivation," 610, citing Arnott, *Corporate Cults*, New York: Amacom, 2000, 72–73.
29. Soltes as cited in Osnos, "The Big House," 20.
30. Osnos, "The Big House," 20.
31. Heath, "Business Ethics and Moral Motivation," 605.
32. Grey and Costas, *Secrecy at Work*, 58.
33. Luban, Strudler, and Wasserman, "Moral Responsibility in the Age of Bureaucracy," 2359.

34. Luban, Strudler, and Wasserman, "Moral Responsibility in the Age of Bureaucracy," 2353.
35. Luban, Strudler, and Wasserman, "Moral Responsibility in the Age of Bureaucracy," 2355.
36. Velasquez, "Debunking Corporate Moral Responsibility," 550.
37. Riesman, Glazer, and Denney, *The Lonely Crowd*, 7.
38. Coffee, "'No Soul to Damn,'" 397.
39. Coffee, "'No Soul to Damn,'" 396.
40. This section again is largely based on information in McLean, Elkind, and Nocera, *Enron: The Smartest Guys in the Room*, with the exceptions noted.
41. Swartz, "How Enron Blew It."
42. Swartz, "How Enron Blew It."
43. Swartz, "How Enron Blew It."
44. McLean, Elkind, and Nocera, *Enron: The Smartest Guys in the Room*, 340.
45. Den Uyl, "The Fortune of Others," 257.
46. Heath, "Business Ethics and Moral Motivation," 611.
47. Heath, "Business Ethics and Moral Motivation," 611.
48. Heath, "Business Ethics and Moral Motivation," 611.

CHAPTER 8

1. Lepore, "Not So Fast."
2. Stewart, *The Management Myth*, 48. The story of Taylor's Bethlehem study comes largely from Stewart's book.
3. Stewart, *The Management Myth*, 49.
4. Stewart, *The Management Myth*, 50.
5. Drucker, *The Practice of Management*, 230.
6. Lepore, "Not So Fast."
7. Lepore, "Not So Fast."
8. Stewart, *The Management Myth*, 56.
9. Lepore, "Not So Fast."
10. Stewart, *The Management Myth*, 56.
11. Moore, *Virtue at Work*, 103.
12. Stewart, *The Management Myth*, 35.
13. Stewart, *The Management Myth*, 101.
14. Stewart, *The Management Myth*, 271.
15. MacIntyre, *After Virtue*, 46.

16. MacIntyre, *After Virtue*, 23.
17. Thaler and Sunstein, *Nudge*, 5.
18. Gardner, *Confucianism*, 34 (Analects 12.19).
19. Kennedy, Kim, and Strudler, "Hierarchies and Dignity," 483.
20. Kennedy, Kim, and Strudler, "Hierarchies and Dignity," 483.
21. Kennedy, Kim, and Strudler, "Hierarchies and Dignity," 483.
22. Gardner, *Confucianism*, 34.
23. Gardner, *Confucianism*, 35.
24. Gardner, *Confucianism*, 37. Confucius, *Analects* 2.3.
25. Smith, "Why You Bought That Ugly Sweater."
26. Vallor, *Technology and the Virtues*, 166.
27. Bowles, *Future Ethics*, 39.
28. Bowles, *Future Ethics*, 4.
29. Bowles, *Future Ethics*, 6.
30. Bayley, *A Dictionary of Idiocy*, loc 177.
31. McLuhan, *The Mechanical Bride*, Preface to the Original Edition.
32. Moriarty, "Business Ethics."
33. Menand, *The Free World*, 281.
34. Drumwright and Murphy, "The Current State of Advertising Ethics," 88.
35. Bowles, *Future Ethics*, 47.

CHAPTER 9

1. Gilbert, "Facebook Legally Can't Roll out Its Suicide Prevention AI in Europe." Some sources question whether GDPR is the real reason Facebook didn't roll it out.
2. Cohen, "How Not to Write a Privacy Law."
3. Cohen, "How Not to Write a Privacy Law."
4. Bowles, *Future Ethics*, 66.
5. Bowles, *Future Ethics*, 65.
6. Klein, "How South America Became a Nazi Haven."
7. Fichte as quoted in Birch and Conway, *Identity Is the New Money*, loc 70.
8. Bowles, *Future Ethics*, 68.
9. Birch and Conway, *Identity Is the New Money*, 176.
10. MacIntyre, *After Virtue*, 33.
11. Bowles, *Future Ethics*, 135.
12. Bowles, *Future Ethics*, 67.
13. Cohen, "How Not to Write a Privacy Law."

CHAPTER 10

1. International Centre for Missing & Exploited Children, "International Centre for Missing & Exploited Children (ICMEC) Expands with Ai, Biometrics, and Ad Tech."
2. AWS Public Sector Blog Team, "An Eye on Science."
3. Bowles, *Future Ethics*, 191.
4. Belofsky, *The Book of Strange and Curious Legal Oddities*, 82.
5. Bowles, *Future Ethics*, 187.
6. Lyons, *Lab Rats*, 164.
7. Vallor, *Technology and the Virtues*, 28.
8. Bowles, *Future Ethics*, 3.
9. Čapek, *R.U.R.*, 9.
10. Čapek, *R.U.R.*, 9.
11. See https://jokojokes.com/a-priest-and-a-rabbi-walk-into-a-bar-jokes .html.
12. Bowles, *Future Ethics*, 115.
13. Kearns and Roth, *The Ethical Algorithm*, 67.
14. Kearns and Roth, *The Ethical Algorithm*, 61.
15. Kearns and Roth, *The Ethical Algorithm*, 78.
16. Kearns and Roth, *The Ethical Algorithm*, 65.
17. Kearns and Roth, *The Ethical Algorithm*, 18.
18. Oates, "Frankenstein's Fallen Angel," 553.
19. Kearns and Roth, *The Ethical Algorithm*, 86.
20. Coeckelbergh, *AI Ethics*, 157, citing Floridi et al., "AI4People—An Ethical Framework for a Good AI Society: Opportunities, Risks, Principles, and Recommendations," 2018, *Minds and Machines* 28, no. 4: 689–707.
21. Coeckelbergh, *AI Ethics*, 158.

CHAPTER 11

1. Aristophanes, *The Clouds*, 31.
2. Schwartz, *A Seat at the Table*, 222.
3. Lyons, *Lab Rats*, 203.
4. Mosley and Irvine, *Making Work Human*, 209.
5. Mosley and Irvine, *Making Work Human*, 224, citing https://rework .withgoogle.com/guides/unbiasing-raise-awareness/steps/watch -unconscious-bias-at-work/.

6. Moore, *Virtue at Work*, 81.

7. Moore, *Virtue at Work*, 85, citing MacIntyre, "Corporate modernity and moral judgement: Are they mutually exclusive?" in Goodpaster and Sayer, *Ethics and Problems of the 21st Century*, Notre Dame, IN: University of Notre Dame Press, 1970, 122–35.

8. Amazon, "Leadership Principles."

9. Lewis as cited in Kim and Strudler, "Workplace Civility," 570.

10. Graeber, *Bullshit Jobs*, 225.

11. Gardner, *Confucianism*, 23.

12. Gardner, *Confucianism*, 25; civility is added in Kim and Strudler, "Workplace Civility," 557.

13. Gardner, *Confucianism*, 25.

14. Kim and Strudler, "Workplace Civility," 567.

15. Vallor, *Technology and the Virtues*, 141 defines technosocial care; I've adapted it more specifically for the workplace.

16. Harvey and Venkatesan, *The Kural*, 59.

17. Vallor, *Technology and the Virtues*, 50.

18. Franklin, *Franklin's Autobiography*, 39.

19. Franklin, *Franklin's Autobiography*, 39.

20. Franklin, *Franklin's Autobiography*, 39.

21. Epstein, *Range*, 21.

22. Epstein, *Range*, 53.

23. Epstein, *Range*, 207.

24. Epstein, *Range*, 103.

25. Epstein, *Range*, 112.

26. Epstein, *Range*, 101.

27. Epstein, *Range*, 178.

28. Harvey and Venkatesan, *The Kural*, 69.

29. Harvey and Venkatesan, *The Kural*, 52.

30. Stewart, *The Management Myth*, 132.

31. Hamel as cited in Stewart, *The Management Myth*, 78.

32. Quinn as cited in Stewart, *The Management Myth*, 186.

33. MacIntyre, *After Virtue*, 75.

34. MacIntyre, *After Virtue*, 76.

35. Collins, *Good to Great*, 12.

36. Stewart, *The Management Myth*, 186.

37. Stewart, *The Management Myth*, 302.

38. Kennedy, Kim, and Strudler, "Hierarchies and Dignity," 486.

CHAPTER 12

1. Graeber, *Bullshit Jobs*, 220.
2. Mumford and Winner, *Technics and Civilization*, 13–14.
3. Graeber, *Bullshit Jobs*, loc 257.
4. Čapek, *R.U.R.*, 20–21.
5. Graeber, *Bullshit Jobs*, 223.
6. Weber, Baehr, and Wells, *The Protestant Ethic and the Spirit of Capitalism*, 116.
7. Graeber, *Bullshit Jobs*, 228.
8. Graeber, *Bullshit Jobs*, 229.
9. Weber, Baehr, and Wells, *The Protestant Ethic and the Spirit of Capitalism*, xiii.
10. Vallor, *Technology and the Virtues*, 226.
11. Mosley and Irvine, *Making Work Human*, 27.
12. Michaelson, Pratt, Grant, and Dunn, "Meaningful Work," 77.
13. Moore, *Virtue at Work*, 86.
14. Terkel, *Working*, 15.
15. Terkel, *Working*, 27.
16. Menand, *The Free World*, 351.

Acknowledgments

I can't tell you how much fun I've had working with Anna Noak, Leah Brown, and Michele Ford on editing this book. I learn constantly from them. Special thanks to all of my colleagues and friends I've driven crazy with questions about ethics when I was thinking through what this book would say. When I was struggling with formulating a point of view on deontology, hats, and pasta, the constant reminders by people I encountered of how important and worthwhile a book on ethics in digital transformation would be kept me going. My fellow enterprise strategists at AWS—Ishit Vachhrajani, Miriam McLemore, Phil Le-Brun, Jonathan Allen, Xia Zhang, Clarke Rodgers, Jake Burns, Tom Godden, John Clark, Gregor Hohpe, Chris Hennesey, and Matthias Patzak—have taught me much. Thanks to the Yale Department of Philosophy, which put up with me for two years and got me to buy the extensive collection of philosophy books on my bookshelves. Thanks to Frankenstein—not Frankenstein, the creature—and the gingerbread man for providing the entertainment. And of course to Jenny, whose support, indulgence, library of books on *Frankenstein*, and chocolate pudding were crucial to the project.

About the Author

M r. Schwartz has been passably ethical in a wide range of organizations, public sector and private sector, large and small, good and evil, benevolent and malevolent. As an enterprise strategist at Amazon Web Services, he works with leaders of the world's largest companies on the challenges of digital transformation: cultural change, organizational structure, governance models, investment strategies, and his favorite topic, overcoming bureaucracy. He has been the CIO of US Citizenship and Immigration Services and Intrax Cultural Exchange and CEO of Auctiva. His four previous books on IT leadership have earned him a passionate following that might very well be in need of ethical instruction. Mr. Schwartz has a BA in computer science and an MA in philosophy from Yale and an MBA in Unethical Studies from Wharton.

Previous Books
by the Author

The Art of Business Value

—

A Seat at the Table
IT Leadership in the Age of Agility

—

War & Peace & IT
Business Leadership, Technology, and Success
in the Digital Age

—

The (Delicate) Art of Bureaucracy
Digital Transformation with the Monkey,
the Razor, and the Sumo Wrestler